NEWMAN'S
BIRDS
BY COLOUR

To Evan and Cailyn, and the next generation
of aspiring birders and nature lovers

NEWMAN'S
BIRDS
BY COLOUR

ILLUSTRATIONS AND TEXT BY
KENNETH NEWMAN

Updated by Nicholas Newman

Published by Struik Nature
(an imprint of Penguin Random House South Africa (Pty) Ltd)
Company Reg. No. 1953/000441/07
The Estuaries, No. 4, Oxbow Crescent, Century Avenue, Century City 7441
PO Box 1144, Cape Town 8000, South Africa

Visit **www.struiknature.co.za** and join the Struik Nature Club for updates,
news, events and special offers.

First published in 2000
Second edition 2008
Third edition 2011
Fourth edition 2024

10 9 8 7 6 5 4 3 2 1

Copyright © in text, illustrations and distribution maps, 2000, 2008, 2011, 2024:
Newman's Children's Trust
Copyright © in published edition, 2000, 2008, 2011, 2024:
Penguin Random House South Africa (Pty) Ltd

Publisher: Pippa Parker
Managing editor: Roelien Theron
Editor: Colette Alves
Designer: Sheryl Buckley
Proofreader: Emsie du Plessis

Reproduction by Dominic Robson
Printed and bound in China by 1010 Printing International Ltd

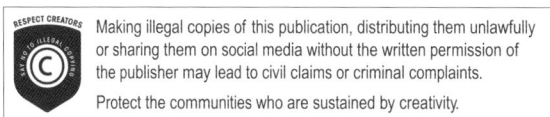

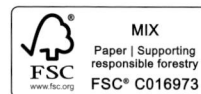

ISBN 978 1 77584 837 0 (Print)
ISBN 978 1 77584 838 7 (ePub)

Also available in Afrikaans as *Newman se Voëls volgens Kleur*
ISBN 978 1 77584 839 4 (Print)
ISBN 978 1 77584 840 0 (ePub)

CONTENTS

FOREWORD

As an ornithologist, I often receive enquiries like, 'I saw this stunning yellow bird, what could it be?' These moments highlight the importance of colour in birdwatching – a vibrant and essential cue for identifying the diverse species around us. *Newman's Birds by Colour* embraces this principle, offering an accessible and rewarding journey to those curious about the wonderful world of birds.

Birdwatching connects us with nature, but it can also be intimidating because of the sheer diversity of bird species. This guide addresses this challenge by focusing on a bird's most striking feature: its colour. Newman's approach simplifies bird identification for both beginners and seasoned birders, inviting readers to observe the world with fresh eyes and understand the biological significance of colour in birds. This book explores the fascinating interplay between colour and avian life, deepening our understanding of how plumage influences behaviours and survival strategies. Every hue, from the iridescence of a sunbird to the camouflage of a nightjar, narrates a story of evolution and adaptation.

Complementing this colour-centric method are thoughtfully designed icons that offer insights into each bird's habitat and relative body size. These icons, alongside vivid photographs, and detailed artwork, significantly enhance the bird identification process. But birdwatching is more than observation; it involves recognising and understanding the environments these birds inhabit. With contributions from experts like Ernst Retief of Birdlife South Africa and Dr Shannon Conradie from the FitzPatrick Institute of African Ornithology, the guide illuminates critical issues in bird conservation. This conservation focus can shift readers from mere observers to active protectors of the avian world.

In my experience, the joy of birding is magnified when shared. *Newman's Birds by Colour* takes a commendable step in this direction by including bird names in several regional languages, including in isiZulu for all South African species. This inclusivity strengthens our birding community, breaking down language barriers and nurturing a shared appreciation for our avian companions.

Newman's Birds by Colour is more than a bird guide; it is a gateway to a lifelong birding adventure. Its distinctive colour-based approach, combined with comprehensive information and a commitment to conservation, makes it an essential companion for anyone eager to explore the enchanting realm of birds. I invite you to begin your journey with this guide and experience the joy and wonder of birdwatching as part of the Newman's family.

C Reynolds

ASSOCIATE PROFESSOR CHEVONNE REYNOLDS
UNIVERSITY OF THE WITWATERSRAND

PREFACE

Newman's Birds by Colour was written with the aim of helping beginner birders by providing simple, practical tips for identifying birds, using key characteristics. This guide serves as a quick reference, focusing on the predominant first impression of colour, size or other easily noticed identifying characteristics. It is not a field guide and was never intended to be. Rather, it was meant to be a companion to the stalwart of the region's birding field guides, *Newman's Birds of Southern Africa* by Kenneth Newman.

This new edition has been updated and enhanced by the addition of photographs, bird names in local languages, and habitat icons. Facilitating correct species identification remains the aim of this new edition. However, it is also hoped that this guide will encourage interest in the conservation plight of birds, and that it will inspire readers to care for the environment and the world in which we live.

NICHOLAS NEWMAN
Visit www.newmansbirds.com

Great Egret

HOW TO USE THIS BOOK

This book is designed to help the beginner identify 'the one that got away'; a briefly seen, tantalising feathered creature that flew off before the birder could focus, leaving only a lasting impression of its predominant colour. Species in this guide are therefore grouped according to first-impression colour. This may not necessarily be the actual colour of the bird, but rather how it may appear in flight at the time of spotting it. For example, a dark brown bird may seem to be black when viewed at a particular angle or in certain light conditions and will therefore appear in both the brown and black sections of the book.

Within each colour section, the species are arranged according to size, with smaller birds at the front and larger birds at the end of the section.

Practically, let's say you've seen an unidentified bird and retained an impression of its predominant colour, for instance red. You can turn to the red-tabbed section to search for the bird there. Check the relative size of the bird and the distribution map to confirm that the bird you saw occurs in the region you are in.

KEY TO HABITAT SYMBOLS

- Human settlements, towns and gardens
- Wetlands
- Succulent karoo and fynbos
- Nama karoo
- Desert
- Rocky areas and cliffs
- Grasslands
- Savanna bushveld
- Forests
- Coastal shores
- Aerial

KEY TO SYMBOLS & ABBREVIATIONS

♂	=	male
♀	=	female
ad.	=	adult
imm.	=	immature
juv.	=	juvenile
br.	=	breeding plumage
non-br.	=	non-breeding plumage

KEY TO LANGUAGE ABBREVIATIONS

A	=	Afrikaans	Z	=	isiZulu
X	=	isiXhosa	Ss	=	Sesotho
Sp	=	Sepedi	Tw	=	Setswana
Ts	=	Xitsonga	Ve	=	Tshivenda
Sw	=	siSwati	Nd	=	isiNdebele
Sh	=	Shona	N	=	Nama
H	=	Herero	G	=	German

THREAT STATUS

EN	=	Endangered
CR	=	Critically Endangered
NT	=	Near Threatened
VU	=	Vulnerable

Distribution map. A dark area indicates where a bird is more common; a pale area indicates where it is less common or present for only part of the year.

Colour tab identifies the colour section you are browsing.

English common name

Text gives the bird's habitat and highlights its identifying features.

Size tab indicates if the species on the page are small, medium, large or extra large.

WHITE STORK
Open grass bushveld. Black and white, with red bill and legs.
117 cm
A: Witooievaar
Z: Unogolantethe
Ss: Mokotatsie O Mosweu
N: !uri oefari
G: Weißstorch

LESSER FLAMINGO
Salt pans and lagoons. Pinkish-white, sometimes fairly white, with red wing feathers, bill and legs.
102 cm
A: Kleinflamink
Z: Ukholwasomncane
Ss: Mmamolalana E Monyenyane
Sp: Tlatšana
Tw: Lekukara
N: ≠khari ǀapaǀnübeb
H: Kakueya Okaṯiṯi
G: Zwergflamingo

Size, from bill tip to tail tip

SADDLE-BILLED STORK
Freshwater bodies. Black-and-white plumage, and red-and-black bill with yellow saddle. 145 cm
A: Saalbekooievaar **Z:** Umadolabomvu
Ss: Molombwe **Ts:** Ngwamhlanga
N: !aroda-am oefari
H: Endongo Otjikaviriro
G: Sattelstorch

GREATER FLAMINGO
Salt pans and lagoons. White plumage, red-and-black wings, pink and black bill, and long, pink legs.
140 cm
A: Grootflamink **Z:** Ukholwasomkhulu
Ss: Mmamolalana E Moholo **Sp:** Tladi
Tw: Tladi **Ts:** Ximinta Ntsengele **N:** kai ǀapaǀnübeb
H: Kakueya **G:** Flamingo

Threat status (see key)

Habitat symbol (see key)

Names in local languages (see key)

Where no symbol is provided, male and female birds do not differ.

Birds may appear in more than one colour section if their plumage is not a single colour or if they have a collar or breast band.

INTRODUCTION

Bird identification can be tricky and frustrating, especially for beginners. A bird often flies away before the birder can get a better look at it, leaving the observer with a fleeting impression – often just a flash of colour - as a clue to its identity. And even that first impression may not be entirely accurate.

In the words of **Kenneth Newman** (1924-2006): 'There is little doubt that the features memorised by most novice birders … are the bird's approximate size and its colour, or the colour that made an impression. There is no doubt whatsoever that colour, no matter how briefly glimpsed, remains in the memory. If one is to assume that the bird seen was indeed red, then the list of possible species will be very short indeed. However, when you delve a little deeper into the problem, it usually transpires that, on second thoughts, it was only its beak, head or tail that was red (or was it green?).'.

This book aims to alleviate this problem by providing a system for identifying birds based on first impression, in other words the colour first noticed.

Long-tailed Paradise Whydah males sport distinctive high contrast coloration and an impressive tail during the breeding season.

IDENTIFYING BIRDS BY FIRST IMPRESSION

There are a number of different systems used by birders to identify birds in the field. This book uses Newman's five-point check for identifying birds by first impression, but there is also another method used by birders called GISS (General Impression of Shape and Size), which may also be helpful (see page 15). We outline both below.

NEWMAN'S FIVE-POINT CHECK

When looking at an unfamiliar bird, make a habit of mentally noting its important features, so that you will remember them once it has flown. By using the formula below, you should be able to make positive identifications. And with a bit of practice, this system will become second nature.

The five key points are:

1. **Colour and markings** – What was your first impression of the bird's coloration?
2. **Size** – What was your first impression of its size?
3. **Habitat** – Where was the bird?
4. **Behaviour and activity** – What was it doing? What time of day was it active?
5. **Distribution** – Is the bird you have tentatively identified commonly found in the area?

1. COLOUR AND MARKINGS

Overwhelmingly, birders notice the general colours and markings on a bird's feathers first. While this is a good starting point for identification, it is also important to pay attention to the colour of specific parts, such as the head, breast, tail and wings, and any distinct patterns or features, such as wingbars or breast bands.

2. SIZE

The easiest way to get a good sense of a bird's size is to compare it with other common birds that you know well. In this book, we consider a **House Sparrow** small (±15 cm), a **Rock Dove** medium-sized (±30 cm), a **guineafowl** large (±50 cm) and a **Hadada Ibis** extra large (70+ cm). Within each colour section, small birds are placed at the beginning and large or extra large birds at the end.

Lilian's Lovebird has distinctive colouring on its body, head and bill. These features should be noted to aid identification.

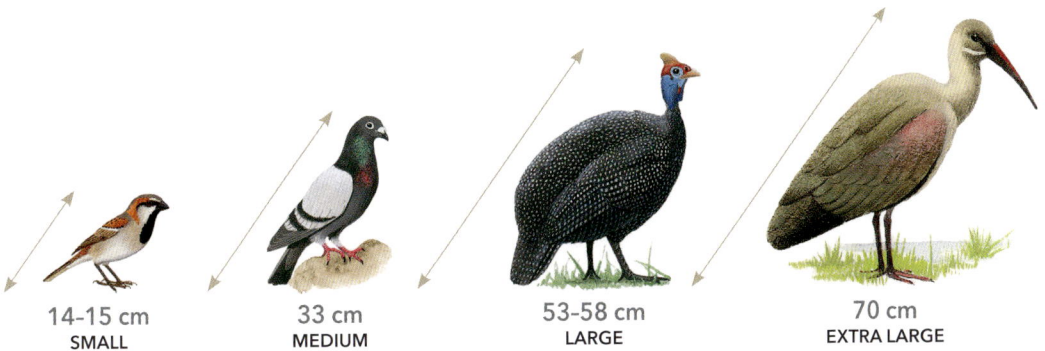

| 14–15 cm | 33 cm | 53–58 cm | 70 cm |
| SMALL | MEDIUM | LARGE | EXTRA LARGE |

Did you know?

A bird is measured by the length of its body, not the height. The bird is measured lying flat, from the tip of its bill to the tip of its tail. If the legs protrude beyond the tail, they are included in the total measurement.

3. HABITAT

A habitat is a place or environment where an organism normally lives. In this guide, we include smaller habitats, such as rocky areas, thickets, gardens or streams, as well as major habitats, such as forests, woodlands and deserts. Birds have different habitat preferences, based on their food and nest requirements. Knowing which birds you are likely to spot in a particular habitat can greatly enhance your birding experience.

The table below gives an overview of these habitats and lists some species that occur in them. It also shows the icons for each habitat, which are used throughout the book.

	Human settlements, towns and gardens Urban environments, especially those with green spaces or that replicate the natural habitat of birds, can support a variety of birdlife. Species commonly seen include **Cape Sparrow, Mourning Dove, Grey Go-away-bird, Blacksmith Lapwing, crows, thrushes, robins** and **weavers**.
	Wetlands Wetlands are areas of land covered by water (fresh or saline) and may be permanent or seasonal. This includes a variety of inland waterways, rivers, marshes, reed beds, farm dams and seasonal pans, as well as coastal wetlands such as estuaries, backwaters and lagoons. Wetlands are home to **herons, ibises, ducks, geese, flamingos** and **storks**, and smaller birds, such as **bishops, weavers** and **warblers**.
	Succulent karoo and fynbos These unique habitats occur in the extreme south and west of the region. They are dominated by evergreen shrubs, bushes and thickets, and have a rich variety of flora, such as proteas, restios and ericas. These habitats are home to several endemic bird species, including **Cape Spurfowl, Victorin's Warbler, Orange-breasted Sunbird** and **Protea Canary**, and other species such as **Ludwig's Bustard** and **Burchell's Courser**.
	Nama karoo This habitat consists of semi-arid stony plains of small scrubs, trees and sparsely dotted succulents and grass. Bird species unique to this habitat include the **Karoo Korhaan, Karoo Chat, Cinnamon-breasted Warbler** and **Black-headed Canary**.
	Desert This habitat is dominated by arid stretches of sandy and rocky areas with sparsely dotted grasses and other plants. Bird species include several of the lark family, such as the **Dune** and **Long-billed larks**, and the **Tractrac Chat**.

Rocky areas and cliffs
Rocky habitat includes cliffs, crags and rocky outcrops.
   This very localised habitat attracts specific birds, including **Bearded Vulture, Mocking Cliff Chat, Cape** and **Drakensberg rockjumpers, Mountain Wheatear, Rockrunner** and **Buff-streaked Chat.**

Grasslands
Grasslands are large open areas where the vegetation is dominated by grasses.
   This habitat harbours numerous interesting birds, from **larks, pipits, widowbirds, korhaans** and **cisticolas** to **francolins** and **cranes.**

Savanna bushveld (thornveld and broad-leaved woodland)
This term is applied to any indigenous wooded region, whether it consists of bushes, trees or a mixture of both. Savanna bushveld covers vast areas of the land. Savanna thornveld is a   drier habitat of predominantly thorn bushes, and is highly attractive to many birds. Savanna broad-leaved woodland consists of large-leaved tree species, such as Mopane and miombo. These trees are well spaced, and the grassy understorey is fairly open.
   Bushveld species include **francolins, guineafowls, sandgrouse, larks, birds of prey, rollers, francolins, flycatchers, bushshrikes, woodpeckers** and **tits.**

Forests (evergreen, riverine and dune)
Evergreen forest is made up of a great variety of indigenous trees, and is found in regions of good rainfall, from the Drakensberg escarpment eastwards to the coastal dune regions and south to the Eastern Cape.
   Riverine forest occurs along waterways. In this habitat, the trees along the river banks receive more water than the surrounding bush, and tend to be larger and evergreen.
   Dune forest consists of dense evergreen vegetation with thick undergrowth and some tall trees. This type of forest grows on sandy soils in a narrow strip along the east and south coasts. Dune and evergreen forests share many characteristics and bird species.
Forest habitats host **robins, thrushes, turacos, flycatchers, apalises, cuckooshrikes, birds of prey,** and **kingfishers.**

Coastal shores
This habitat occurs where the sea meets the land, and includes beaches, bays and dunes. Common shorebird species are **Cape Gannet, African Penguin, Cape Cormorant, Kelp Gull** and **Greater Crested Tern.**

Aerial
Birds that are mostly seen in flight, and perform essential activities such as feeding, in the air, are considered to have aerial habitats.
   Aerial birds include the **African Palm Swift, Greater Striped Swallow, Barn Swallow** and **Common Martin.**

The African Swamphen walks across floating vegetation and wades in shallow water.

4. BEHAVIOUR AND ACTIVITY

Pay attention to what the bird is doing. A bird's behaviour is another important clue to its identity. Is it walking or hopping (starling or thrush), swimming (duck), wading (heron), or probing the mud (ibis)? If it is flying, is it feeding in the air (swift or swallow)? If the bird is in a tree, then what is it doing in the tree? It could be feeding in the outer leaves of the canopy (warbler), or perching on the top of a tree (flycatcher, shrike or drongo) or on the side of a tree (roller or kingfisher). The bird could be pecking at the tree trunk or a branch (woodpecker or barbet).

Note the time of day you saw the bird. Birds are generally most active during the morning, from dawn until about 10h30, and in the evening, from about 16h30 till last light. In the middle of the day they tend to rest, or are less active, especially in hot weather. Exceptions are the high-flying eagles and vultures, but even these are most active during the first half of the day. Nocturnal birds – owls, nightjars and thick-knees – are most active between dusk and midnight, and longer when the moon is bright. Nightjars do much of their feeding during the first few hours of darkness and can be seen flying at dusk.

Check if the bird is a resident or migrant. The majority of birds are present throughout the year, but a few are seasonal migrants that arrive in spring and depart again in late summer. If the bird is a migrant, it is unlikely to be seen between mid-April and mid-September.

5. DISTRIBUTION

If you are still uncertain about the bird's identification, the final step is to check the distribution map to see if the bird occurs in the area in which you saw it. While migration patterns are slowly changing due to climate change and other factors, you are still guaranteed to see birds in their natural distribution areas.

GISS: GENERAL IMPRESSION OF SIZE AND SHAPE

GISS, which stands for General Impression of Size and Shape (pronounced 'jizz'), is a universally accepted method for identifying birds, and refers to the initial overall impression gathered when the bird is first seen. Such impressions are usually formed by shape and size, rather than specific details, which combine to make a bird recognisable at a glance.

For example, we know that the **Western Cattle Egret** belongs to the heron family, not only because it has a long neck and long legs (features found in other bird families as well), but also because of the characteristic posture of this bird group: their GISS. Similarly, most people know what a **wagtail** looks like and how it walks. If you were to come across a bird with vibrant blue or pink hues that had the strutting gait and bobbing tail movements of a wagtail (its GISS), you would be able to identify it as such.

Closely related bird species often exhibit resemblances in body shape, size and even postures, such as tail-up positions or sudden, alert movements. Becoming acquainted with various groups of similar-looking birds aids in discerning species and expediting identification. For example, if you observe ducks, you will notice how most of them stand in an almost horizontal position with their legs spaced widely apart, resulting in a waddling walk. This distinctive walking style, in conjunction with their bill shape, contributes to the recognisable GISS of birds in this particular group. Conversely, whistling ducks such as the **White-faced** and **Fulvous whistling ducks** are more akin to geese and display a different GISS. They exhibit an upright stance, and walk without waddling because their legs are less widely spaced and are positioned further back on their bodies.

In some cases, it is necessary to pay attention to the combination of plumage colouring, GISS and behavioural traits in order to identify the bird. With **shrikes**, for example, you will notice that they have robust bodies, prominent heads and sturdy, hooked beaks. However, shrikes can be categorised into four distinct groups, with behavioural differences. True shrikes, including the **Southern Fiscal** and **Souza's Shrike**, often perch conspicuously on trees or wires, employing a still-hunting approach to capture ground-dwelling insects. **Boubous** and **bushshrikes** prefer to find sustenance among tree and bush canopies. **Tchagra shrikes** predominantly forage on the ground or in lower strata, while **Helmetshrikes** move in groups between trees.

Other characteristics that contribute to GISS include beaks and bills (see page 21), legs and feet (see page 24) and feather arrangements and colours (see page 18).

Robin

Sunbird

Bee-eater

Starling

Woodpecker

Chat

Thrush

Whistling duck

Dabbling duck

WHAT IS A BIRD?

It may be tempting to define a bird as something that flies. However, some birds such as ostriches are·flightless, and flight is therefore not a defining characteristic. A bird is a warm-blooded, egg-laying vertebrate that is distinguished from other creatures by an important structural difference – its unique covering of feathers. Birds' feathers are believed to have evolved from the scales of ancient reptilians.

The earliest and most primitive known avian dinosaur, named *Archaeopteryx*, (illustration top right), lived in the late Jurassic period (150–155 million years ago). *Archaeopteryx* had characteristics of both a bird and a reptile, with feathers all over its body, facilitating flight. It also had teeth, claws on its wings and a bony, reptilian tail.

CLASSIFICATION AND NAMING OF BIRDS

In this book, only common names are used to refer to bird species. However, all birds (and other organisms) have unique scientific names, which conform to an international system of classification that is used by all countries, irrespective of the local language. Within this system, birds are grouped into families, and within the families are one or more genera (genus in the singular). Each genus (e.g., *Passer*, a genus of sparrows) has within it one or more species (e.g., *Passer melanurus*, the Cape Sparrow). A species can also be divided further into subspecies.

What is a species? A species is best defined as a type of organism that can only reproduce with other members of its kind. During courtship, species are prevented from interbreeding in various natural ways. Voice certainly plays an important role in mate recognition. Plumage colour and markings are also important for courtship and territorial defence.

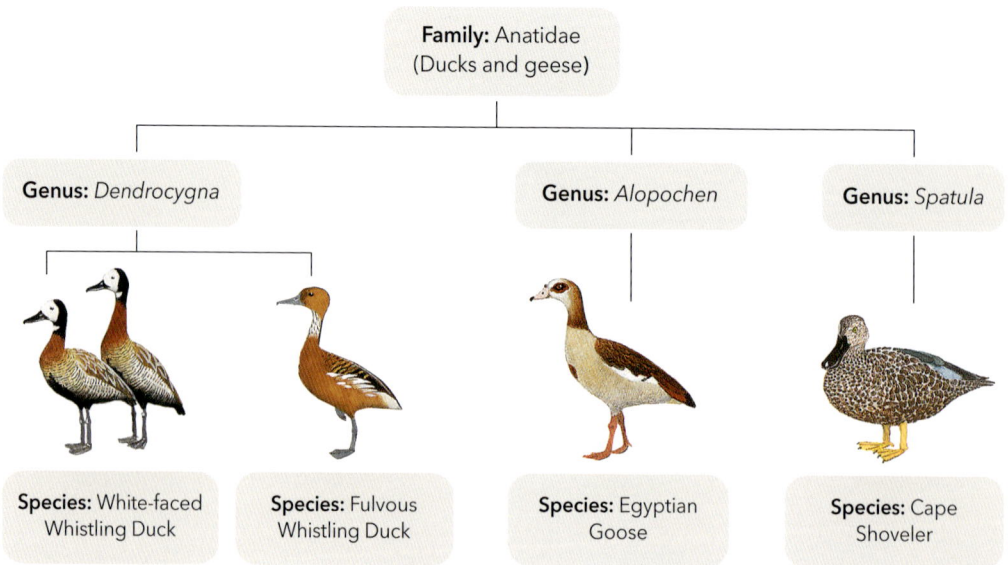

Family: Anatidae
(Ducks and geese)

Genus: *Dendrocygna*

Genus: *Alopochen*

Genus: *Spatula*

Species: White-faced Whistling Duck

Species: Fulvous Whistling Duck

Species: Egyptian Goose

Species: Cape Shoveler

ANATOMY OF A BIRD

It is advisable to become familiar with the various parts of a bird, so that you can understand the terminology used in bird guides, as well as the sometimes perplexing bird names. You may wonder, for example, why the **White-fronted Bee-eater** is so called when it obviously doesn't have a white breast. However, if you check the anatomy diagram below you will see that the 'front' of a bird is not its chest but its forehead. It is therefore useful to understand terms such as secondaries, primaries, coverts, tarsus and orbital ring, and how they relate to bird names and identifying characteristics.

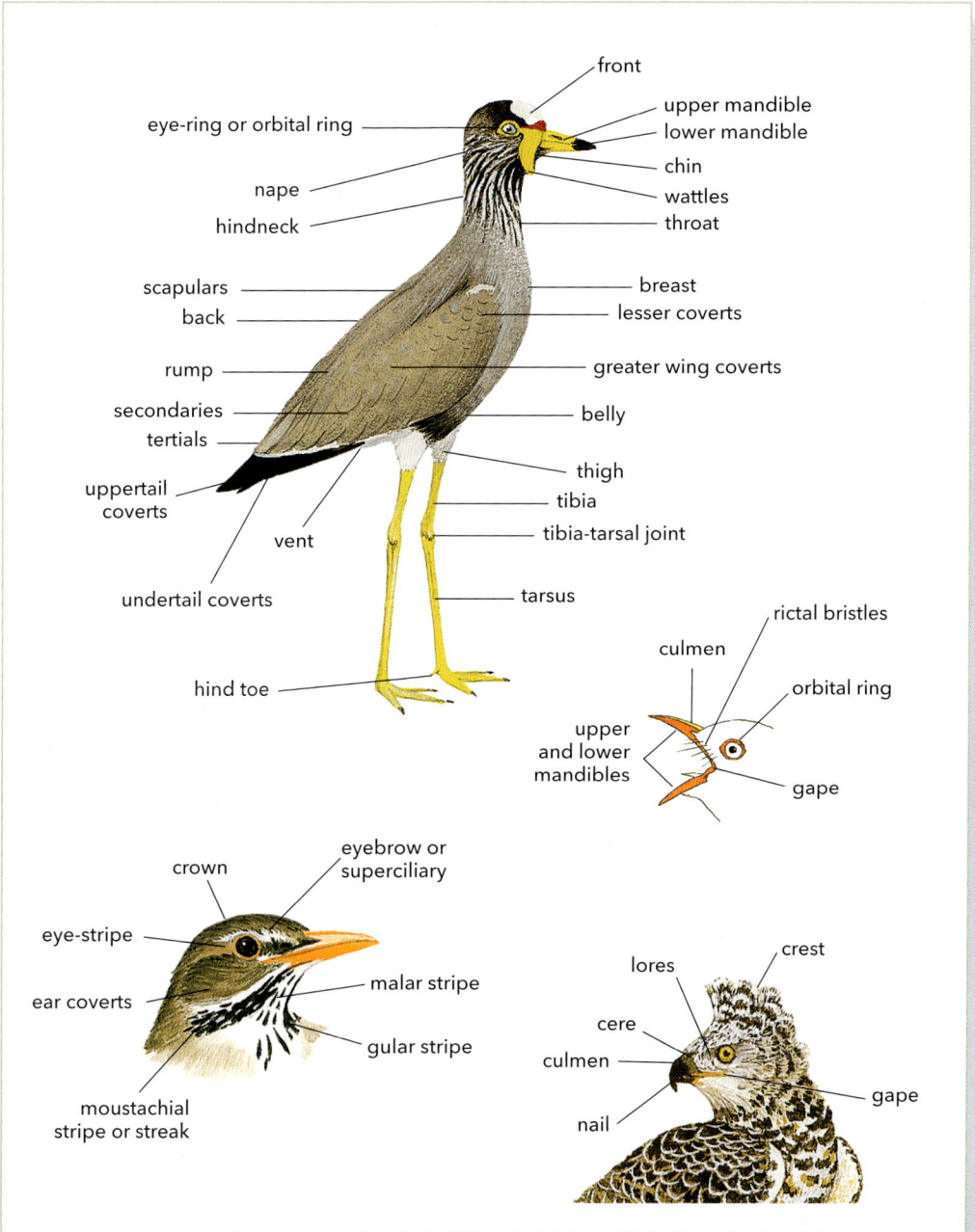

PHYSICAL FEATURES AND CHARACTERISTICS

When trying to identify birds, it is useful to have knowledge of physical features, such as the types of feathers on the wings and how they are arranged, or the type of bill or feet that is particular to a certain group.

FEATHERS

Feathers are an integral structural part of a bird, and are used for a variety of functions, from flight to insulation and courtship displays.

Feather structure

A typical feather consists of a central shaft and a vane. The shaft has two parts: the calamus, which extends under the skin into the follicle, and the rachis, the flexible tube above the skin, from which paired barbs grow. The barbs have a series of tiny filaments called barbules, which have hooklets that link the barbs. This creates the firm, smooth surface of the vane, which pushes against the air during flight. At the base of some feathers there may be downy barbs, which are softer, as they do not have interlocking hooklets.

Types of feathers

There are many different types of feathers, from the large, structured tail and wing feathers to the soft and fluffy down feathers and small filoplumes.

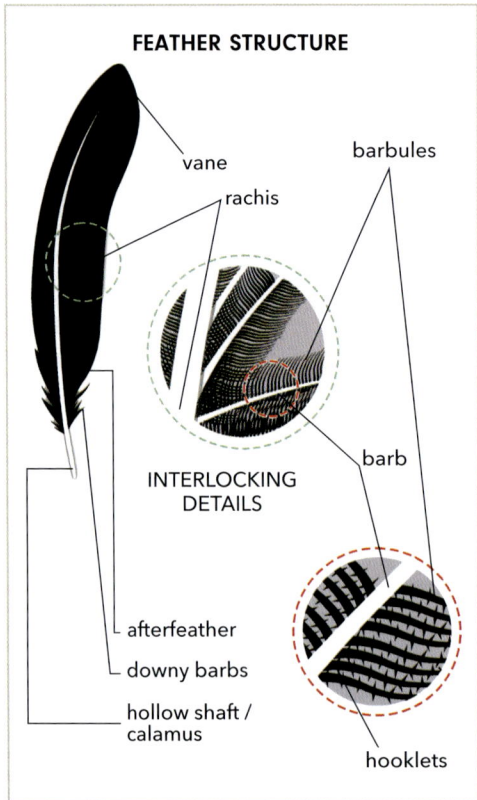

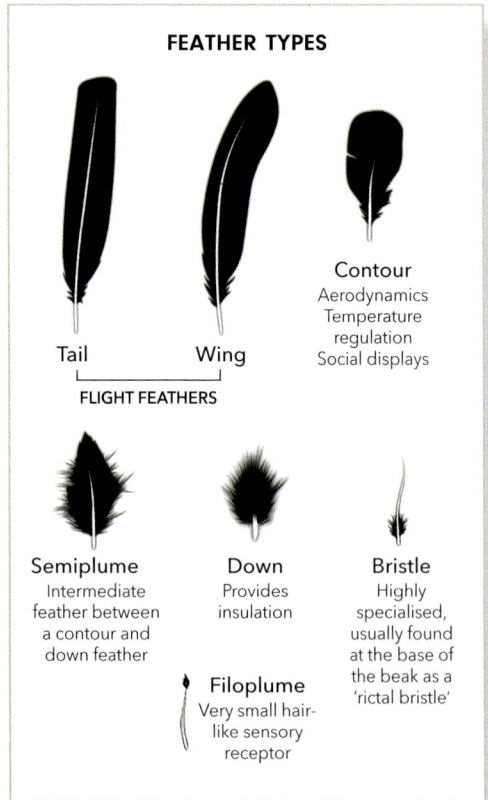

FEATHER STRUCTURE

vane
rachis
barbules

INTERLOCKING
DETAILS

barb

afterfeather

downy barbs

hollow shaft /
calamus

hooklets

FEATHER TYPES

Tail   Wing

FLIGHT FEATHERS

Contour
Aerodynamics
Temperature
regulation
Social displays

Semiplume
Intermediate
feather between
a contour and
down feather

Down
Provides
insulation

Bristle
Highly
specialised,
usually found
at the base of
the beak as a
'rictal bristle'

Filoplume
Very small hair-
like sensory
receptor

The Spotted Eagle-Owl has an impressive wingspan and is able to fly slowly and silently.

Wing feathers

The most noticeable feathers are those of the wings, and reference is often made to these when plumage characteristics are described. The main feathers of the wing are the flight feathers, which are made up of:

- **Outer primary feathers**, attached to the 'hand'.
- **Secondary feathers**, attached to the 'forearm'.
- **Tertials or coverts,** attached to the humerus or 'upper arm'.
- **The small bastard wing or alula**, which helps create lift and prevents stalling in slow flight.

THE UPPER WING OF A BIRD

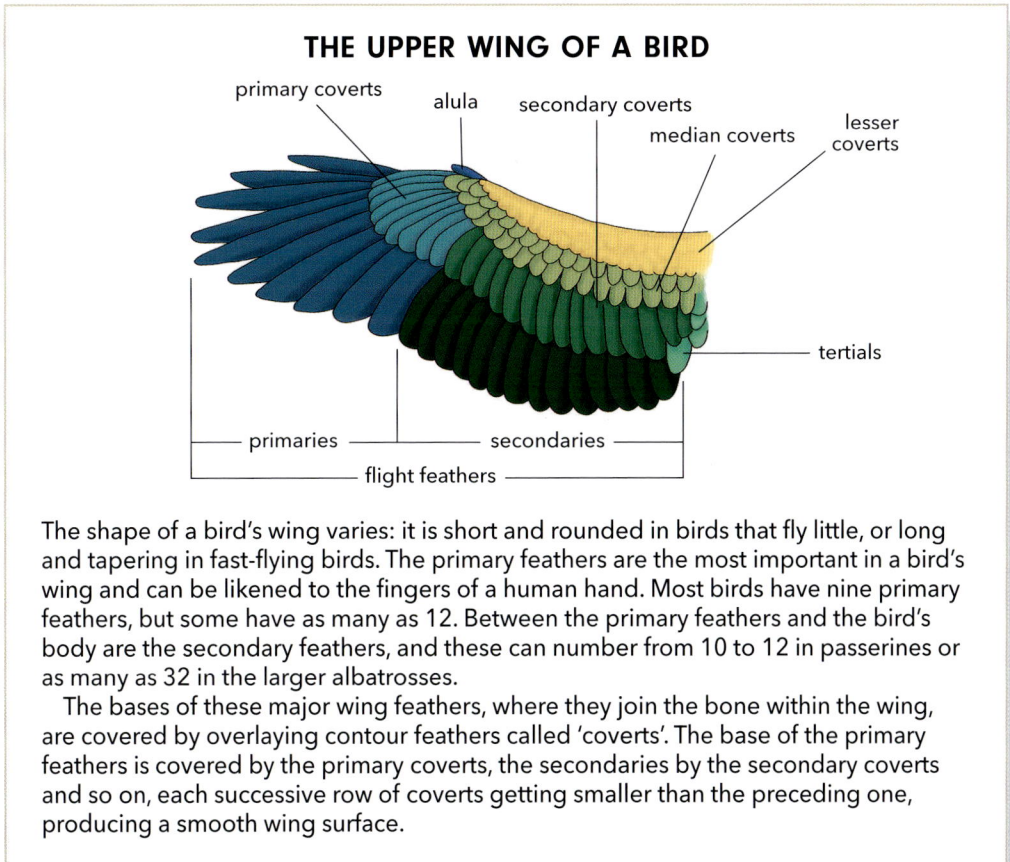

The shape of a bird's wing varies: it is short and rounded in birds that fly little, or long and tapering in fast-flying birds. The primary feathers are the most important in a bird's wing and can be likened to the fingers of a human hand. Most birds have nine primary feathers, but some have as many as 12. Between the primary feathers and the bird's body are the secondary feathers, and these can number from 10 to 12 in passerines or as many as 32 in the larger albatrosses.

The bases of these major wing feathers, where they join the bone within the wing, are covered by overlaying contour feathers called 'coverts'. The base of the primary feathers is covered by the primary coverts, the secondaries by the secondary coverts and so on, each successive row of coverts getting smaller than the preceding one, producing a smooth wing surface.

Migration

Birds that migrate into Africa from the northern hemisphere (the Palaearctic region), such as the **Garden Warbler**, do so at the onset of the northern winter. At this time, temperatures drop to well below freezing, especially within the Arctic Circle. With waters frozen over and the land deep in snow, there is little food for birds. The great southward movement to warmer, food-rich regions involves countless millions of birds of every description, large and small. These northern visitors arrive in Africa in the months of September and October and return north again in March and April. This migration takes place over a wide front, and while millions move into Africa, others migrate to India, China and Australia.

How do birds find their way?

Navigation for day-flying migrants is based on inherent instinct and a visual memory of well-used routes. Many smaller birds navigate by observing the position of the sun. Although they rest sometimes, there is little opportunity for feeding; instead, they rely on their fat reserves, and many birds have often lost a third of their body weight by the time they reach southern Africa.

Shorebirds and seabirds tend to follow coastlines or rivers and lakes. They fly fast and non-stop, day and night, until sighting a convenient shoreline or estuary, where they may spend several days feeding before continuing their migration.

Threats

These extraordinary annual journeys are not without danger. While many birds fall victim to natural perils such as predators or weather events, by far the most serious threats they face are illegal hunting and trapping. Each year millions of birds on flyways between Europe and Africa are killed by hunters, poachers and trappers. These birds are usually hunted for food, for sport, or for sale in the illegal wildlife trade. Migratory birds also die from eating poisoned bait, usually laid out for other animals such as foxes and wolves.

Energy-efficient flight

Heavy-bodied birds, such as **vultures**, **eagles** and **storks**, have greater wing loading, and must therefore flap vigorously to remain airborne. In order to remain aloft without becoming exhausted, these large birds seek out upward currents of warm air. These currents (thermals) are a result of sunlight warming surfaces such as ploughed fields, buildings and sheltered valleys, which causes bubbles of warm air to rise. Since the bubbles are warmer than the surrounding air, they rise quickly. By circling in these thermals, large birds are able to gain height without flapping their wings, and also to travel cross-country up to 400 km in a day.

Feather colour

Birds exhibit a vast array of coloration, from subtle, plain shades to bright, iridescent greens and blues. These splendidly varied colours in feathers are mainly produced in two ways: pigments or feather structure, known as structural coloration.

Pigmentation in birds comes from three pigment groups: carotenoids, melanin and porphyrins. Pigments are formed or absorbed on a cellular level within the bird's underlying feathers.

Carotenoids: These pigments are derived from plants and are responsible for red, yellow and orange hues in feathers. Birds acquire carotenoids by consuming the plants directly or by eating insects or animals that have consumed these pigments.

Melanin: This pigment is produced naturally by the bird's own pigment cells (melanocytes). It can produce a range of colours, including black, dark brown, light brown and rufous.

Porphyrins: These pigments are responsible for vibrant reds, greens, pinks and browns. Each porphyrin pigment has its own chemical structure and ultraviolet tendencies.

Structural coloration arises from the physical structure of the feathers. Microscopic structures on the feather surface interact with light, creating dynamic colours, which may change depending on the angle at which they are viewed. These structures can be iridescent or non-iridescent in form. Structural colours are commonly found in birds with blue or iridescent colouring.

Pigments are responsible for the rich colour of the European Bee-eater's feathers.

BEAKS AND BILLS

The words 'beak' and 'bill' are synonymous. In this book, both are used: beak for the smaller ones and bill for the larger.

The size and shape of a bird's beak or bill is related to the bird's food and feeding habits. Understanding the functions of different beaks and bills will help with identifying the type of bird, and the habitat it prefers. The diagram overleaf shows the various shapes of beaks and bills and their function.

SOME SPECIALISED BILLS

The **Trumpeter Hornbill** has a hollow casque on its bill, enabling it to amplify sound.

Insectivorous birds often have short, slender bills.

Rollers feed on large grasshoppers, beetles, scorpions, lizards and small frogs.

The **African Spoonbill** moves its partially open bill through the water in a sideways, sweeping motion to catch small aquatic creatures.

Short, stout bills are used for crushing seeds.

Kingfishers have sharp, dagger-like bills, allowing them to catch and hold fish.

A **skimmer** uses its longer lower mandible to plough through surface water while flying. On contact with a fish, the bill snaps shut.

The huge, hooked bill of a large **vulture** is a tool for tearing the tough hide of animals killed by four-legged predators.

The slender, curved bill of **sunbirds**, coupled with their long tongues, enables them to probe deep into flowers to reach the nectar.

The powerful hooked bills of raptors are used for tearing the flesh of their prey.

Many ocean birds have external, tubular nostrils through which excess sea salt is expelled.

Many insectivorous birds have long, curved bills with which they probe soft ground.

The **Great White Pelican** has an extendible pouch below its bill that is used as a scoop for catching fish.

The huge **Saddle-billed Stork** has a large and colourful bill with a yellow 'saddle', which it uses to stab at prey.

Many waterbirds have flat bills with tooth-like edges that are used to strain food from water.

The **Lesser Moorhen**, in common with many of its relatives, has a colourful 'frontal shield' on its forehead.

Parrots' powerful bills are adapted for cracking large, hard-shelled seeds and extracting the kernels.

The **Pied Avocet** uses its recurved bill to sweep the water's surface for small organisms.

LEGS AND FEET

We see very little of the true leg in most birds because the upper sections of the leg, the bird's 'knee' and tibia, are covered by feathers. What we see as the backward-bending 'knee' is equivalent to our ankle joint, while the lower 'leg' is actually the ankle. Technically then, a bird's foot extends from what appears to be the 'knee' (the tibiotarsal joint) down to the toes. Below are a few common types of bird feet.

EXAMPLES OF SPECIALISED FEET

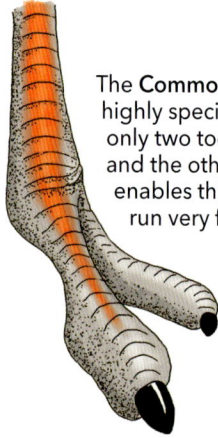

The **Common Ostrich** has a highly specialised foot with only two toes – one large and the other small – which enables this flightless bird to run very fast.

Ducks and geese such as the **South African Shelduck** have webbed, paddle-like feet that aid swimming and diving under water to reach food.

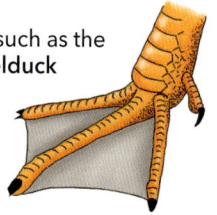

The African Jacana has the longest toes of all, with greatly elongated claws that prevent it from sinking while walking over water lilies.

Swifts have very small feet with all four toes facing forwards, enabling them to cling to the rough surfaces of rocky cliffs (or buildings), where they roost and nest. As a result, they cannot perch on trees or telephone wires.

Birds of prey have very powerful feet, especially the inner and rear toes, which are used for grasping, piercing and holding prey. The most powerful talons in Africa are found on the **African Crowned Eagle** and the **Martial Eagle**.

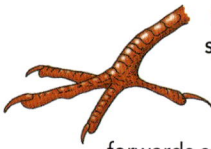

Passerines such as **sparrows** typically have all four toes joined at the same level: three facing forwards and one backwards. This helps the bird remain on its perch, even in bad weather.

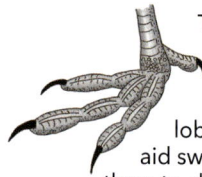

The **Little Grebe, Red-knobbed Coot** and **African Finfoot** have semi-webbed or lobed feet that serve to aid swimming but also allow them to clamber over and on floating plant matter.

Parrots such as the **Cape Parrot** have feet with short toes and sharp claws, which are used for clinging to and scrambling along branches, often at peculiar angles, to reach fruit. The foot is also used like a hand when feeding.

Perhaps the strangest foot of all also has the strangest name: the zygodactyl or yoke-toed foot, which is found in **woodpeckers, barbets** and **cuckoos**. This type of foot has two toes facing backwards, which facilitates climbing on trees.

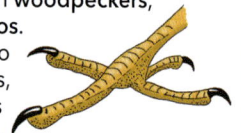

PASSERINES VS NON-PASSERINES

PASSERINES

Passerines are also known as songbirds or perching birds, and represent more than 50% (5,400 species) of the roughly 10,000 or more bird species in the world. Passerines are small to medium-sized land birds, and include robins, thrushes, white-eyes and wagtails – all birds that are commonly found in our gardens. e largest passerines are the crows.

A passerine's foot has four toes, which are all set at the same level. Three toes face forwards and one backwards, and they are all unwebbed. This configuration allows these little birds to roost even on a windy night. When the bird crouches, its feet locks onto the perch and can only relax and unlock when the bird flexes its legs to stand.

Passerines such as this Cape White-eye have four toes at the same level, which allows them to clutch their perch even in windy conditions.

NON-PASSERINES

All birds that do not have locking feet are classified as non-passerines. This is a large and diverse group of birds that do not share any other distinguishing features. There is great variation in leg length and foot shape, with members of the group ranging from those with webbed feet to those with talons. This group includes birds such as **seabirds**, **bustards**, **raptors**, **pigeons**, **parrots**, **nightjars** and **woodpeckers**, to name just a few.

A SIMPLIFIED DIAGRAM OF A PERCHING FOOT

To settle securely on a small branch or slender wire, the bird's flexion leg tendons are automatically tightened as the leg is folded.

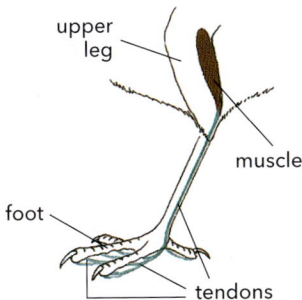

upper leg | muscle | foot | tendons

upper leg | muscle | tendons

muscle | tendons

1 The typical passerine foot has all four toes joined at the same level, three facing forwards and one backwards.

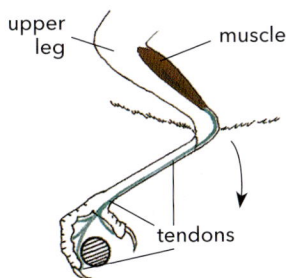

2 As the bird begins to settle, the tendons start to tighten.

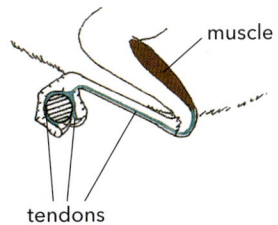

3 When the leg is fully folded, the toes are locked onto the perch and can only be unlocked when the bird stands.

WHAT DO YOU NEED TO GO BIRDING?

Birding is an entertaining and educational pastime that surprisingly requires very little equipment and is easy to get involved in. You only need a couple of items to start you off on your birding journey.

BINOCULARS

When it comes to equipment, one item reigns supreme – a pair of binoculars. Without this item, observing distant or diminutive birds becomes nearly impossible. Nowadays, the market offers a wide range of makes and models, catering to various budgets. While prices can soar into the thousands, there are plenty of affordable yet highly functional binoculars available. Spend as generously as your budget allows; it will undoubtedly prove to be a valuable investment. When selecting binoculars, consider the following key principles:

- Binoculars should feel comfortable in your hands and not be overly heavy, ensuring a steady grip.
- Optimal binoculars for birdwatching typically fall within the 8 x 25, 8 x 32, and 10 x 42-50 range. The first number denotes the magnification, meaning 8 x binoculars enlarge the bird eightfold. The second number represents the diameter of the front lens in millimetres. For example, in 8 x 35 binoculars, each front lens has a diameter of 35 mm. Larger front lens diameters offer a broader field of view and brighter images due to increased light-gathering capability. Brightness is particularly crucial when observing birds in low-light conditions, while a wider field of view aids in locating birds, especially during flight, through the binoculars. For these reasons, a 10 x 40 or 10 x 50 pair of binoculars is recommended.

Roof-prism binoculars

Barrel-type binoculars

CAMERAS

Over the years, birdwatching has evolved, and a camera has become a valuable addition to the birder's kit. With a reasonable camera you can capture images of fast-moving birds for later examination, which is useful for identifying species and fostering familiarity. Although not necessary initially, there may come a time when you might wish to invest in a scope to capture close-ups of more distant birds such as shorebirds. The guidelines for selecting a scope are much the same as for binoculars. In addition, you may also want to purchase a tripod for stability.

BOOKS AND APPS

A field guide, whether in the form of a book or a specialised birding app, is the next indispensable tool in the birder's arsenal. The primary objective of a field guide is to facilitate quick species identification through illustrations and concise descriptions of plumage and song. An app, such as *Newman's Birds* app, offers the most compact and concise identification resource for on-the-go birding. In addition to species information and illustrations, apps provide quick access to photographic images and bird calls, aiding in the identification process. For dedicated birders, a field guide typically serves as a supplementary resource to a more comprehensive bird handbook. These comprehensive references, though bulky and unwieldy for fieldwork, offer in-depth insights into bird characteristics and behaviour, making them ideal for leisurely study.

PEN AND PAPER

The final piece of equipment you should arm yourself with is a small notebook and a pencil or ballpoint pen. Cultivate the habit of making notes of the birds you have seen, particularly when you are not sure what you've spotted. A simple sketch, no matter how crude, with notes about beak shape, leg colour, habitat, etc. will prove essential when you page through your field guide that evening, trying to identify 'the one that got away' or 'the bird that isn't in Newman's book'.

JOIN A BIRD CLUB

The quickest way to learn about birds is to go into the field with helpful, more experienced birders. Bird clubs, with their weekend and day outings, provide this essential service. If there's a club near you, it's a great idea to go along. Bird clubs usually offer evening lectures by more experienced members, with interesting audiovisual content, and many produce a quarterly magazine, as well as newsletters about forthcoming club activities. To get more information on connecting with a club near you, go to **www.newmansbirds.com**

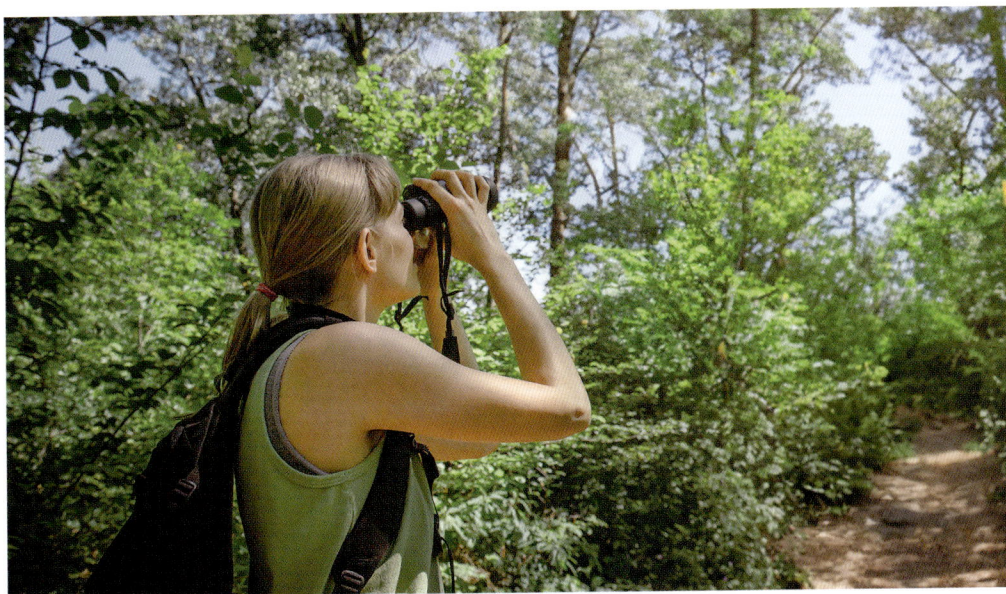

Binoculars are essential for observing birds in the distance.

Greater Double-collared Sunbird

DESCRIBING BIRDS BY COLOUR

KEY TO IDENTIFICATION

⬤	BLACK PLUMAGE	**30-49**
◑	BLACK-AND-WHITE PLUMAGE	**50-79**
⬤	GREY PLUMAGE	**80-107**
◯	WHITE PLUMAGE	**108-113**
⬤	BLUE PLUMAGE	**114-127**
⬤	RED PLUMAGE	**128-145**
⬤	ORANGE PLUMAGE	**146-155**
⬤	YELLOW PLUMAGE	**156-173**
⬤	GREEN PLUMAGE	**174-185**
⬤	PURPLE PLUMAGE	**186-191**
⬤	RUFOUS PLUMAGE	**192-213**
⬤	DARK BROWN PLUMAGE	**214-247**
⬤	LIGHT BROWN PLUMAGE	**248-273**
⬤	SPECKLED PLUMAGE	**274-283**
⬤	COLLARS AND BREAST BANDS	**284-297**

BLACK PLUMAGE

Black plumage is the result of a dark pigment called melanin, which also gives rise to brown, grey and reddish-brown coloration. Dark plumage serves a variety of functions and can benefit a bird in a number of ways.

How does black plumage serve a bird?

Camouflage: Very dark plumage can help a bird blend into its environment or into the shadows. The African Black Oystercatcher is difficult to spot when it is feeding on mussel-covered rocks, and it is almost invisible in its nest among the dried kelp at the high-water mark when incubating its eggs. For smaller birds, their dark plumage (often in the upper feathers) makes them difficult to detect in the dark interiors of dense bushes, trees and rocks.

Warning coloration: It is thought that black birds have distasteful flesh, and are therefore not sought after by predators. The black coloration is thus a signal to potential predators and could explain why black drongos can brazenly pester eagles and other large raptors, even pecking them in flight, with no repercussions.

Heat retention: Black plumage absorbs sunlight and can help birds retain heat. Verreaux's Eagle nests on the shady side of mountain cliffs during the cold winter months, but in such conditions its dark coloration limits heat loss.

Strength, durability and flight performance: Black plumage is stronger and more resistant to wear and tear than pale plumage and black feathers are often found in the primaries (wing tips or leading edges of a bird's wing). In flight, dark upperwings heat more quickly than the underwings, which is known to decrease friction and increase flight performance.

Aerial feeders, such as swifts and swallows, have little need for camouflage, but they do need their wing feathers to be strong and durable for flight. Some swifts spend over a year flying and sleeping on the wing without ever landing before they become mature enough to breed and nest on land.

Note: In the context of this book it should be understood that the word 'black' also covers birds that are dark brown, but appear black when seen from a distance.

WHITE-RUMPED SWIFT

Common in towns. Black, with white crescent shape on lower back, and forked tail. Fast flyer. **15 cm**

A: Witkruiswindswael
Z: Unonqane
Ss: Lehaqasi La Nkotosweu
Tw: Phetla Ya Mokotosweu
N: !uri|nana sōsowob
G: Weißbürzelsegler

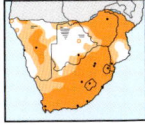

BLACK SAW-WING

Lowlands and escarpment. Black, with long, forked tail. Slow, low flight. **15 cm**

A: Swartsaagvlerkswael
Z: Inkonjanemnyama
G: Erzschwalbe

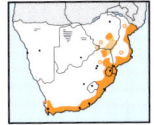

LITTLE SWIFT

Common in towns; nests under bridges. Black, with large white patch on rump visible from side, and square tail. Quite noisy 'chittering' in flight.
14 cm

A: Kleinwindswael
Z: Umakhalelilanga
Ss: Lehaqasi Le Lenyenyane
Tw: Phetla E Nnye
N: ≠khari sōsowob
H: Okandiri Kambepo
G: Haussegler

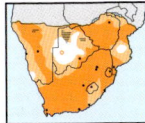

AFRICAN PALM SWIFT

Common in towns, in vicinity of palm trees. Small, slender-winged brown swift with deeply forked tail.
17 cm

A: Palmwindswael **Z:** Ijiyankomelimlotha
Ss: Lehaqasi La Palema **Tw:** Phetla Ya Mokolwane
N: !unihai sōsowob **G:** Palmensegler

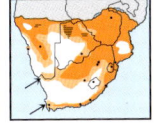

ALPINE SWIFT

Mountains. Comparatively larger swift with dark brown breast band, and white chin and belly. 22 cm

A: Witpenswindswael Z: Inhlolazulu X: Irulumente
Ss: Lehaqasi La Mpasweu Tw: Phetla Ya Mpasweu
N: !ur-!nã sõsowob G: Alpensegler

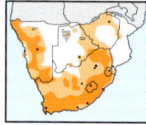

DUSKY INDIGOBIRD (br. ♂)

Bushveld. Glossy black; when breeding, whitish bill and reddish legs distinguish it from Village and Purple indigobirds. 11 cm

A: Gewone Blouvinkie Z: Umfelokazomlomomhlophe
Ss: Mohlolohadi-Lomotshweu G: Purpur-Atlaswitwe

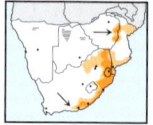

PURPLE INDIGOBIRD (br. ♂)

Bushveld. Glossy black; when breeding, whitish bill distinguishes it from Village and Dusky indigobirds. 11 cm

A: Witpootblouvinkie Z: Umfelokazonsomi
G: Weißfuß-Atlaswitwe

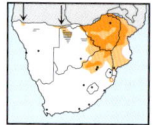

VILLAGE INDIGOBIRD (br. ♂)

Bushveld. Glossy black; when breeding, red bill and legs distinguish it from Dusky and Purple indigobirds. 11 cm

A: Staalblouvinkie Z: Umfelokazomlomobomvu
Ss: Mohlolohadi-Lomofubedu G: Rotschnabel-Atlaswitwe

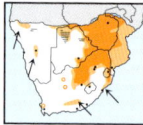

BLACK-EARED SPARROW-LARK ♂

Scrublands. Black, with rufous upperparts, and white bill. 12–13 cm

A: Swartoorlewerik
Z: Intakajolwanemnyama
G: Schwarzwangenlerche

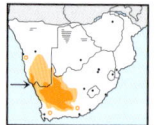

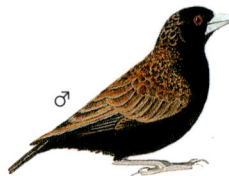

AMETHYST SUNBIRD ♂

Woodland. All black except for iridescent throat and forehead. 15 cm

A: Swartsuikerbekkie **Z:** Insusha
G: Amethyst-Glanzköpfchen

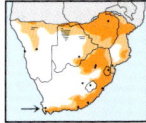

SOUTHERN BLACK TIT

Woodland. Black, with much white in wings; female has greyer underparts. 16 cm

A: Gewone Swartmees **Z:** Isicukujeje
X: Isichukujeje **G:** Mohrenmeise

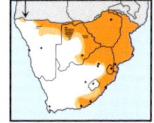

SCARLET-CHESTED SUNBIRD ♂

Woodland. Mainly black, with iridescent green on forehead and red breast (visible when bird is perched). 15 cm

A: Rooiborssuikerbekkie **Z:** Usifubabomvu
H: Otjiondaosondu **G:** Rotbrust-Glanzköpfchen

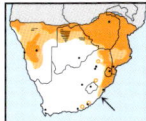

CARP'S TIT

Woodland. Like Southern Black Tit, but smaller, with more extensive white in wings. 14 cm

A: Ovamboswartmees **G:** Rüppellmeise

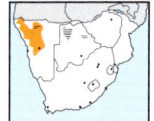

YELLOW BISHOP (br. ♂)

Marshy regions. Black, with yellow rump and shoulder; retained by non-br. **15 cm**

A: Kaapse Flap **Z:** Umambathilanga
X: Amabalengwe **Ss:** Thaha-Thekatshehla
G: Samtweber

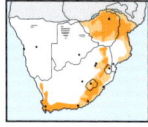

br. ♂

YELLOW-CROWNED BISHOP (br. ♂)

Wetlands and reed beds. Black, with yellow crown, nape and back, and pink legs. **12 cm**

A: Goudgeelvink **Z:** Intakanyosi **Ss:** Thaha-Tshehla
Sp: Rramakgatho **G:** Tahaweber

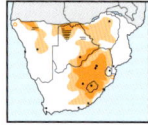

br. ♂

SOUTHERN RED BISHOP (br. ♂)

Wetlands. Red upperparts, breast and vent, and black face and underparts. **14 cm**

A: Rooivink **Z:** Ibomvana **X:** Intakomlilo
Ss: Thaha-Kgube **G:** Oryxweber

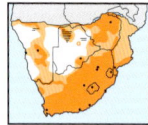

br. ♂

WHITE-WINGED WIDOWBIRD (br. ♂)

Bushveld and marshy areas. Black, with white on wings and yellow shoulder; retained by non-br. **15–19 cm**

A: Witvlerkflap
Z: Intakemaphikamhlophe
G: Spiegelwida

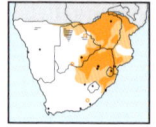

♂

FAN-TAILED WIDOWBIRD (br. ♂)

Reed beds and marshy areas. Black, with red shoulder; retained by non-br. **19 cm**

A: Kortstertflap
Z: Umangube
X: Isahomba
Ss: Molepe-Hetlafubedu
G: Stummelwida

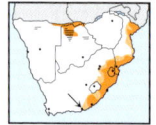

br. ♂

THICK-BILLED WEAVER ♂

Reed beds, riverine edges and valleys. Dark brown, with white spot on forehead when breeding.
18 cm

A: Dikbekwewer
Z: Usiqhophokezi
G: Weißstirnweber

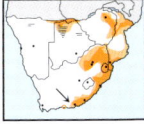

♂

RED-COLLARED WIDOWBIRD (br. ♂)

Bushveld vleis. Black, with red collar (often difficult to see unless bird is perched).
40 cm (incl. tail)

A: Rooikeelflap **Z:** Ujojo
Ss: Molepe-Lalafubedu **G:** Schildwida

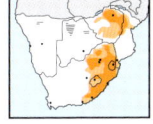

br. ♂

♀

YELLOW-MANTLED WIDOWBIRD (br. ♂)

Highveld grasslands near water. Black, with yellow shoulder and mantle; br. in summer only. 22 cm

A: Geelrugflap
G: Gelbschulterwida

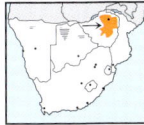

♂

LONG-TAILED WIDOWBIRD (br. ♂)

Moist grasslands and valleys. Black, with red tail and shoulder. 60 cm (incl. tail)

A: Langstertflap **Z:** Ibhaku **X:** Isakabula
Sp: Lekphaka **G:** Hahnschweifwida

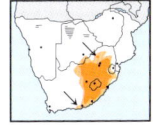

br. ♂

non-br. ♂

♀

SHAFT-TAILED WHYDAH (br. ♂)

Thornveld. Black upperparts, buffy underparts, and red bill and legs, and long tail shafts. **34 cm (incl. tail)**

A: Pylstertrooibekkie
Z: Ibhakelimsilosihlaku
G: Königswitwe

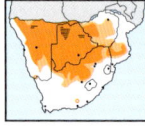

br. ♂

ANT-EATING CHAT

Well-grazed grasslands. Often perched on fence or mound. Dark brown; male darker; pale wing feathers visible in flight.
18 cm

A: Swartpiek
Z: Indlantuthwane
Ss: Thoromedi-Thokwa
G: Termitenschmätzer

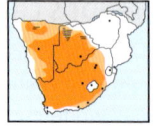

♂

LONG-TAILED PARADISE WHYDAH (br. ♂)

Acacia thornveld. Black head and upperparts, creamy buff nape and underparts, and rufous breast. **60 cm (incl. tail)**

A: Gewone Paradysvink **Z:** Ibhaku Lehlanze
G: Spitzschwanzparadieswitwe

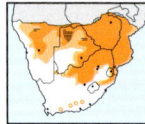

br. ♂

MOUNTAIN WHEATEAR ♂

Rocky grasslands, hills and suburbia. Male all grey, in some areas plumage varies from dark grey to even black, with white shoulder and vent; in dry areas may have white belly; wings black.
17–20 cm

A: Bergwagter
Z: Ikhwelentabeni
Ss: Kgalodi
G: Bergschmätzer

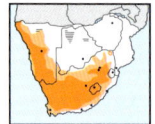

♂

ARNOT'S CHAT

Mopane woodland. Black, with white shoulders; male has white cap; female has white throat. 18 cm

A: Bontpiek **Z:** Umbexe Wezihlahla
Ss: Sethwena-Hlohotshweu **G:** Arnotschmätzer

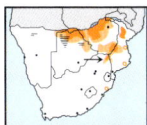

BOULDER CHAT

Rocky regions. Black, with white spots on upperwing and tail tip.
23-27 cm

A: Swartberglyster **Z:** Umbexe Wamadwala
G: Steindroßling

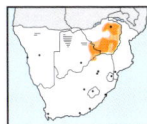

MOCKING CLIFF CHAT

Rocky regions and suburbia. Dark upperparts; female has dull red underparts but seems black; male has chestnut belly and white shoulder patches. 20-23 cm

A: Dassievoël **Z:** Isikhwelemaweni **Ss:** Sethwena-Nketsisane
Sp: Leseka **G:** Rotbauchschmätzer

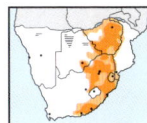

BLACK CRAKE

Inland waters. Small, dark body with long red legs and yellow bill. Walks on floating vegetation.
20-23 cm

A: Swartriethaan
Z: Isiqhanazana
Ss: Kgoholelhaka E Nthso
Sp: Kgogolelhaka Ye Ntsho
Tw: Kgogoletlhaka E Ntsho
Sh: Chinyamukutuku
N: ≠nū ≠ā-anib
G: Mohrenralle

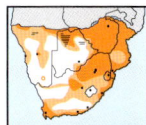

DWARF BITTERN

Wetlands. Dark grey-black upperparts and grey-streaked underparts. 25 cm

A: Dwergrietreier **Z:** Umabhumfashane
Tw: Kgapu Ya Kotswana **N:** |hai ||nowab
G: Sturms Zwergrohrdommel

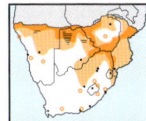

LESSER MOORHEN

Secluded inland waters. Dark body, with mostly yellow bill, and red shield and culmen. 23 cm

A: Kleinwaterhoender
Z: Inkukhumezane
Ss: Kgohometswana
Tw: Kgogonokana
N: ≠khari ‖gamanib
G: Zwergteichhuhn

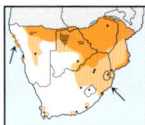

BLACK-NECKED GREBE

Saline waters and dams. Blackish-brown above with red eyes; br. ad. has golden ear coverts and flanks; non-br. ad. whitish below. 28 cm

A: Swartnekdobbertjie **Z:** Ivukelintamemnyama
Ss: Thoboloko E Molalantsho **Tw:** Senwedi Sa Molalantsho
N: ≠nū-!ao dûb **G:** Schwarzhalstaucher

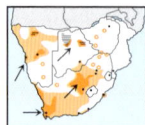

non-br.

br.

COMMON MOORHEN

Inland waters. Blackish with white flank marks, red frontal shield and bill, and yellow bill tip and legs. 30-36 cm

A: Grootwaterhoender **Z:** Inkukhayamanzi
Ss: Kgohometsi **Tw:** Kgogonoka **Sh:** Deranyoro
N: kai ‖gamanib **H:** Ohunguriva Yomewa **G:** Teichhuhn

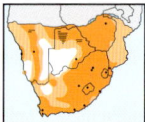

SOUTHERN BLACK FLYCATCHER

Woodland. Glossy black, with dark eyes; tail with small indentation. Quiet bird. 19-22 cm

A: Swartvlieëvanger
Z: UmMbesi
G: Drongoschnäpper

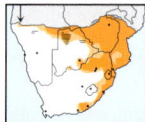

COMMON SQUARE-TAILED DRONGO

Forest and dense river fringes. Glossy black, with wine-red eyes; tail shallowly forked. Noisy.
19 cm

A: Kleinbyvanger
Z: Uhlakayiya
X: Intengwana
Ss: Thekwana

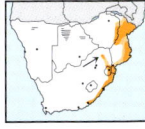

BLACK CUCKOOSHRIKE ♂

Woodlands. Glossy black, sometimes with yellow shoulder spot and orange-yellow gape; tail rounded.
22 cm

A: Swartkatakoeroe
Z: Inhlangu
X: Usasa
Ss: Rankwetsidi
G: Kuckuckswürger

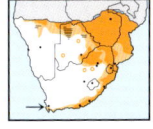

FORK-TAILED DRONGO

Broad-leaved and acacia bushveld. Glossy black, with ruby-red eyes; forked tail diagnostic. Noisy and conspicuous.
25 cm

A: Mikstertbyvanger
Z: Intengu
X: Intengu
Ss: Theko
Tw: Kuamose
Sh: Nhegure
N: güdarub
G: Trauerdrongo

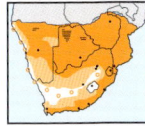

BLACK CUCKOO

Well-wooded and suburban areas. All black. Perches and calls in same tree for long periods. Diagnostic call 'I'm so SICK'.
30 cm

A: Swartkoekoek
Z: Undodosibona
Ss: Lehopoho Le Lentsho
Sh: Madhodho
N: ≠nū hōhōseb
G: Schwarzkuckuck

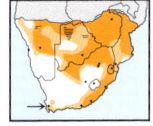

RETZ'S HELMETSHRIKE

Broad-leaved and riverine woodland. Black, with white vent and tail tips, and red eye-rings, bill and legs.
22 cm

A: Swarthelmlaksman
Z: Impevelimehlabomvu
G: Dreifarb-Brillenwürger

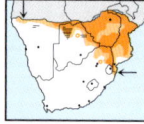

COMMON STARLING

Towns and farmlands. Green-black, with a purple sheen on upper breast and mantle. 20–22 cm

A: Europese Spreeu **Z:** Ikhwinsi LaseYurobhu
Ss: Lehodi-Papapa **G:** Star

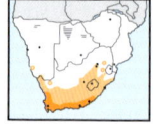

PIED STARLING

Grassveld and karoo. Blackish-brown with orange-yellow gape, and pale eyes, belly and vent. 25–27 cm

A: Witgatspreeu **Z:** Ingwangwa
X: Iqiyogiyo **Ss:** Lehodi-Phatshwa **G:** Zweifarbenstar

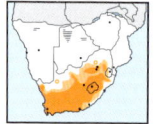

RED-BILLED BUFFALO WEAVER

Thornveld. Male darker than female; both told by red bill. 24 cm

A: Buffelwewer
Z: Usoqhawomnyama
G: Büffelweber

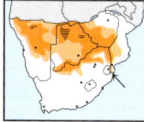

PALE-WINGED STARLING

Rocky regions. Glossy black, with white wing panels with an orange tinge, and orange eyes. Often in small flocks. 26 cm

A: Bleekvlerkspreeu **Z:** Isomelimaphikamhlophe
Ss: Lehodi-Ihlofubedu **G:** Bergstar

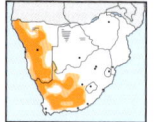

RED-WINGED STARLING

Widespread. Glossy black, with brick-red wings in flight; female has grey head and mantle. 27-28 cm

A: Rooivlerkspreeu
Z: Insomi
Ss: Letshomila
Sp: Lebutswa
Tw: Letsopi
Sh: Sviho
G: Rotschwingenstar

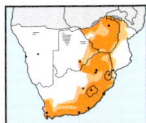

♀

♂

GREEN WOOD HOOPOE

Woodland and suburbia. Glossy green-black, with curved, red bill and long tail. Loud, cackling call. In small flocks. 30-36 cm

A: Rooibekkakelaar
Z: Inhlekabafazi
X: Umkulunga
Ss: Pekadifate E Tala
Tw: Foofoo
N: !am hai‖nūres
G: Steppenbaumhopf

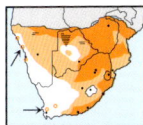

COMMON SCIMITARBILL

Woodland and thornveld. All dark; told by very curved black beak. 24-28 cm

A: Swartbekkakelaar
Z: Unosungulo
Ss: Sebodu
Sp: Kuela
Tw: Sebodu
Sh: Shokosha
N: ≠nū-am hai‖nūres
G: Sichelhopf

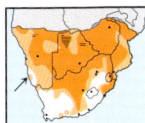

VIOLET WOOD HOOPOE

Namibian woodland. Dark violet-blue and black plumage, and red bill and legs. 40-42 cm

A: Perskakelaar
Tw: Letsheganoga
N: ≠hoa‖awa hai‖nūres
G: Damarabaumhopf

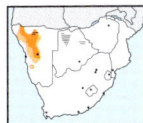

JACOBIN CUCKOO

Mixed woodland. Black upperparts and white underparts. All-black form has white in wings only. Noisy and active. 33–34 cm

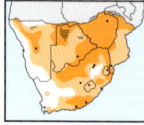

A: Bontnuwejaarsvoël
Z: Inkanku
X: Igwabalelunga
Ss: Lekeokiri La Mmetsosweu
N: |hõ hõhõseb
G: Jakobinerkuckuck

MAGPIE SHRIKE

Mixed woodland. Black, with white wing stripe; female has shorter tail.
40–50 cm

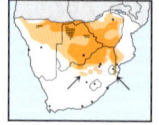

A: Langstertlaksman
Z: UmQonqotho
Sp: Motsilodi
G: Elsterwürger

GABAR GOSHAWK
(melanistic morph)

Mixed woodland. Black form uncommon. All black, with striped tail, and bright red cere and legs. Small, fast flying. 30–34 cm

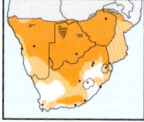

A: Kleinsingvalk
Z: Uheshomlotha
Ss: Mamphoko
N: !uri-|nana anitsēbeb
H: Oharukoze Okaapa
G: Gabarhabicht

HOUSE CROW

Commensal with humans. Introduced. Has grey mantle and breast but looks all black. 43 cm

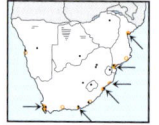

A: Huiskraai
Z: Igwababa Ledolobha
G: Glanzkrähe

CAPE CROW

Farmlands, open country, often on telephone poles. Entirely black.
48–53 cm

A: Swartkraai **Z:** Ingwababane
X: Unomyayi **Ss:** Mokgwabane
Sp: Legogobane **Tw:** Lehukubu
Ts: Xikhunguba
Nd: Ingwababane
Sh: Chikangubuya
N: ≠nūnâeb
H: Otjikwarikoko
G: Kapkrähe

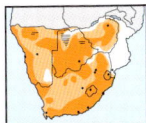

PIED CROW

Widespread. Black, with white breast and collar.
46–52 cm

A: Witborskraai
Z: Igwababa
G: Schildrabe

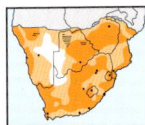

WHITE-NECKED RAVEN

Hilly regions. Black, with white patch on hind neck. Heavy bill.
50–54 cm

A: Withalskraai
Z: Iwabayi
X: Ihlungulu
Ss: Lekgwaba
Sp: Mmankgoro
Tw: Mokgomilo
G: Geierrabe

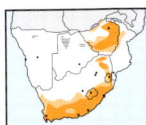

BAT HAWK

Well-wooded rivers. Dark brown with whitish eyes, legs and chin. Flies at dusk. 45 cm

A: Vlermuisvalk
Z: Umahlwthilulwanei
Ss: Fiolo Ya Mmankgane
Tw: Segodi Sa Mmamathwane
G: Fledermausaar

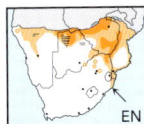

BLACK SPARROWHAWK

Well-developed and riverine woodlands; often in poplar stands near human settlements. Black, with variable white underparts; dark morph uncommon. 45–58 cm

A: Swartsperwer
Z: Uheshanomnyama
Ss: Fiolo E Ntsho
Tw: Segodi Se Sentsho
N: ≠nū ani!khāb
G: Mohrenhabicht

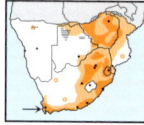

LONG-CRESTED EAGLE

Lowland, hilly regions. Brownish black. Long crest diagnostic. 53–58 cm

A: Langkuifarend
Z: Isiphungumangathi
X: Isiphunguphungu
Ss: Mokui
N: gāxū!amxadana !khās
G: Schopfadler

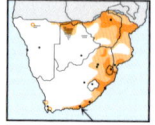

BLACK HARRIER

Farmlands and grasslands. Black, with yellow cere, eyes and legs; underwings show white when hovering. 48–53 cm

A: Witkruisvleivalk
Z: Umamhlangenomnyama
Ss: Mmankgodimohlaka E Montsho
N: ≠nū !khuwihīsabes
G: Mohrenweihe

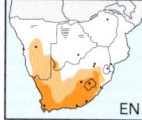

EN

CRESTED GUINEAFOWL

Lowland riverine forests and dune forests. Black, with white spots, pale beak, and black head tuft and neck. 50 cm

A: Kuifkoptarentaal
Z: Impangelejwayelekile
Ss: Kgaka Ya Motlwenya
Sh: Hangatoni
N: !amxadana |khenas
G: Kräuselhauben-Perlhuhn

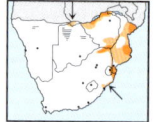

HELMETED GUINEAFOWL

Bushveld and grassland. Blue-grey with white spots, appearing black from a distance, with bluish face, and bony casque. 53–58 cm

A: Gewone Tarentaal
Z: Impangele Lehlathi
Ss: Kgaka Ya Lenaka
Nd: Intendele
Sh: Hanga
N: ||nâxa |khenas
H: Onganga
G: Helmperlhuhn

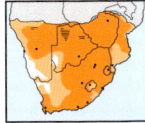

AFRICAN OYSTERCATCHER

Coastal bird on rocky shores. Red bill and legs. 51 cm

A: Swarttobie
Z: Unozila
Ss: Sejakgofu Se Sentsho
N: ≠nü döbas
G: Schwarzer Austernfischer

RED-KNOBBED COOT

Inland waters. All-black body; told by white bill and frontal shield. 43 cm

A: Bleshoender
Z: Intuntwane
X: Unonkqayi
Ss: Tshumu
G: Kammbleßhuhn

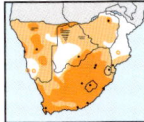

AFRICAN BLACK DUCK

Rivers. Dark brown with white-spotted upperparts, bluish wing patch, grey bill, and orange legs.
51–54 cm

A: Swarteend **Z:** Idadelimnyama **Ss:** Letata La Noka
Sp: Letata **Tw:** Sehudi Se Sentsho **Sw:** Lidada Lemfula
N: ≠nü ≠naras ombaka ondurozu **G:** Schwarzente

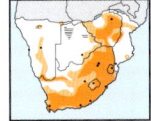

SOUTHERN POCHARD

Deep fresh water. Male dark brown with bronze sheen; female dark on upperparts only. 51 cm

A: Bruineend
Z: Isankawu
Ss: Letata La Leihlofubedu
Tw: Pidipidi Ya Leitlhohubidu
N: ǀawamû ≠naras
G: Rotaugenente

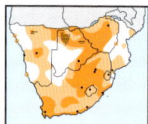

BLACK HERON

Inland waters. Differs from Slaty Egret in having yellow on feet only. Mantles its wings when feeding. 66 cm

A: Swartreier
Z: Inhlangu
Ss: Leholotsiane Le Lentsho
Tw: Sekhuko
N: ≠nū gai-!noab
G: Glockenreiher

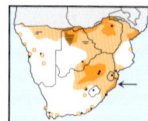

RUFOUS-BELLIED HERON

Inland waters. Appears all black but has rufous belly and wings, and yellow legs, bill and facial skin. 58 cm

A: Rooipensreier **Z:** Umacuthomnyama
Ss: Kokolofitwe Ya Mpafubedu **Sp:** Kokolofute Ya Mpahwibidu
N: ǀawa-!nā ǀgurikhoeseb **G:** Rotbauchreiher

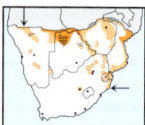

SLATY EGRET

Lagoons and backwaters. Very dark grey; told by yellow legs and feet and tawny throat. 60 cm

A: Rooikeelreier
Z: Ingeklenengilebomvu
Ss: Leholotsiane La Mmetsofubedu
N: ǀawa-dom gai-!noab
G: Braunkehlreiher

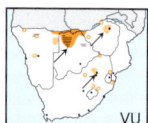

CAPE CORMORANT

Coastal waters. Dark, with yellow gular patch. Flocks fly over the sea in long, undulating lines.

64 cm

A: Trekduiker
Z: Iwonde Lasolwandle
Ss: Ntodi Ya Lebopo
Tw: Ntodi Ya Letshitshi
N: !huni-dom ≠nū-anis
G: Kapkormoran

REED CORMORANT

Inland and coastal waters. Brown-speckled wings; tail longer than in Crowned Cormorant.

60 cm

A: Rietduiker
Z: Iphishamanzi
Ss: Ntodi Ya Lehlaka
N: ≠ā ≠nū-anis
G: Riedscharbe

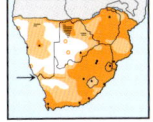

CROWNED CORMORANT

Coastal waters. Glossy black; tail shorter and crest more prominent than in Reed Cormorant. 54 cm

A: Kuifkopduiker
Z: Iwondelimqhele
Ss: Ntodi Ya Motlwenya
N: !amxadana ≠nū-anis
G: Wahlbergscharbe

BANK CORMORANT

Coastal waters. All dark; br. ad. has white rump. Roosts in small groups on islands and rocks.

75 cm

A: Bankduiker
Z: Iwondelimhlanomhlophe
Ss: Ntodi Ya Bophirimela
N: !uri-ǁā ≠nū-anis
G: Küstenscharbe

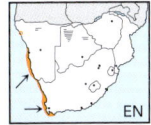

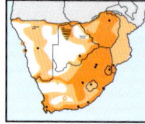

AFRICAN DARTER

Inland waters. Very dark brown crown and body; front of neck rufous in male, sandy in female.
79 cm

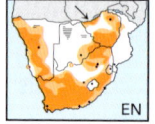

A: Slanghalsvoël
Z: Inyoninyoka
X: Ivuzi
Ss: Timeletsane
Sh: Chigwikwi
N: |ao|haros
G: Schlangenhalsvogel

VERREAUX'S EAGLE

Mountains, cliffs. Black, with white 'V' mark on the back, and yellow cere and feet.
84 cm

EN

A: Witkruisarend
Z: Ukhozolumnyama
X: Untsho
Ss: Lejapela
Tw: Ntsu
N: !âu!khās
G: Felsenadler

WHITE-BREASTED CORMORANT

Inland and coastal waters. Dark brown upperwings and tail, black-edged wing feathers and white throat and breast.
90 cm

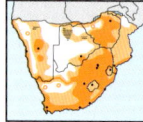

A: Witborsduiker
Z: Iwondelimhlope
X: Umxwiqa
Ss: Ntodi Ya Sefubasweu
N: !uri||khaib
G: Weißbrustkormoran

BATELEUR

Savanna bushveld, in game parks. Mostly black; told by red face and legs, short tail and rocking flight action.
55–70 cm

EN

A: Berghaan
Z: Ingqungqulu
X: Ingqanga
Ss: Petleke
Sp: Kgwadira
N: !nuwu-≠are !khās
G: Gaukler

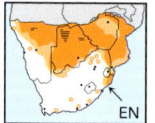

SOUTHERN GROUND HORNBILL

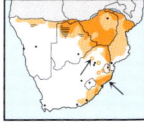

Savanna bushveld. Mostly black, with red facial and neck skin; white in wings visible in flight. 90 cm

A: Bromvoël
Z: Insigizi
X: Intsikizi
Ss: Lekgotutu
Sp: Lehututu
N: !hükököseb
G: Hornrabe

SPUR-WINGED GOOSE

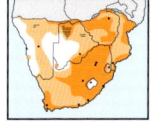

Inland waters. Blackish upperparts with green sheen, white underparts, and pink bill and legs. 102 cm

A: Wildemakou
Z: Ihhoye
X: Ihoye
Ss: Letshikgwi
Sp: Moselamotlaka
Tw: Letsukwe
N: ||khü||gawo !kharas
G: Sporngans

AFRICAN OPENBILL

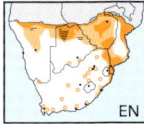

Inland waters. All dark, with tawny bill with gap between mandibles. 94 cm

A: Oopbekooievaar
Z: Isigqobhammenke
Ss: Molomobutse
Sp: Molomobutšwe
N: |ō-am!nâ oefari
G: Klaffschnabel

EN

BLACK STORK

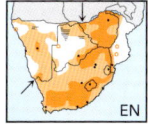

Wetlands. Glossy black, with white belly, and red bill and legs. 122 cm

A: Grootswartooievaar
Z: Unowanga
X: Unocofu
Ss: Mokorwane
Sp: Lentlopodi
N: ≠nü oefari
G: Schwarzstorch

EN

BLACK-AND-WHITE PLUMAGE

When the black and white areas of an animal's colouring are roughly the same size, the animal is said to be pied, hence the names Pied Kingfisher, Pied Crow and Pied Babbler. However, this term does not apply when either black or white is dominant, as is often the case with birds. For example, Verreaux's Eagle has little white on its back and is therefore not considered a pied eagle.

How does black-and-white plumage serve a bird?

Camouflage: Many seabirds, such as the Kelp Gull, have white underparts and blackish upperparts. This coloration is known as countershading, and acts as a sort of camouflage. While hunting for fish, a bird with countershading will not easily be detected by its prey, as its white belly will be hard to distinguish from the brightness of the water surface when seen from below. Seen from above, the bird's dark upperparts will make it hard to detect against the dark sea.

MELANISTIC BIRDS

While there are many black bird species, individual birds with abnormally black or dark brown plumage for their species are occasionally encountered. This condition is known as melanism, and it can manifest as partially or entirely blackish plumage. This phenomenon occurs in a range of species.

There are two main causes for melanism. First, an excess of a black or brown feather pigment called melanin can cause the loss of normal feather colouring. When this happens, the bird's usual feather colouring is darkened and may completely mask normal plumage patterns. Second, it can be inherited from parents who have the genetic makeup to be a dark morph.

What is a dark morph? Species that commonly exhibit melanistic tendencies are referred to as having a dark morph within the species. **Dark morphs** are common in about 3.5% of all bird species. In hawk species alone, such as the **Gabar Goshawk** and **Black Sparrowhawk**, and other raptors, such as **Wahlberg's Eagle**, dark morphs constitute about 25% of the population.

BRONZE MANNIKIN

Grass and scrub. Black head and breast, white underparts and dull brown upperparts. 9 cm

A: Gewone Fret
Z: Amadojeyanajwayelekile
X: Ingxenge
Sp: Sejamoroko
Sh: Zadzsaga
G: Kleinelsterchen

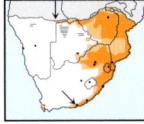

DUSKY SUNBIRD ♂

Dry woodland and scrub. Upperparts and breast black with coppery iridescence; belly white. 10–12 cm

A: Namakwasuikerbekkie
Z: Incwincwemthuthu
G: Rußnektarvogel

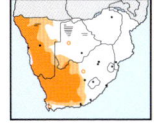

RED-BACKED MANNIKIN

Bush and seeding grasses. Black head and breast, white underparts and rufous upperparts. 10 cm

A: Rooirugfret
Z: Amadojeyanabomvu
G: Glanzelsterchen

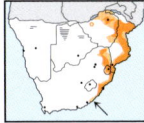

RED-FRONTED TINKERBIRD

Woodland. Black-and-white upperparts, red forehead and pale yellow underparts. 10.5 cm

A: Rooiblestinker
Z: Unkovuka
X: Unogandilanga
Ss: Modisatsatsi Wa Phatlafubedu
Sp: Tetengwa Ya Phatlahwibidu
G: Feuerstirn-Bartvogel

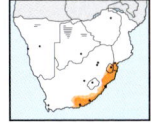

YELLOW-FRONTED TINKERBIRD

Woodland. Black-and-white upperparts, yellow forehead and pale yellow underparts.
10.5 cm

A: Geelblestinker
Z: Unkovuka WaseNyakatho
Ss: Modisatsatsi Wa Phatslasehla
Sp: Tetengwa Ya Phatslasehla
Tw: Mothudi
Sh: Chivangazuva
G: Gelbstirn-Bartvogel

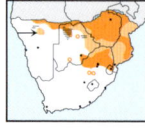

GREEN TWINSPOT

Forest fringes. Green upperparts and white-spotted black underparts.
10 cm

A: Groenkolpensie **Z:** Intiyaneluhlaza
G: Grüner Tropfenastrild

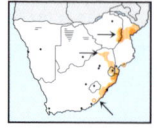

PINK-THROATED TWINSPOT ♂

Dense scrub. Pink face, breast and rump with cinnamon wings and back, with white-spotted black belly. 12 cm

A: Rooskeelkolpensie **Z:** Umagumejana **G:** Perlastrild

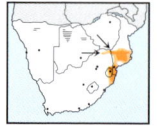

PIN-TAILED WHYDAH (br. ♂)

Bush and suburbia. Small pied bird with red beak and very long tail.
11–12 cm (br. male 34 cm)

A: Koningrooibekkie **Z:** Uhlekwane
G: Dominikanerwitwe

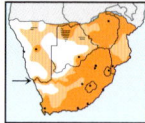

br. ♂

RED-THROATED TWINSPOT ♂

Dense bush. Cinnamon wings and back, with white-spotted black belly; male with red face, breast and rump 12.5 cm

A: Rooikeelkolpensie **Z:** Umagumejanobomvu
G: Rotkehl-Tropfenastrild

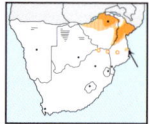

SCALY-FEATHERED WEAVER

Thornveld. Pale brown with black-and-white scaling on wing feathers.
11 cm

A: Baardmannetjie
Z: Usontshetshana
G: Schnurrbärtchen

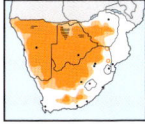

BLACK-EARED SEEDEATER

Woodland. Black mask, dark grey upperparts, with streaking on head.
13–14 cm

A: Swartoorkanarie
G: Schwarzwangengirlitz

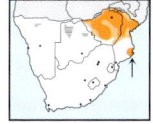

SOCIABLE WEAVER

Dry acacia woodland. Scaled pale grey-brown above with pale brown cap, black lores and chin, and white underparts. 14 cm

A: Versamelvoël
Z: Unosidlekekazi
G: Siedelweber

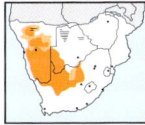

CAPE SPARROW ♂

Suburbia and farmlands. Black-and-white head and breast, and chestnut mantle.
15 cm

A: Gewone Mossie
Z: Undlunkulu
X: Unondlwane
Ss: Serobele-Hlohophatshwa
Sp: Lemphorokgohlo La Kapa
Ve: Malegeni
Sw: Njolwane
H: Oyatuhere RwaKapa
G: Kapsperling

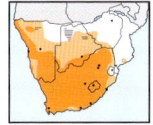

CHESTNUT-BACKED SPARROW-LARK ♂

Short grassland. Black head and body with white ear-patch and bill. 12–13 cm

A: Rooiruglewerik
Z: Intakajolwane
Ss: Mmadiberwane-Nkatakgunong
G: Weißwangenlerche

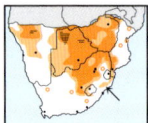

♂

AFRICAN STONECHAT

Vleis. Mainly black upperparts, white rump and half-collar and rufous breast. 14 cm

A: Gewone Bontrokkie
Z: Isichegu
X: Inchaphe
Ss: Tlhatsinyane
Sp: Thisa
Sw: Indayi
Sh: Mujesi
G: Schwarzkehlchen

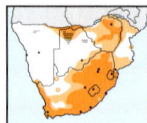

♀

♂

GREY-BACKED SPARROW-LARK ♂

Scrublands and desert. Black head and underparts, white-edged feathers, and white ear-patch, bill and legs. 12–13 cm

A: Grysruglewerik
Z: Intakajolwane Yasehlane
Ss: Mmadiberwane-Nkataputswa
G: Nonnenlerche

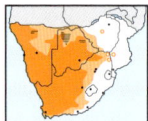

♂

PALE BATIS

Miombo woodland. Black and white with grey cap and yellow eyes; female with pale rufous breast band. 10 cm

A: Mosambiekbosbontrokkie
G: Sansibarschnäpper

♀

♂

PRIRIT BATIS

Thornveld. Black and white with grey cap and yellow eyes; female with pale buff throat and breast. **12 cm**

A: Priritbosbontrokkie
Z: Incwaba YaseNtshonalanga
Ss: Swamahlaku-Sa-Bophirima
G: Priritschnäpper

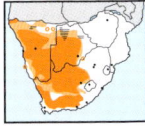

♀

♂

ASHY TIT

Thornveld. Black and white, with grey mantle and body. **14 cm**

A: Akasiagrysmees **Z:** Unongilemnyama WaseNyakatho
Ss: Seteatea-Sa-Bophirima **G:** Aschenmeise

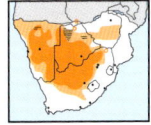

CHINSPOT BATIS

Woodland. Black and white with grey cap and yellow eyes; female with rufous breast and chin-spot. **12-13 cm**

A: Witliesbosbontrokkie **Z:** Incwaba **X:** Unondyola
Ss: Swamahlaku-Sa-Bokone **G:** Weißflankenschnäpper

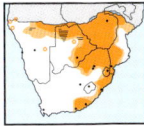

♀

♂

CARP'S TIT

Woodland. Small black bird with much white in wings. **14 cm**

A: Ovamboswartmees **G:** Rüppellmeise

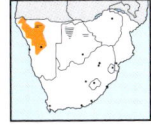

CAPE BATIS

Forest fringes. Black head with yellow eyes and red eye-rings; male has black chest; female has rufous throat and breast band and white underparts. **12-13 cm**

A: Kaapse Bosbontrokkie **Z:** Udokotela
Ss: Swamahlaku-Sa-Kapa **G:** Kapschnäpper

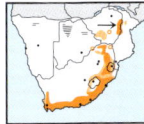

♀

♂

MIOMBO TIT

Miombo woodland. Black-and-white bird with grey mantle. **14 cm**

A: Miombogrysmees **G:** Miombomeise

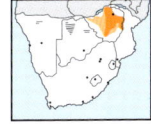

GREY TIT

Karoo scrub, rocky hills and gorges. Grey-brown and black with tawny appearance and short tail. 15 cm

A: Piet-tjou-tjou-grysmees
Z: Unongilemnyama WaseNingizimu
G: Rotbauchmeise

SOUTHERN BLACK TIT

Woodland. Small black bird with white-edged wings. 16 cm

A: Gewone Swartmees **Z:** Isicukujeje
X: Isichukujeje **G:** Mohrenmeise

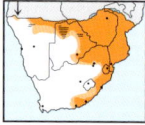

BRUBRU

Woodland. Black-and-white wingbar, rufous flanks and white underparts; female has brown cap. 15 cm

A: Bontroklaksman **Z:** Usacingo **G:** Brubru

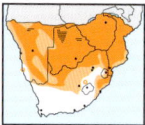

CINNAMON-BREASTED BUNTING

Rocky koppies. Cinnamon-brown with black-and-white streaked head (blacker in male). 13-14 cm

A: Klipstreepkoppie **Z:** Usokhandamidwa Wamatshe
X: Undenjenje **Ss:** Motweditwedi **Tw:** Kwabebe **Ts:** Vontiyo
Sh: Mvemvere **G:** Bergammer

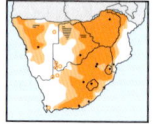

CAPE BUNTING

Various arid habitats. Black-and-white streaked head, rufous upperparts and grey-brown-washed underparts. 16 cm

A: Rooivlerkstreepkoppie **Z:** Usokhandamidwonsundu
Ss: Mmaborokwane-Nyaopedi **G:** Kapammer

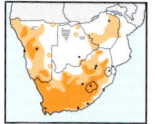

GOLDEN-BREASTED BUNTING

Woodland. Black-and-white streaked head, brown mantle, white shoulder patch, yellow breast and white belly. 16 cm

A: Rooirugstreepkoppie **Z:** Usokhandamidwombalabala **X:** Intsasa
Ss: Mmaborokwane-Petatshehla **G:** Gelbbauchammer

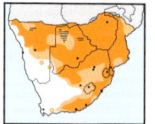

BLACK-HEADED CANARY ♂

Dry scrublands. Black head, breast and belly, and rufous upperparts.
15 cm

A: Swartkopkanarie
Z: Umbhalanokhandelimnyama
Ss: Tswere-Hlohontsho
G: Alariogirlitz

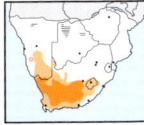

ARNOT'S CHAT

Mopane woodland. Black with white shoulders; male has white cap; female has white throat.
18 cm

A: Bontpiek
Z: Umbexe Wezihlahla
Ss: Sethwena-Hlohotshweu
G: Arnotschmätzer

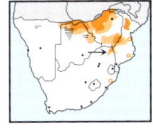

BUFF-STREAKED CHAT ♂

Rocky grassland. Striking black and pale buff plumage; lively, demonstrative behaviour. 15-17 cm

A: Bergklipwagter **Z:** Inkolotsheni
Ss: Sethwena-Majweng
Sp: Tantabe
D: Fahlschulterschmätzer

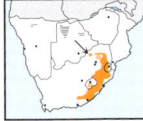

FAIRY FLYCATCHER

Dry shrubby areas. Grey cap and upper body, black-and-white mask and wings, black tail and pinkish lower breast.
12 cm

A: Feevlieëvanger **Z:** Uqholompunga
G: Livingstones Rotschwanzschnäpper

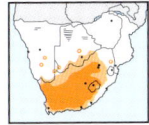

BLUE-MANTLED CRESTED FLYCATCHER ♂

Forest fringes. Crested head, dark upperparts, white wing-bar and underparts; male has black throat and breast; female has finely spotted breast. 17–18 cm

A: Bloukuifvlieëvanger
Z: Uqholwane **X:** Igotyi
G: Blaumantel-Schopfschnäpper

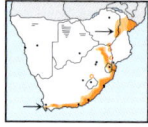

♂

LITTLE SWIFT

Common in towns; nests under bridges. Black, with large white patch on rump visible from side; square tail. Quite noisy 'chittering' in flight. 14 cm

A: Kleinwindswael
Z: Umakhalelilanga
Ss: Lehaqasi Le Lenyenyane
Tw: Phetla E Nnye
N: ≠khari sōsowob
H: Okandiri Kambepo
G: Haussegler

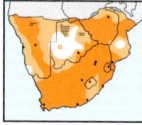

WHITE-RUMPED SWIFT

Common in towns. Black, with white crescent shape on lower back, and forked tail. Fast flyer. 15 cm

A: Witkruiswindswael **Z:** Unonqane
Ss: Lehaqasi La Nkotosweu **Tw:** Phetla Ya Mokotosweu
N: !uri|nana sōsowob **G:** Weißbürzelsegler

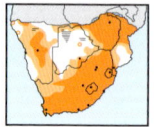

ALPINE SWIFT

Mountains. Dark brown head and breast band, and white chin and belly. 22 cm

A: Witpenswindswael **Z:** Inhlolazulu **X:** Irulumente
Ss: Lehaqasi La Mpasweu **Tw:** Phetla Ya Mpasweu
N: !ur-!nä sōsowob **G:** Alpensegler

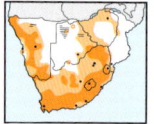

BLACK SAW-WING

Lowlands and escarpment. Black with long, forked tail; NE race has white underwing coverts. Slow, low flight. 15 cm

A: Swartsaagvlerkswael **Z:** Inkonjanemnyama
G: Sundevalls Sägeflügelschwalbe

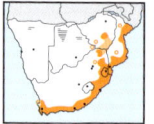

WHITE-EARED BARBET

Lowland tree canopies. Dark brown, but appears black and white, with black bill and legs. **17 cm**

A: Witoorhoutkapper **Z:** Intunjana
Ss: Mankotlo Wa Tsebesweu
Tw: Mogorosi Wa Tsebesweu
G: Weißohr-Bartvogel

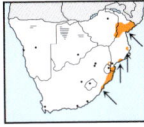

BLACK-BACKED PUFFBACK

Woodland. Pied with red eyes. Displaying male puffs out white back. **18 cm**

A: Sneeubal
Z: Isicivo
X: Unomaswana
Ss: Tshemedi-Hlahlankata
G: Schneeballwürger

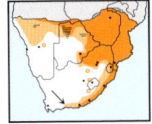

ACACIA PIED BARBET

Woodland. Black upperparts with yellow markings, red forehead, black throat and white underparts.
17–18 cm

A: Bonthoutkapper
Z: Unomunga
Ss: Serokolo
Sp: Kokonya
Tw: Tlholabaeng
Ts: Xitsemahangoni
N: |hõ kurib toas
H: Ombonde
G: Rotstirn-Bartvogel

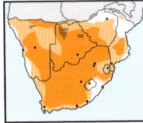

BLACK-THROATED WATTLE-EYE

Riverine and coastal thickets. Red eye-wattle, black upperparts and white underparts; female has all-black breast; male has narrow black breast band.
18 cm

A: Beloogbosbontrokkie
Z: Umashiyabomvu
G: Schwarzkehl-Lappenschnäpper

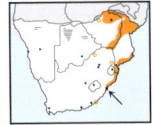

CAPPED WHEATEAR

Open veld. Pied terrestrial bird with rufous upperparts and flanks.
18 cm

A: Hoëveldskaapwagter
Z: Uqolomhlophe
G: Erdschmätzer

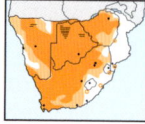

CAPE WAGTAIL

Wetlands and suburbia. Greyish-brown with white throat and black chest band. 18 cm

A: Gewone Kwikkie
Z: Umncishu
Ss: Motjodi-Thokwana
G: Kapstelze

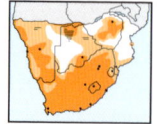

MOUNTAIN WAGTAIL

Fast-flowing forest streams. Grey and white with black chest band.
19-20 cm

A: Bergkwikkie
Z: UmVemventabe
G: Langschwanzstelze

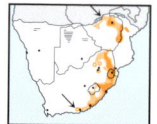

MOUNTAIN WHEATEAR

Rocky koppies, dry gullies. Black with whitish cap, white vent and shoulders.
17-20 cm

A: Bergwagter
Z: Ikhwelentabeni
Ss: Kgalodi
G: Bergschmätzer

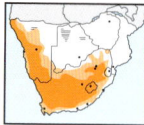

♂

AFRICAN PIED WAGTAIL

Lowland rivers. Small pied bird with bobbing tail.
20 cm

A: Bontkwikkie
Z: UmVemvolunga
Ss: Motjodi-Phatshwa
Sp: Moselakatane
Sh: Kamujana
G: Witwenstelze

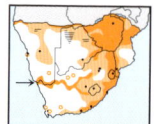

STRIPED KINGFISHER

Woodland. Black and white with blue on back, tail and wings, and red lower mandible and feet. 18–19 cm

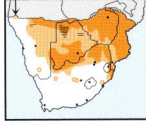

A: Gestreepte Visvanger
Z: Unongozolwane
Ss: Seinodi Sa Metjhato
Tw: Seinwedi Sa Meeledi
N: daoxa ǁaudīb
G: Streifenliest

FISCAL FLYCATCHER

Woodland. Male black and white; female brown and white. 20 cm

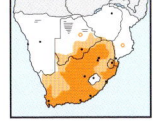

A: Fiskaalvlieëvanger **Z:** Isaqola **X:** Icola
Ss: Kapantsi-Patshwa **G:** Würgerschnäpper

SANDERLING

Coast and wetlands. Very white appearance with dark black shoulder patch. 19 cm

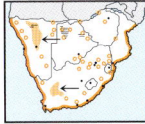

A: Drietoonstrandloper **Z:** Umaphithizela
Ss: Seyalelebopo Sa Maotoraro **N:** !nona-≠aiǀkhunu huri-am!gûb
G: Sanderling

br.   non-br.

SOUTHERN FISCAL ♂

Mixed bushveld and suburbia. Completely pied, with stout hooked beak. 23 cm

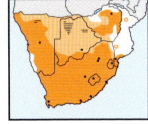

A: Fiskaallaksman
Z: Iqola
X: Inxanxadi
Ss: Tshemedi-Phatshwa
Sp: Tšokatšokane
Tw: Setomelamitlwa
Ve: Dzhuga
Sw: Lilunga
Nd: Ilunga
Sh: Korera
G: Fiskalwürger

♂

WHITE-TAILED SHRIKE

Arid woodland. Black and white with grey mantle and flanks, and yellow eyes. 15 cm

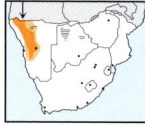

A: Kortstertlaksman
G: Drosselwürger

WHITE-CRESTED HELMETSHRIKE

Bushveld. Pied with grey crown, and orange-yellow eye-wattles and legs. 22 cm

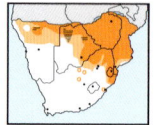

A: Withelmlaksman
Z: Abayeni
G: Brillenwürger

LESSER GREY SHRIKE

Bushveld. Black and grey upperparts, white underparts, and stout hooked beak. 20–22 cm

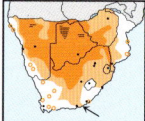

A: Gryslaksman
Z: Unolunga
Ss: Tshemedi-Thokwa
G: Schwarzstirnwürger

SOUTHERN WHITE-CROWNED SHRIKE

Woodland. Dark upperparts, lores and ear coverts, white crown and pale underparts. 23–25 cm

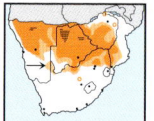

A: Kremetartlaksman
Z: Unomqhelomhlophe
Sp: Leagakametlwa
Ts: Ghengele
G: Weißscheitelwürger

COMMON MYNA

Towns. Brown bird with black head, mantle and breast, black-and-white wings and white vent.
25 cm

A: Indiese Spreeu
Z: Usothathizwe
Ss: Lehodi-Tlabotjha
G: Hirtenmaina

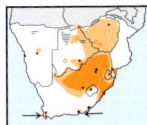

TROPICAL BOUBOU

Woodland. Black upperparts with white wingbar, cinnamon-washed underparts.
21 cm

A: Tropiese Waterfiskaal
Z: Ibhobhoni Lethafa

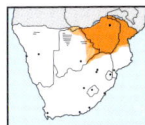

SWAMP BOUBOU

Riverine woodland. Black upperparts with white wingbar, white underparts.
22–23 cm

A: Moeraswaterfiskaal **G:** Zweifarbenwürger

SOUTHERN PIED BABBLER

Woodland. White bird with black wings and tail, and orange eyes. 26 cm

A: Witkatlagter
Z: Ihlekehlelimhlophe
H: Onḑera Otjiapa
G: Südlicher Rattenschwätzer

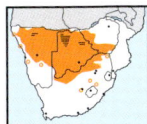

SOUTHERN BOUBOU

Woodland. Black upperparts with white wingbar, white throat, cinnamon belly and vent. 23 cm

A: Suidelike Waterfiskaal **Z:** Ibhoboni
X: Igqubusha **Ss:** Sehweletsane **Sp:** Malobe **Ts:** Xighigwa
Sh: Chinhanga **G:** Flötenwürger

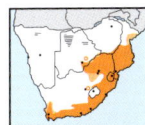

PIED STARLING

Karoo and grasslands. Blackish with white under-belly and vent, whitish eyes and orange gape.
25–27 cm

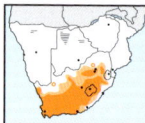

A: Witgatspreeu
Z: Ingwangwa
X: Iqiyogiyo
Ss: Lehodi-Phatshwa
G: Zweifarbenstar

PIED KINGFISHER

Waterbodies. Pied bird with stout black bill. Hovers over water before plunging.
28–29 cm

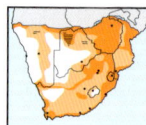

A: Bontvisvanger **Z:** Ihlabahlabane
Ss: Seinodi Se Setjhekeho
Sp: Seinodi Se Sethomo
Tw: Mmatlhapi Yo Monala
Ts: N'warikwenyana
N: |hō ||audīb
H: Ongambura Mahundju Ombonde
G: Graufischer

NAMAQUA DOVE ♂

Farmlands. Light brown above with purple wing spots, black breast, whitish underparts and maroon-red legs. 27 cm

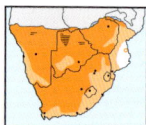

A: Namakwaduifie
Z: Unkombose
X: Isavukazana
Ss: Mokgorwane
Sp: Mmankwetla
Tw: Mokgwarinyane
Ts: Xivhambalana Xa Ncila
Sh: Dzembe
N: flōb
G: Kaptäubchen

BLACK-WINGED KITE

Grasslands. Grey upperparts, black shoulder patches and wing tips, and white underparts. 30 cm

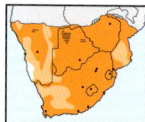

A: Blouvalk **Z:** Udemezane
X: Isitshisane **Ss:** Segootsane
Tw: Segootsane **Ts:** Nwarikapanyana
H: Orukoze Rovivava Ovizorondu
G: Gleitaar

BLACKSMITH LAPWING

Wetlands and open grass. Black and white with grey wings, and black bill and legs. 30 cm

A: Bontkiewiet **Z:** Indudumela **Ss:** Mootlatshepe
Sp: Kokolofute **Tw:** Lethulatshipi **N:** ||gī||gīb
H: Orukungwini Oruzoronou **G:** Schmiedekiebitz

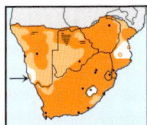

LONG-TOED LAPWING

Marshes and flooded areas. Black-and-white head and breast, white wings in flight, and red bill and legs. 30 cm

A: Witvlerkkiewiet **Z:** Ititihoye Lamazibu
Tw: Lerrane La Dikubu **G:** Langzehenkiebitz

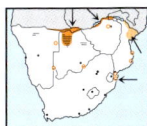

WHITE-CROWNED LAPWING

Sandbanks. Grey head, white crown and underparts, black-and-white wings, and yellow bill, wattles and legs. 30 cm

A: Witkopkiewiet **Z:** Ititihoyelimqhelomhlophe
Sp: Thapšane Ya Lerethetelele **Tw:** Lerrane La Lebodulelele
G: Langspornkiebitz

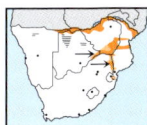

GREY PLOVER (non-br.)

Tidal flats. Mottled upperparts, white forehead and eyebrows, black 'armpits' in flight. 30 cm

A: Grysstrandkiewiet
Z: Umakhwaphamnyama
G: Kiebitzregenpfeifer

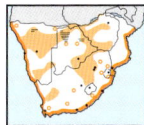

non-br.

BLACK-WINGED STILT

Inland waters. Black-and-white wader with long, straight bill and long, red legs. 38 cm

A: Rooipootelsie
Z: Uduku
Ss: Mmamenotwana
Tw: Mmotlanakane
N: gāxü|nüb
G: Stelzenläufer

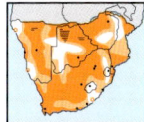

PIED AVOCET

Coastal and inland waters. Black-and-white wader with distinctive long, upturned bill and long, white legs.
43 cm

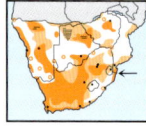

A: Bontelsie
Z: Usipheshula
Ss: Motume
Sp: Motume
Tw: Motume
N: ≠om‖nao-ams
G: Säbelschnäbler

AFRICAN SKIMMER

Inland waters. Dark upperparts, white under-parts, large red bill and short red legs. Skims water, bill immersed. 38 cm

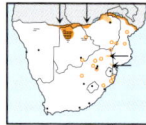

A: Waterploeër
Z: Unokhukhula
Ss: Selemametsi Sa Afrika
Sh: Chiururo
G: Afrikascherenschnabel

WHISKERED TERN

Inland waters. Br. bird grey with black cap; non-br. bird pale grey above, with white underparts and a black line behind the eye. 23 cm

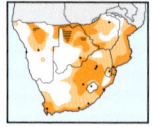

A: Witbaardsterretjie **Z:** Umachibini **Ss:** Lepheulane La Ditedusweu **N:** !uri-‖hō-am ‖au!khōb **G:** Weißbart-Seeschwalbe

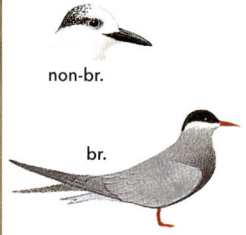

non-br.

br.

WHITE-WINGED TERN (non-br.)

Inland waters. Grey upperparts, black speckles on crown, white underparts, and a black spot behind the eye. 23 cm

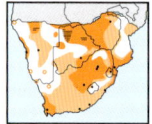

A: Witvlerksterretjie **Z:** Unochibi **Ss:** Lepheulane La Lepheosweu **Tw:** Lepheulane La Lefukasweu **N:** !uri-‖gawo ‖au!khōb **G:** Weißflügel-Seeschwalbe

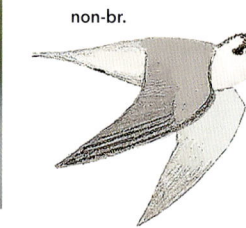

non-br.

LITTLE TERN (non-br.)

Coastal shores. Grey upperparts, mottled black cap, white forehead, black legs and bill. 22–24 cm

A: Kleinsterretjie
Z: Unonklilwane

non-br.

DAMARA TERN

Coastal shores. Grey upperparts, white underparts, and black cap, legs and long, slender bill.
21–23 cm

A: Damarasterretjie
Z: Unonklilwane WakwelaBathwa
G: Damaraseeschwalbe

ANTARCTIC TERN (non-br.)

Coastal shores. Grey upperparts, white underparts, black cap, and dark red bill. 34–40 cm

A: Grysborssterretjie **Z:** Insukakude Yeqhwa
G: Gabelschwanz-Seeschwalbe

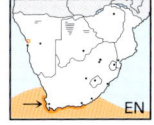

non-br.

COMMON TERN (non.br)

Coastal shores. Grey upper-parts, white underparts, black cap and dark red bill.
35–38 cm

A: Gewone Sterretjie **Z:** Unontenteza
Ss: Lepheulane La Hlapi **N:** swawel ||au!khōb
G: Flußseeschwalbe

non-br.

SANDWICH TERN

Coastal shores. White with pale grey upperparts, black cap, and long, slender yellow-tipped black bill.
40 cm

A: Grootsterretjie **Z:** Unonkliyo **Ss:** Lepheulane Le Leholo
N: kai ||au!khōb **G:** Brandseeschwalbe

br.

non-br.

JACOBIN CUCKOO

Woodland. Pied form has black upperparts, white underparts and crested head. 33–34 cm

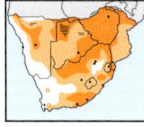

A: Bontnuwejaarsvoël **Z:** Inkanku **X:** Igwabalelunga
Ss: Lekeokiri La Mmetsosweu **Tw:** Phetlhamedupe La Mometso
Ts: Nkata Mangovo **H:** Ondera Yomburombe **G:** Jakobinerkuckuck

LEVAILLANT'S CUCKOO

Woodland. Completely pied with streaked breast and crested head. 38–40 cm

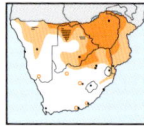

A: Gestreepte Nuwejaarsvoël **Z:** Inknkemidwa
Ss: Lekeokiri La Mmetsometjhato
Tw: Phetlhamedupe Ya Mometso
H: Ondera Yomburombe Yotjungora **G:** Kapkuckuck

GREAT SPOTTED CUCKOO

Woodland. White-spotted black upperparts, pale underparts, and grey crested head. 38–40 cm

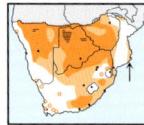

A: Gevlekte Koekoek **Z:** Unozalashiyomabala
Ss: Lekeokiri La Mmetsosehla **Tw:** Phetlhamedupe La Mometsosetlha
Ts: Hunyi **N:** kai höhöseb **G:** Häherkuckuck

MAGPIE SHRIKE

Woodland. Black with bold white wingbar and long tail. 40–50 cm

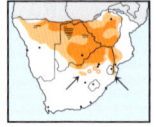

A: Langstertlaksman
Z: UmQonqotho
Sp: Motsilodi
Tw: Motsulodi
Ts: Ncilongi
G: Elsterwürger

GIANT KINGFISHER

Inland waters. Black and white with rufous breast (male) or belly (female), and large black bill. 43–46 cm

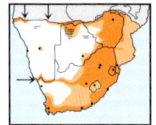

A: Reusevisvanger
Z: Isivuba
X: Uxomoyi
Ss: Seinodi Se Seholo
Tw: Mmatlhapi Se Mogolo
Ts: N'wancakini
G: Riesenfischer

SOUTHERN RED-BILLED HORNBILL

Savanna. Black and white with large, bright red bill. 42–50 cm

A: Rooibekneushoringvoël
Z: Umkholwane
Ss: Korwe Ya Molomofubedu
Tw: Korwe Ya Molomohubidu
Ts: Manon'wana
G: Mopanetoko

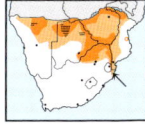

SOUTHERN YELLOW-BILLED HORNBILL

Mixed savanna. Black-and-white bird with large yellow bill. 48–60 cm

A: Geelbekneushoringvoël
Z: Uzazu
Ss: Korwe Ya Molomosehla
Tw: Mokgothopitsi
Nd: Ukoro
H: Etoko Rotjinjotjingara
G: Rotringtoko

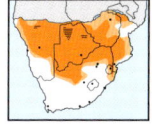

AFRICAN GREY HORNBILL

Thornveld. Dark grey bill and upperparts, mottled brown wings, white underparts, distinctive eyebrow stripe, and cream patch on bill. Most vocal of the hornbills. 43–48 cm

A: Grysneushoringvoël
Z: Umkholwanomlotha
Ss: Korwe Ye Putswa
Tw: Korwemodimo
Ts: Manteveni
H: Etoko Evahe
G: Grautoko

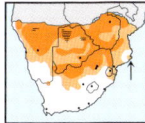

CROWNED HORNBILL

Riverine forest. Blackish upperparts, white underparts, and large red bill with yellow base. 50–57 cm

A: Gekroonde Neushoringvoël
Z: UmKhololwane
X: Umkholwane
Sp: Kgoropo Ya Kgare
Ts: Nkorhonyarhi
Sh: Woto
G: Kronentoko

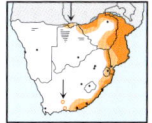

TRUMPETER HORNBILL

Riverine forest. Large pied hornbill with huge bill and casque. 58–65 cm

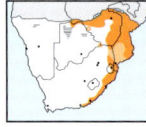

A: Gewone Boskraai
Z: Imemela
X: Ilithwa
Sp: Kgoropo Ya Thamahwibidu
Ts: Nkorhondlopfu
Sh: Gakamira
G: Trompeter-Hornvogel

SOUTHERN CRESTED GUINEAFOWL

Lowland riverine forests and dune forests. Black with white spots, black tufted head and neck, and pale beak. 50 cm

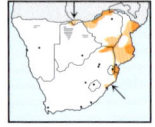

A: Kuifkoptarentaal
Z: Impangelejwayelekile
Tw: Kgaka Ya Setlopo
Ts: Mangoko
Sh: Hangatoni
G: Sambesi-Haubenperlhuhn

PIED CROW

Towns and human settlements. Black, with white breast and collar. 46–52 cm

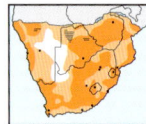

A: Witborskraai
Z: Igwababa
X: Igwangwa
Ss: Mohakajane
Sp: Legokobu
Tw: Mohoghobu
Ts: Qigwana
Ve: Tshihungu-hurwa
Sh: Gunguwo
H: Otjikuara
G: Schildrabe

HELMETED GUINEAFOWL

Grasslands and bush. White-spotted dark body, blue neck, red helmet, and horn-coloured casque and bill. 53–58 cm

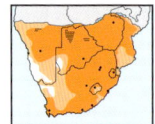

A: Gewone Tarentaal
Z: Impangele Lehlathi
Ss: Kgaka Ya Lenaka
Ts: Mhangela
Sh: Hanga
N: ||nâxa |khenas
H: Onganga
G: Helmperlhuhn

RED-CRESTED KORHAAN ♂

Woodland. Brown upperparts with cream chevrons, and black belly with white border; crest visible only during courtship.
53 cm

A: Boskorhaan
Z: UmNgqithi
Sp: Kgwarakgwara
Tw: Khoba
H: Etuva
G: Rotschopftrappe

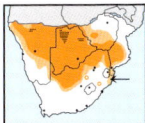

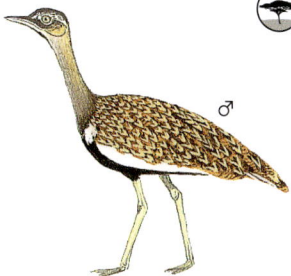

NORTHERN BLACK KORHAAN ♂

Karoo and savanna scrub. Black with white patches, buffy barring on upperparts, red bill and bright yellow legs.
53 cm

A: Witvlerkkorhaan
Z: Iseme Lethafa
Ss: Tlatlawe Ya Leboya
Tw: Tlatlawe Ya Bokone
N: ||haragas
H: Etatewe
G: Weißflügeltrappe

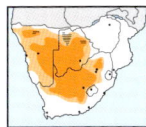

SOUTHERN BLACK KORHAAN ♂

Karoo renosterveld. Black with white patches, buffy barring on upperparts, red bill and bright yellow legs. 53 cm

A: Swartvlerkkorhaan
Z: Iseme LaseKapa
X: Ikhalukhalu
Ss: Tlatlawe Ya Borwa
G: Gackeltrappe

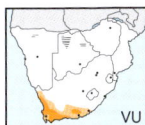

BLACK-BELLIED BUSTARD ♂

Grasslands. Tawny upperparts and neck with black markings, black-and-white head marking, black belly and pale yellow legs.
58–65 cm

A: Langbeenkorhaan
Z: Ufumba
Ss: Lekakarane La Mpantsho
Tw: Mokgweba
Ts: Xicololwa Leyi Kulu
Sh: Gunja
G: Schwarzbauchtrappe

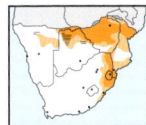

AUGUR BUZZARD

Wooded hills. Dark brown upperparts, white underparts and chestnut tail.
44–53 cm

A: Witborsjakkalsvoël
Sp: Segodi
Tw: Ntswana Ya Sehubasweu
Sh: Nyamudzura
N: !uri-ǀgã anitsēbeb
G: Augurbussard

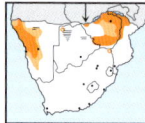

OSPREY

Inland waters and coastal lagoons. Dark upperparts and face mask, white underparts and legs, long wings. 55–63 cm

A: Visvalk
Z: Inkwazana
Ss: Phakwehlapi
Sp: Sepekwahlapi
Tw: Phakwetlhapi
N: ǁauhīsabes
G: Fischadler

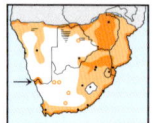

BLACK HARRIER

Moist grasslands. Black with yellow legs; pale underwings visible in flight.
48–53 cm

A: Witkruisvleivalk
Z: Umamhlangenomnyama
Ss: Mmankgodimohlaka E Montsho
N: ≠nū !khuwihīsabes
G: Mohrenweihe

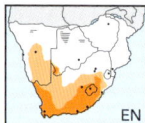

EN

PALM-NUT VULTURE

Coastal shores. White with black wings and tail, and horn-coloured bill and legs.
60 cm

A: Witaasvoël
Z: Inqemvuma
Sp: Lenong La Mopaleme
Tw: Lenong La Mokolwane
Ts: Gungwa
N: !uri ǁgananis
G: Palmengeier

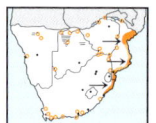

BLACK SPARROWHAWK

Tall trees. White form blackish above, white below with long yellow legs. 46–58 cm

A: Swartsperwer **Z:** Uheshanomnyama **Ss:** Fiolo E Ntsho
Sp: Matsenelela Yo Moso **Tw:** Segodi Se Sentsho
N: ≠nū ani!khāb **G:** Dominohabicht

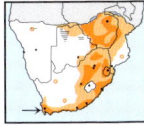

white form

melanistic form

AFRICAN HAWK-EAGLE

Savanna and riverine forests. Dark brown upperparts, white underparts with heavy spotting. 60–65 cm

A: Grootjagarend **Z:** Ukhozolumidwayidwa
Ss: Ntsutjheke E Kgolo **Tw:** Ntsukgweba E Kgolo
N: kai-anxa !khās **G:** Habichtsadler

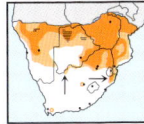

BLACK-CHESTED SNAKE EAGLE

Bushveld and grasslands. Dark brown upperparts, pale underparts and bare legs; pale underwings visible in flight. 63–68 cm

A: Swartborsslangarend **Z:** Indlanyokemnyama **Ss:** Lejanoha La Sefubantsho **Tw:** Lejanoga La Sehubantsho **Ts:** Xithaklongwa
N: ≠nū-lgā lao!khas **G:** Schwarzbrust-Schlangenadler

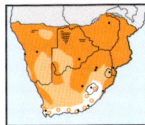

GREATER CRESTED (SWIFT) TERN

Coastal shores. Grey upperparts, white underparts and a yellow bill. 50 cm

A: Geelbeksterretjie
Z: Unolwandle
N: !huni-am ‖au!khōb
G: Eilseeschwalbe

CASPIAN TERN

Inland waters, coastal lagoons and estuaries. Grey upperparts, white underparts, black cap and large black-tipped red bill. 52 cm

A: Reusesterretjie **Z:** Ubhaklakliyo
Ss: Lepheulane Le Leholoholo
N: !nau-am ‖au!khōb
G: Raubseeschwalbe

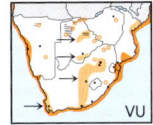

VU

BLACK-CROWNED NIGHT HERON

Inland waters; roosts in reeds or trees. Black upperparts, grey wings, white underparts and yellow legs.
56 cm

A: Gewone Nagreier
Z: Usiba
Ss: Kokolofitwe Ya Bosiu
Tw: Kokolohutwe Ya Bosigo
H: Etuva Routuku
G: Nachtreiher

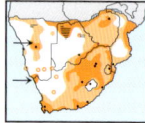

AFRICAN PENGUIN

Coastal shores. Black breast band on white underparts diagnostic. 63 cm

A: Brilpikkewyn
Z: Inguzambongolo
Ss: Phenkwine Ya Afrika
Sp: Phenkwine Ya Afrika
Tw: Phenkwine Ya Aforika
N: Afrika xoros
G: Brillenpinguin

KELP GULL

Coastal shores. Black upperwings, white body and yellow bill. 63 cm

A: Kelpmeeu
Z: Unochweba
Ss: Mmamawatle Wa Mokokotlontsho
N: kai gao≠oaxas
G: Dominikanermöwe

WHITE-FACED WHISTLING DUCK

Large dams and pans, and estuaries. Black head, white face, and rufous neck and upper breast. 48 cm

A: Nonnetjie-eend
Z: Umabhomfushane
Ss: Lewewe La Leramasweu
Sp: Lewewe La Sehubašweu
Ts: Xiyahkokeni
N: !uri-ai ≠naras
H: Ombaka Yomurungu Omuvapa
G: Witwenente

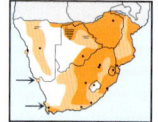

KNOB-BILLED DUCK ♂

Inland waters. Black-speckled head and neck, white underparts, dark blue-green upperparts appear black. 64–79 cm

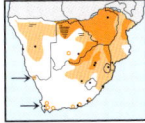

A: Knobbeleend **Z:** Unosimila
Ss: Letata La Kotjwana
Ts: Xikuvikuvi **Sh:** Pura
H: Ombaka Yotjinyo Otjiputuputu
G: Glanzente

SPUR-WINGED GOOSE

Inland waters. Black bird with white on face and belly, and pink bill and legs. 102 cm

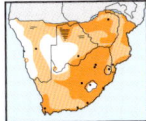

A: Wildemakou
Z: Ihhoye
X: Ihoye
Ss: Letshikgwi
Tw: Letsukwe
N: ||khū||gawo !kharas
G: Sporngans

MARTIAL EAGLE

Bushveld. Dark brown above, appearing black, with pale spotted underparts and well-feathered legs; dark underwings visible in flight. 78–83 cm

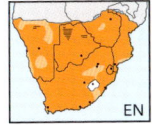

A: Breëkoparend **Z:** Isihuhwa **Ss:** Ntsu E Kgolo **Tw:** Ntsu
Ts: Manole **N:** !ari!khās **G:** Kampfadler

WHITE-HEADED VULTURE

Bushveld. Dark brown plumage, red bill, pink and blue face, and pink legs. 85 cm

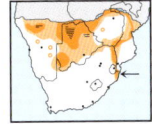

A: Witkopaasvoël **Z:** Ukhandelimhlope **Ss:** Lenong La Hlohosweu **Tw:** Lenong La Tlhogosweu **Ts:** Khoti Mpenyani **N:** !uri-dana kai-anis **G:** Wollkopfgeier

LAPPET-FACED VULTURE

Bushveld. Dark brown upperparts, white underparts, yellowish bill, and red head and neck. 115 cm

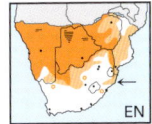

A: Swartaasvoël **Z:** Indlangamandla **Ss:** Letlakapipi
Tw: Bibing **Ts:** Khoti Mfumo **Sh:** Gohora **N:** ≠nü kai-anis
G: Ohrengeier

AFRICAN SACRED IBIS

Inland waters. White bird with black head and neck and long, decurved bill. 89 cm

A: Skoorsteenveër
Z: Inkankanelunga
Ss: Lehalanyane
N: ≠khani‖khâbams
G: Heiliger Ibis

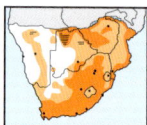

WHITE-BREASTED CORMORANT

All waters. Adult has dark upperparts, and white throat and breast; immature is entirely white below. 90 cm

A: Witborsduiker
Z: Iwondelimhlope
X: Umxwiqa
Ss: Ntodi Ya Sefubasweu
Tw: Ntodi Ya Sehubasweu
Ts: Ngulukwani
N: !uri‖khaib
G: Weißbrustkormoran

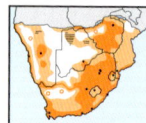

CAPE GANNET

Coastal waters. Black legs, tail and wing feathers, white body, and buffy-yellow head. 84–94 cm

A: Witmalgas
Z: Isicibamanzi
X: Umkholonjane
Ss: Seqwelo Sa Kapa
N: ‖ui !handas
G: Kaptölpel

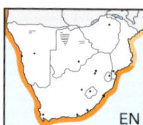

LUDWIG'S BUSTARD

Karoo and Namib plains. Dark foreneck and upperwings, and white belly. 75–90 cm

A: Ludwigpou
Z: Iseme Lasehlane
Ss: Kgupa Ya Mmetsosootho
Tw: Kgupa
N: ≠gamadom !huib
G: Ludwigstrappe

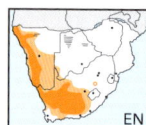

DENHAM'S BUSTARD

Hilly grasslands. Ash-grey foreneck, black cap, black-and-white upperwings. 86–110 cm

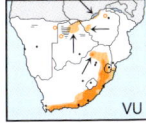

A: Veldpou
Z: iSeme
Ss: Kgupa Ya Mmetsoputswa
Tw: Kgorithamaga
G: Stanleytrappe

BLACK-HEADED HERON

Grasslands. Black cap, hind-neck and flight feathers, white throat, and grey body, bill and legs. 97 cm

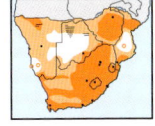

A: Swartkopreier
Z: Unokilonkolikhandamnyama
Ss: Kokolofitwe Ya Hlohontsho
H: Etuva Rotjiuru Otjizorunda
G: Schwarzkopfreiher

KORI BUSTARD

Woodland and grasslands. Brown upperparts with grey neck and head crest, black-and-white upperwings, white underparts, and pale yellow legs. 134 cm

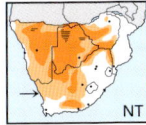

A: Gompou
Z: Isemelikhulu
Ss: Kgori
Ts: Mithisi
Nd: Itjeme
Sh: Ngomanyuni
N: kai !huib
G: Riesentrappe

GREY HERON

Inland waters. Grey upperparts, grey-white underparts, black band on head, and yellow bill and legs. 100 cm

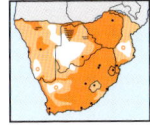

A: Bloureier **Z:** Unokilonkojwayelekile
Ss: Kokolofitwe Ya Putswa **Tw:** Sengwepe **H:** Etuva Evahe
G: Graureiher

ABDIM'S STORK

Grassveld and bushveld.
Black bird with white belly
and rump, and whitish legs;
bill horn-coloured in summer.
76 cm

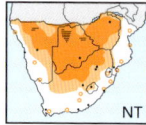

A: Kleinswartooievaar
Z: Umahlombamhlophe
Ss: Lekololwane
Sh: Ngauzani
N: ≠hoa-ai oefari
G: Abdimsstorch

YELLOW-BILLED STORK

Inland waters. White bird
with black flight feathers;
told by yellow bill, red
face and red legs.
97 cm

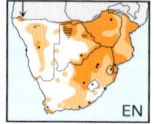

A: Nimmersat
Z: Unomlomophuzi
Tw: Lenompoo
Ts: Ghumba Leri Kulu
G: Nimmersatt

AFRICAN WOOLLY-NECKED STORK

Wooded wetlands. Dark
brown with white head
and neck, and dark red
bill and legs. 86 cm

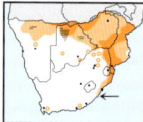

A: Wolnekooievaar
Z: Isithandamanzi
Sp: Leakabosane
Tw: Mokotatsie Wa Molalasweu
N: !uri-!ao oefari
G: Wollhalsstorch

WHITE STORK

Grassveld and bushveld.
Black and white with red bill
and legs. 117 cm

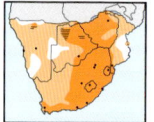

A: Witooievaar
Z: Unogolantethe
Ss: Mokotatsie O Mosweu
N: !uri oefari
G: Weißstorch

BLACK STORK

Freshwater bodies. All black except for white belly, and red bill and legs.
122 cm

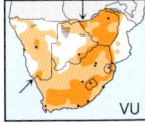

A: Grootswartooievaar
Z: Unowanga
X: Unocofu
Ss: Mokorwane
Tw: Lelentsho
N: ≠nū oefari
G: Schwarzstorch

MARABOU STORK

Bushveld and wetlands. Massive bill, bare head and neck with large throat pouch.
152 cm

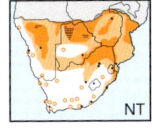

A: Maraboe
Z: Inqelendlovu
X: Usilwangula
Ss: Ghube
Tw: Ghube
Ts: Qandlopfu
Sh: Svorenyama
N: aurairi
G: Marabu

SADDLE-BILLED STORK

Freshwater bodies. Massive red-and-black bill with yellow saddle diagnostic. 145 cm

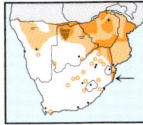

A: Saalbekooievaar
Z: Umadolabomvu
Ss: Molombwe
Ts: Ngwamhlanga
N: !aroda-am oefari
G: Sattelstorch

COMMON OSTRICH ♂

Bushveld and arid lands. Unmistakable tall black-and-white bird with buff, grey or white tail. 2 m

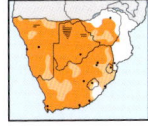

A: Volstruis
Z: Intshe
X: Inciniba
Ss: Mpshe
Tw: Ntshe
Ts: Yinca
Ve: Mphwe
Nd: Intshe
Sh: Mhou
N: ǀamib
H: Ombo
G: Strauß

GREY PLUMAGE

There are few completely grey birds in the region, but numerous species have partially grey plumage or a combination of grey and other colours. Birds often referred to as 'grey' are frequently grey-brown or dull brown (for example, the Hadada Ibis), and one should take care to distinguish between these two colours.

How does grey plumage serve a bird?

Grey upperparts can help camouflage birds such as gulls, the Caspian Tern and Dark Chanting Goshawk, making them less conspicuous to predators when viewed from above.

ACCIPITERS AND THEIR RELATIVES

Accipiter is Latin for hawk, and it is the generic name for the group of raptors known as **sparrowhawks** and **goshawks**. Sparrowhawks have long, slender legs and feet and an elongated central toe. The larger species are called goshawks, and are basically similar, but lack the long central toe. The chanting goshawks are related to the accipiters, but are in a different genus, *Melierax*. The three species of chanting goshawk are the **Dark Chanting Goshawk**, **Pale Chanting Goshawk** and **Gabar Goshawk**. These birds are moderately large hawks with reddish ceres and long, orange-red legs.

Accipiters can be difficult to identify, since their upperparts are grey or dark brown, depending on age and sex. It is easier to distinguish them by the colour of the eyes, cere and legs, and the patterns on their underparts.

Eye, cere and leg colour: Eye colour may be yellow, deep red or dark brown, and the cere may be yellow, red or grey. The combination of red eye, cere and legs is found only in the adult **Gabar Goshawk**. Yellow is the most common leg colour among accipiters, while orange is common to adult **goshawks** and the **Ovambo Sparrowhawk**.

Barring or streaking: Most adult goshawks and sparrowhawks have close rufous or grey barring on their underparts, and some have a plain grey upper breast. Immature **Shikra** and **Gabar Goshawk** have a streaked upper breast and a barred belly, while immature **Little Sparrowhawks** and **African Goshawks** have heavily spotted underparts. The **Rufous-breasted Sparrowhawk**, the immature **Black Sparrowhawk** and some immature **Ovambo Sparrowhawks** stand apart in having an entirely uniform rufous breast and belly.

GREY PENDULINE TIT

Woodland. Dark grey-green upperparts, pale grey breast, and buff-coloured face, belly and vent. 8–9 cm

A: Gryskapokvoël
Z: Iklosi
X: Unogushana
G: Kapbeutelmeise

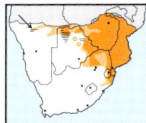

SWEE WAXBILL

Wooded streams. Grey head, olive-green upperparts, whitish breast, red rump and tail coverts, yellow belly and vent; male has black mask. 9–10 cm

A: Suidelike Swie
Z: UbuSukuswane
X: Utsoyi
Ss: Borane-Swaswi
G: Kapgrünastrild

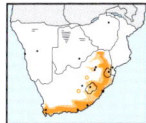

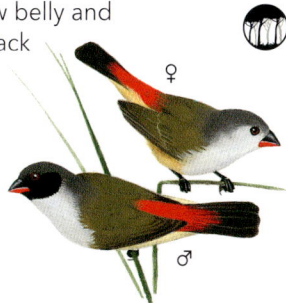

GREY WAXBILL

Woodland thickets. Dark grey upperparts, pale grey underparts, and red eyes, rump and uppertail base. 11 cm

A: Gryssysie
Z: Ivuzigazi
Sp: Rramphitlimphitli
G: Schwarzschwanzastrild

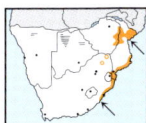

NEDDICKY (S & SE races)

Woodland and thickets. Rufous cap, brown upperparts, and blue-grey underparts. 10–11 cm

A: Neddikkie
Z: Incede
X: Incede
Ss: Motintinyane-O-Moputswa
Sp: Setwaneng
G: Braunkopf-Zistensänger

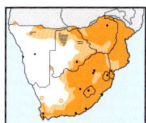

LONG-BILLED CROMBEC

Bushveld. Grey upperparts and buff-orange underparts; appears almost tailless. 10–12 cm

A: Bosveldstompstert
Z: Inkashana
G: Langschnabel-Sylvietta

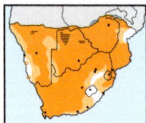

YELLOW-BELLIED EREMOMELA

Mixed bushveld or scrub. Grey-brown upperparts, pale grey breast, with a variable yellow belly. 9–10 cm

A: Geelpensbossanger
Z: Imbuzanephuzi
G: Gelbbauch-Eremomela

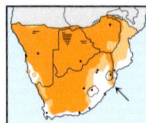

BURNT-NECKED EREMOMELA

Acacia woodland. Grey-brown upperparts, pale eyes, yellow-buff underparts, and brown throat bar (may be indistinct or absent). 12 cm

A: Bruinkeelbossanger
Z: Imbuzane Yomnqawe
G: Rostband-Eremomela

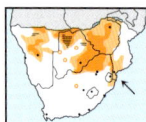

GREY-BACKED CISTICOLA

Fynbos and scrubland. Dark rufous head, grey back with black streaking, and pale buff underparts. 12–13 cm

A: Grysrugtinktinkie
Z: Intinga YaseKapa

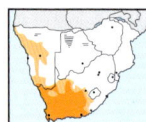

GREY-BACKED CAMAROPTERA

Bushveld. Dark grey upperparts, olive-green wings, pale greyish throat, and creamy grey-white underparts. 12 cm

A: Grysrugkwêkwêvoël
Z: Imbuzanemhlanempunga
G: Graurücken-Grasmücke

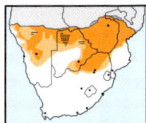

GREEN-BACKED CAMAROPTERA

Bushveld. Dull olive-green upperparts and white underparts; tail usually raised. 12 cm

A: Groenrugkwêkwêvoël
Z: Ibhoyi **X:** Unomanyuku
Sp: Lellakakwana
Ts: Xime-memee
G: Grünmantel-Bogenflügel

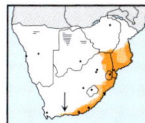

GREEN-BACKED HONEYBIRD

Woodland. Greenish-grey upperparts, yellow-edged flight feathers, and slender bill. 11.5 cm

A: Dunbekheuningvoël
Ss: Modisadinotshi Wa Mokokotlotala
Tw: Tshetlho Ya Mokotlatalatlhaga
N: !am-||ā dani!khōdanab
G: Zwerghoniganzeiger

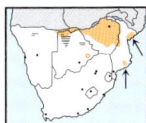

FAIRY FLYCATCHER

Karoo bushveld. Grey, with pink central breast, black tail, and black mask and wings with white bar. 12 cm

A: Feevlieëvanger **Z:** Uqholompunga
G: Livingstones Rotschwanzschnäpper

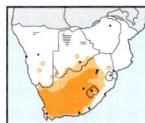

GREY TIT-FLYCATCHER

Woodland. Grey upperparts, white underbelly, blackish wings, and black tail with white outer feathers.
14 cm

A: Waaierstertvlieëvanger
Z: Umantuluza
G: Meisenschnäpper

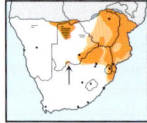

LAYARD'S WARBLER (TIT-BABBLER)

Fynbos and mountain scrub. Dark grey upperparts, white underparts, spotted breast, and pale eyes.
15 cm

A: Grystjeriktik
Z: Ihlekehleke Lasehlane
G: Layards Meisensänger

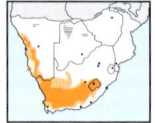

ASHY FLYCATCHER

Riverine woodland. Grey upperparts, pale grey underparts and blackish wings. 14–15 cm

A: Blougrysvlieëvanger **Z:** Usikhothamlotha
G: Schieferschnäpper

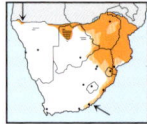

CHESTNUT-VENTED WARBLER (TIT-BABBLER)

Thornveld thickets. Mostly dark grey, with chestnut vent, spotted breast, and pale eyes. 15 cm

A: Bosveldtjeriktik
Z: Ihlekehleke
Ss: Pharalanku-Tonofubedu
G: Meisensänger

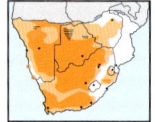

GREY SUNBIRD

Coastal forests. Entirely grey, darker above, with slender, decurved beak. 14 cm

A: Gryssuikerbekkie
Z: Incwincwemphungana
G: Graunektarvogel

ASHY TIT

Thornveld. Grey mantle and underparts, and black cap, throat, belly and tail.
14 cm

A: Akasiagrysmees
Z: Unongilemnyama WaseNyakatho
Ss: Seteatea-Sa-Bophirima
G: Aschenmeise

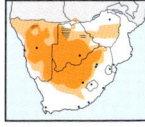

SOUTHERN GREY-HEADED SPARROW

Woodland. Plain grey head, chestnut upperparts, whitish underparts and stout black or horn-coloured bill.
15–16 cm

A: Gryskopmossie
Z: Ujolwanokhandaphunga
G: Graukopfsperling

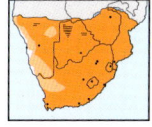

CAPE SPARROW ♀

Suburbia and farmlands. Grey-and-white head and breast, chestnut mantle, black-and-white wings, whitish underparts and stout black bill. 15 cm

A: Gewone Mossie **Z:** Undlunkulu **X:** Unondlwane
Ss: Serobele-Hlohophatshwa **Sp:** Lemphorokgohlo La Kapa
Ve: Malegeni **H:** Oyatuhere RwaKapa **G:** Kapsperling

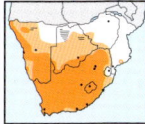

♀

PROTEA CANARY

Protea woodland. Mainly drab grey with pale wingbars and heavy, grey bill. 16 cm

A: Witvlerkkanarie
Z: Umbhalane Wesiqalaba
G: Proteagirlitz

STREAKY-HEADED SEEDEATER

Woodland. Grey-brown upperparts, streaky crown, white eyebrows, pale underparts, and stout, blackish bill.
16 cm

A: Streepkopkanarie
Z: UmBhalanonsundu
Ss: Tswere-Hlohokgwaba
G: Brauengirlitz

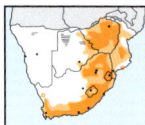

MOUNTAIN WHEATEAR ♂

Rocky hills. Body plumage varies from grey to black, with black wings, and white shoulder and vent; in arid areas belly may be white.
17–20 cm

A: Bergwagter
Z: Ikhwelentabeni
Ss: Kgalodi
G: Bergschmätzer

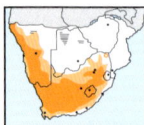

KAROO CHAT

Karoo scrub. Mostly grey with white belly, and blackish wings and upper tail; Namibian race paler, buffy.
15–18 cm

A: Karoospekvreter
Z: Umbexe Wasehlane
G: Bleichschmätzer

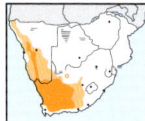

SCALY-THROATED HONEYGUIDE

Forest and bushveld. Grey upperparts with yellow bars on wings, streaky head, scaly throat with yellowish tinge, and paler underparts.
19 cm

A: Gevlekte Heuningwyser
Z: Inhlavana
Ss: Tsetlo Ya Dirothi
G: Gefleckter Honiganzeiger

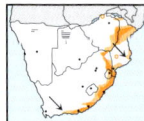

LESSER HONEYGUIDE

Woodland. Dark greenish-grey upperparts, paler-edged wing feathers, dusky grey underparts, and white outer tail feathers. 15 cm

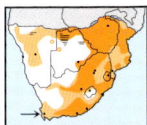

A: Kleinheuningwyser **Z:** Ingedana **Ss:** Tsetlo E Nnyenyane
N: ≠khari dani!khōdanab **G:** Kleiner Honiganzeiger

MOUNTAIN WAGTAIL

Mountain streams. Grey and black upperparts, white underparts, black chest band, and very long tail. 19–20 cm

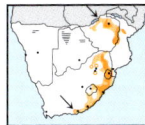

A: Bergkwikkie
Z: Umvemventabe
G: Langschwanzstelze

CAPE WAGTAIL

Wetlands and suburbia. Greyish upperparts, pale underparts, white chin and throat, and black chest band. 18 cm

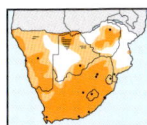

A: Gewone Kwikkie
Z: Umncishu
Ss: Motjodi-Thokwana
G: Kapstelze

AFRICAN SCOPS OWL

Woodland. Black-streaked grey plumage, resembling tree bark, yellow eyes, and prominent ear tufts. 18 cm

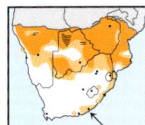

A: Skopsuil
Z: Umadletshana
Ss: Makgohlwana
Tw: Sekopamarumo
Sh: Chimbori
N: ≠gae |honnes
H: Okasivi Kautui Outiṭi
G: Afrikanische Zwergohreule

SHORT-TOED ROCK THRUSH

Rocky hills. Grey back, mantle and throat, whitish cap, and dull orange underparts.
18 cm

A: Korttoonkliplyster **Z:** Inhlaletshenekhandalimhlophe
G: Kurzzehenrötel

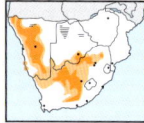

MIOMBO ROCK THRUSH

Miombo woodland. Grey head and upperparts with black flecks, dull orange breast, and pale white belly.
18 cm

A: Angolakliplyster **G:** Miomborötel

LITTLE STINT

Wetlands. Non-br. birds grey-brown with white-edged feathers, white underparts, and black bill and legs. 14 cm

A: Kleinstrandloper **Z:** Unothwayizana **Ss:** Tsititsiti
N: ≠khari huri-am!gûb **G:** Zwergstrandläufer

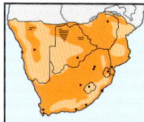

SENTINEL ROCK THRUSH

Rocky hills and grasslands. Grey head, chest and mantle, and dull orange underparts.
21 cm

A: Langtoonkliplyster
Z: Ikhwelemarsheni
X: Umganto
Ss: Thume-Kokotloputswa
G: Langzehenrötel

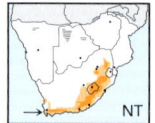

CAPE ROCK THRUSH

Cliffs. Grey head and dull orange body.
21 cm

A: Kaapse Kliplyster
Z: Isihlalamatsheni
X: Unomaweni
Ss: Thume-Hlohoputswa
Sp: Mmaratasebilo
G: Klippenrötel

AFRICAN PARADISE FLYCATCHER

Woodland and suburbia. Deep blue-grey head, grey breast, chestnut upperparts, and blue eye-ring and bill. 23 cm female, 41 cm male

A: Paradysvlieëvanger
Z: Inzwece **X:** Ujejane
Ss: Kapantsi-Ya-Meru
Tw: Mothwapea
Ts: Xiavava
Nd: Eve **Sh:** Kateredemu
G: Paradiesschnäpper

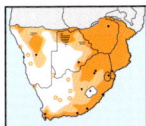

WATTLED STARLING

Open bushveld. Pale grey with black flight feathers and tail; br. male has black and yellow head ornamentation. 21 cm

A: Lelspreeu
Z: Impofazana
X: Unowambu
Ss: Lehodi-Le-Mekadi
Ts: Khwezu Elimhlope
G: Lappenstar

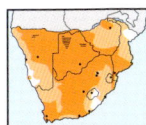

RED-BACKED SHRIKE

Bushveld. Grey cap and nape, chestnut back, black mask, wings and tail, white underparts, and hooked beak. 18 cm

A: Rooiruglaksman **Z:** Umathithibala **X:** Ihlolo
Ss: Tshemedi-Kgunong **G:** Neuntöter

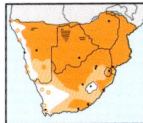

LESSER GREY SHRIKE

Bushveld. Grey and black upperparts, white underparts, and stout, hooked beak. 20–22 cm

A: Gryslaksman **Z:** Unolunga **Ss:** Tshemedi-Thokwa
G: Schwarzstirnwürger

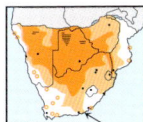

GREY CUCKOOSHRIKE

Forest fringes. Dark grey, with black tail and flight feathers. 27 cm

A: Bloukatakoeroe **Z:** Iklebedwane **X:** Umsimpofu
Ss: Mmaselakgwasa **G:** Waldraupenfänger

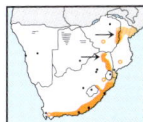

PYGMY FALCON

Thornbush savanna. Grey upperparts (female with rufous mantle) and white underparts. **19.5 cm**

A: Dwergvalk **Z:** Uklebenyana **Ss:** Phakwana
N: ≠khari ǀaub **H:** Orukoze Okaṭiṭi **G:** Zwergfalke

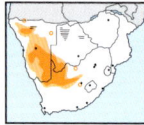

STRIPED KINGFISHER

Woodland. Blue back, tail and wings, black wing coverts, brown streaking on cap and white underparts, and dark brown-and-red bill. **18–19 cm**

A: Gestreepte Visvanger
Z: Unongozolwane
Ss: Seinodi Sa Metjhato
Sp: Senwamorula Sa Mela
N: daoxa ǁaudīb
G: Streifenliest

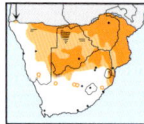

GREY-HEADED KINGFISHER

Mixed woodland. Grey head and mantle, royal blue back, tail and wings, black wing coverts, chestnut belly and all-red bill. **20 cm**

A: Gryskopvisvanger **Z:** Isiphikelelesikhandampunga
Ss: Seinodi Sa Hlohoputswa **Tw:** Seinwedi Sa Tlhogokotswana
N: ǀhai-dana ǁaudīb **G:** Graukopfliest

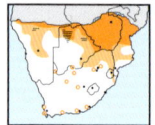

WOODLAND KINGFISHER

Woodland. Turquoise upperparts, black wing coverts, greyish-white underparts, and red-and-black bill. **23–24 cm**

A: Bosveldvisvanger **Z:** Imbuyelelo
Ss: Seinodi Sa Moru **Tw:** Thathadikoma
Ts: Ncocololo **N:** haiǀgom ǁaudib
H: Ongambura Mahundju YaAngola
G: Senegalliest

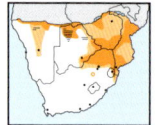

BROWN-HOODED KINGFISHER

Woodland. Blue rump and tail, blue-and-black upperwings, brownish-streaked head and mantle, white underparts and red bill. **23–24 cm**

A: Bruinkopvisvanger **Z:** Isiphikeleli **G:** Braunkopfliest

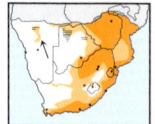

BOKMAKIERIE

Suburbia. Grey crown and mantle, olive upperparts, yellow underparts and bold black breast band.
23 cm

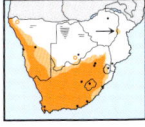

A: Bokmakierie
Z: Inkovu
X: Ingqwangi
Ss: Ptjemptjete
Sp: Mpherwane
G: Bokmakiri

MEYER'S PARROT

Woodland. Brown head, mantle and wings, pale blue back and rump, and green underparts.
23 cm

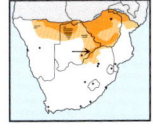

A: Bosveldpapegaai
Z: Isikhwenenesimahlombaphuzi
Tw: Heka Ya Phatlasetlha
N: !huni-!ū ‖giririb
G: Goldbugpapagei

GREY-HEADED BUSHSHRIKE

Woodland. Grey head, green upperparts, orange breast, yellow eyes and underparts, and heavy, hooked bill.
25–27 cm

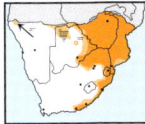

A: Spookvoël
Z: Usipoki
X: Umbankro
G: Graukopfwürger

RÜPPELL'S PARROT

Woodland. Grey-brown, with blue rump, underbelly and vent.
23 cm

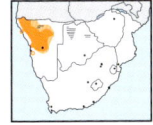

A: Bloupenspapegaai
Sh: Hwenga
N: ≠hoa-!nā ‖giririb
Ss: Heka Ya Mpatalalehodimo
G: Rüppellpapagei

LAUGHING DOVE

Varied habitats. Pinkish head; cinnamon blotched back, blue-grey wings, cinnamon breast with black flecks, and dark pink legs. 25 cm

A: Rooiborsduifie **Z:** Ukhonzane
X: Icelekwane **Ss:** Mofubetswana
Sp: Mphephane **Tw:** Lephoi
Ts: Serhu **Sh:** Mhetura
N: |apa!ao≠nais
H: Ohanda
G: Palmtaube

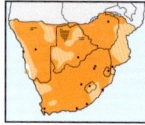

MOURNING COLLARED DOVE

Riverine woodland. Grey head, black collar, and yellow eyes with red eye-ring. 30 cm

A: Rooioogtortelduif
Z: Ihobhelililayo
Ss: Mokuru Wa Leihlosehla
Sp: Mokuru Wa Leihlosehla
Tw: Mokuru Wa Leitlhosetlha
N: !huni-mû ≠nais
G: Angolaturteltaube

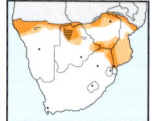

RED-EYED DOVE

Woodland and suburbia. Pinkish-grey with a broad black collar, and red eyes. 33–36 cm

A: Grootringduif **Z:** Ihobhelimehlabombu
X: Indlasidudu **Tw:** Letseba **Ts:** Khopola
Sh: Bvukutirwo **N:** |awa-mû ≠nais **G:** Halbmondtaube

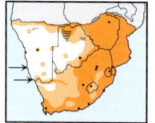

RING-NECKED DOVE

Varied habitats. Greyest of the collared doves, with black collar and bill, and dark red legs. 28 cm

A: Gewone Tortelduif
Z: Usamdokwe
X: Untamnyama
G: Gurrtaube

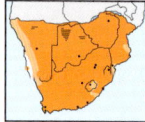

ROCK DOVE (FERAL PIGEON)

Urban areas. Variable plumage; typically grey with black wingbars, many individuals with glossy green neck feathers. 33 cm

A: Tuinduif **Z:** Ijuba Ledolobha **G:** Haustaube

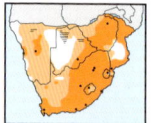

SPECKLED MOUSEBIRD

Bushveld and suburbia. Brown upperparts, pale brown crest and underparts, black mask and upper mandible, white lower mandible, and black legs. 30–35 cm

A: Gevlekte Muisvoël
Z: Indlazi
X: Indlazi
Sp: Letswiokoko
Tw: Moririmothlofe
Ts: Nhlazi
G: Braunflügel-Mausvogel

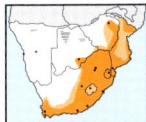

WHITE-BACKED MOUSEBIRD

Dry bush and suburbia. Grey upperparts and upstanding crest, white back, buff underparts, black-tipped white bill, and red legs. 30–34 cm

A: Witkruismuisvoël **Z:** Indlazemhlanomhlophe **Sp:** Letshee
Tw: Marungwane **N:** !uri-|nana |khenni
G: Weißrücken-Mausvogel

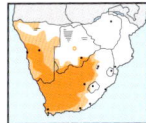

RED-FACED MOUSEBIRD

Thornveld and suburbia. Greyish-brown upperparts, grey-white rump and underparts, blue eyes, black bill, and red mask and legs. 32–34 cm

A: Rooiwangmuisvoël **Z:** UmTshivovo **X:** Intshili **Sp:** Letswiababa
Ts: Ncivovo **Sh:** Swenya **N:** |awa-ai |khenni **G:** Rotzügel-Mausvogel

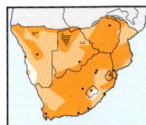

RED-CHESTED CUCKOO

Woodland and suburbia. Grey upperparts, rufous breast, banded underparts, and yellow eye-ring, ower mandible and legs. 28 cm

A: Piet-my-vrou
Z: Uphezukomkhono
X: Uphezukomkhono
Ss: Tlo-Nke-Tsoho
Sp: Bjalapeu
Ts: Ngwafalantala
N: |awa|gä höhöseb
G: Einsiedlerkuckuck

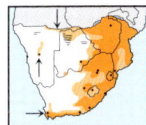

BLACK-WINGED LAPWING

Grassveld. Grey head, neck and upper breast, white forehead, brown back, and white underparts.
29 cm

A: Grootswartvlerkkiewiet
Z: Ititihoye
G: Schwarzflügelkiebitz

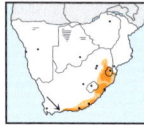

BLACKSMITH LAPWING

Wetlands, grasslands and fields. Black-and-white bird with grey wings.
30 cm

A: Bontkiewiet
Z: Indudumela
Ss: Mootlatshepe
N: ||gī||gīb
G: Schmiedekiebitz

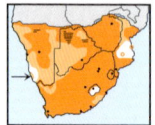

SENEGAL LAPWING

Grassveld and woodland. Brown upperparts, grey head, neck and upper breast, and white forehead and underparts. 23 cm

A: Kleinswartvlerkkiewiet
Z: Umahambehlala
G: Trauerkiebitz

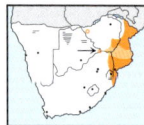

WHITE-CROWNED LAPWING

Sandbanks of major rivers. Grey head and neck, white crown and underparts, black-and-white wings, and yellow bill, wattles and legs.
30 cm

A: Witkopkiewiet
Z: Ititihoyelimqhelomhlophe
Tw: Lerrane
N: !uri-gao-ao|gapa xaixais
G: Langspornkiebitz

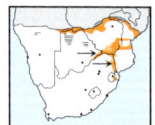

LITTLE SPARROWHAWK

Woodland. Dark grey upperparts, white rump, two white spots on tail, rufous-banded underparts, and yellow, eyes, bill, cere and legs. 23–25 cm

A: Kleinsperwer
Z: Uheshanyana
Ss: Fiolo E Nnyenyane
N: ≠khari ani!khāb
G: Zwergsperber

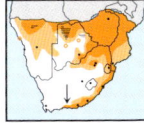

RED-FOOTED FALCON ♂

Grasslands. Dark grey with rufous vent, and red eye-ring, cere and feet. 28–30 cm

A: Westelike Rooipootvalk
Z: Uklebonyawobomvu
Ss: Phakwe Ya Leotofubedu
N: huri ǀawa-≠ai ǀaub
G: Rotfußfalke

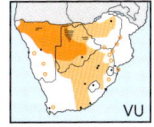

AMUR FALCON

Grasslands. Grey upperparts, red or orange eye-ring, cere and legs; male has pale grey underparts and rufous vent; female has white, spotted underparts. 28–30 cm

A: Oostelike Rooipootvalk **Z:** Oklebeklebe **Tw:** Phakalane
N: ai≠oa ǀawa-≠ai ǀaub **G:** Amur-Rotfußfalke

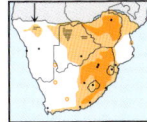

SOUTHERN WHITE-FACED OWL

Woodland. Grey with dark streaks, black-bordered white facial disc, and orange eyes. 25–28 cm

A: Witwanguil
Z: Umandubulu
Tw: Kukuruma
Nd: Umandubulo
N: !uri-ai ǀhonnes
G: Weißgesicht-Ohreule

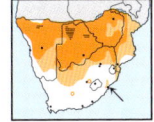

BLACK-WINGED KITE

Woodland. Grey upperparts, black carpal patches and wing tips, and white underparts. **30 cm**

A: Blouvalk **Z:** Udemezane **X:** Isitshisane
Ss: Segootsane **Ts:** Nwarikapanyana
N: ≠nũ-‖gawo hĩsabes **H:** Gleitaar

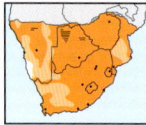

ROCK KESTREL ♂

Hills. Rufous body, grey head and tail, black tip on tail, and yellow eye-ring, cere and legs.
30–33 cm

A: Kransvalk
Z: Umathebethebana Wamadwala
X: Uthebethebana
Tw: Phakwe Ya Lefika
N: ‖hoa ǀaub
G: Turmfalke

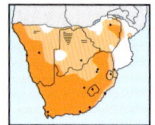

LESSER KESTREL ♂

Grassland. Rufous body, grey head, back, greater coverts and tail, and yellow eye-ring, cere and legs. **28–30 cm**

A: Kleinrooivalk
Z: Umathebethebanomncane
Ss: Seotsanyana Se Senyenyane
Tw: Phakalane E Nnye
N: ≠khari ǀawa ǀaub
G: Rötelfalke

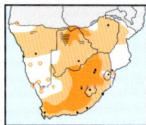

SHIKRA

Woodland. Plain grey upperparts, rufous-banded underparts, deep red eyes, and yellow cere and legs.
30–34 cm

A: Gebande Sperwer
Z: Uheshomidwayidwa
Tw: Segodi Sa Moeledi
N: daoxa aniǃkhāb
G: Schikra

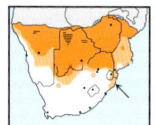

GABAR GOSHAWK

Woodland. Grey upperparts and breast, bold white rump, and red eyes, cere and legs. 30–34 cm

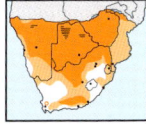

A: Kleinsingvalk
Z: Uheshomlotha
Ss: Mamphoko
N: !uri-ǀnana anitsēbeb
H: Oharukoze Okaapa
G: Gabarhabicht

OVAMBO SPARROWHAWK

Woodland. Grey upperparts, grey-banded underparts, dark eyes, red cere and orange legs. 33–40 cm

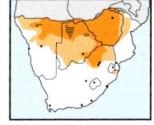

A: Ovambosperwer   **Z:** Uheshosaklebe
Ss: Fiolo Ya Ovambo   **N:** ǀhai-daoxa aniǃkhāb
H: Orukoze Yovambo   **G:** Ovambosperber

LIZARD BUZZARD

Woodland. Grey upperparts and chest, banded underparts, black throat stripe, bold white bar on black tail, and red cere and legs. 35–37 cm

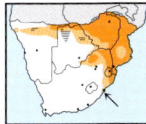

A: Akkedisvalk
Z: Usozi
Tw: Segodi Sa Mokgatitswane
N: ≠nowo hīsabes
H: Orukoze Roviturukuhu
G: Sperberbussard

PEREGRINE FALCON

Woodland and near cliffs. Grey upperparts and barred underparts. 34–40 cm

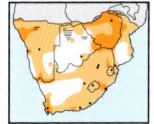

A: Swerfvalk
Z: Uklebosikhweshekweshe
G: Wanderfalke

WHISKERED TERN (br.)

Inland waters. Grey body, black cap, white cheeks, and red bill and legs. **23 cm**

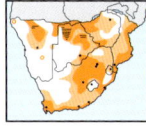

A: Witbaardsterretjie **Z:** Umachibini
Ss: Lepheulane La Ditedusweu **N:** !uri-ǀhō-am ǁau!khōb
G: Weißbart-Seeschwalbe

br.

LITTLE TERN (non-br.)

Coastal shores. Grey upperparts, mottled black cap, white forehead and underparts, and black bill and legs. **22–24 cm**

A: Kleinsterretjie **Z:** Unonklilwane

non-br.

WHITE-WINGED TERN (non-br.)

Inland waters. Grey back and upperwings, black nape, black spot behind eye, and white upper tail. **23 cm**

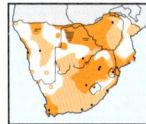

A: Witvlerksterretjie
Z: Unochibi
Ss: Lepheulane La Lepheosweu
N: !uri-ǁgawo ǁau!khōb
G: Weißflügel-Seeschwalbe

non-br.

DAMARA TERN

Coastal shores. Pale grey back, wings and short tail, white underparts, black cap, and long black bill. **21–23 cm**

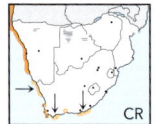

A: Damarasterretjie **Z:** Unonklilwane WakwelaBathwa
G: Damaraseeschwalbe

ANTARCTIC TERN
(non-br.)

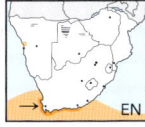

Coastal shores. Grey upperparts, white underparts and dark red bill; larger than Common Tern.
34–40 cm

A: Grysborssterretjie
Z: Insukakude Yeqhwa
G: Gabelschwanz-Seeschwalbe

non-br.

SANDWICH TERN

Coastal shores. Mostly white, with shaggy black cap, pale grey back and wings, and long, slender yellow-tipped black bill. 40 cm

A: Grootsterretjie **Z:** Unonkliyo **Ss:** Lepheulane Le Leholo
N: kai ǁau!khōb **G:** Brandseeschwalbe

br.

non-br.

COMMON TERN
(non-br.)

Coastal shores. Grey upperparts, white underparts and black bill; smaller than Antarctic Tern. 35–38 cm

A: Gewone Sterretjie **Z:** Unontenteza **Ss:** Lepheulane La Hlapi
N: swawel ǁau!khōb **G:** Flußseeschwalbe

non-br.

AFRICAN RAIL

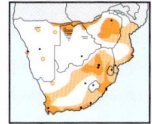

Reed beds. Grey head and underparts, rufous upperparts, and red bill and legs. 36 cm

A: Grootriethaan **Z:** Isizinzi **Ss:** Mopakapaka
Ts: Nwatsekutseku **N:** kai ≠ā-anib **G:** Kapralle

HARTLAUB'S GULL

Coastal shores. Grey upperwings and back, white body, and red bill and legs.
38 cm

A: Hartlaubmeeu
Z: Unochweba WaseKapa
Ss: Mmamawatle Wa Bophirimela
N: !khawaga ≠kharigaos **G:** Hartlaubsmöwe

GREY-HEADED GULL

Inland waters and coastal shores. Grey head, back and upperwings, and red bill and legs. 42 cm

A: Gryskopmeeu **Z:** Indewula
Ss: Mmamawatle Wa Hlohoputswa
N: |hai-dana ≠kharigaos **G:** Graukopfmöwe

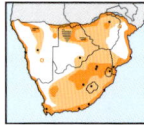

GREEN-BACKED (STRIATED) HERON

Inland waters. Grey mantle and underparts, black cap, dark wings and tail, and orange legs. 41 cm

A: Groenrugreier **Z:** Umacutholuhlaza **N:** !am-||â |gurikhoeseb
G: Mangrovenreiher

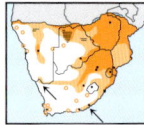

AFRICAN GOSHAWK

Forests. Grey upperparts, rufous-banded underparts, grey cere, and yellow eyes and legs.
40 cm

A: Afrikaanse Sperwer **Z:** ushomheshe
X: Ukholo **Ss:** Fiolo Y Afrika
Tw: Segodi Sa Aforika
G: Afrikahabicht

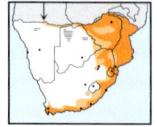

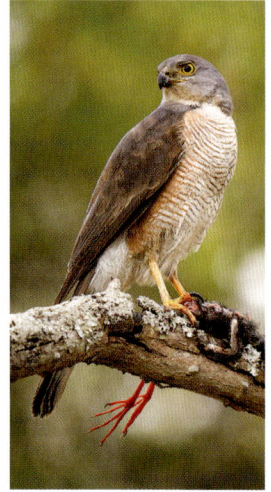

LANNER FALCON

Woodland. Grey upperparts, russet crown, buffy-white underparts, and yellow eye-rings, cere and legs.
40–45 cm

A: Edelvalk
Z: Uklebemawa
Ss: Phakwe Ya Kgosi
Nd: Uhelwane
N: gaob |aub
G: Lannerfalke

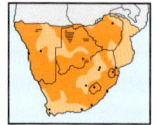

MONTAGU'S HARRIER ♂

Grasslands. Grey upperparts and chest, black primaries and wingbar, white belly and rufous-streaked underwings. 40–47 cm

A: Blouvleivalk Z: Unohlohlweni
N: |hai !khuwihīsabes G: Wiesenweihe

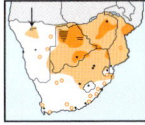

GREY GO-AWAY-BIRD

Woodland. All grey with crested head, long tail and black bill and legs. 47–50 cm

A: Kwêvoël Z: UmKlewu Ss: Mokowe
Ts: Kwenyana Sh: Kuwe N: kôeb
H: Ongurukwena G: Graulärmvogel

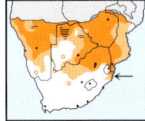

HOUSE CROW

Commensal with humans. Glossy black, with grey head, breast and mantle.
43 cm

A: Huiskraai
Z: Igwababa Ledolobha
G: Glanzkrähe

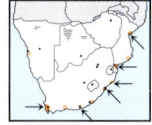

BLUE KORHAAN ♂

Grassveld. Blue-grey neck and body, and tawny upperparts. 50–58 cm

A: Bloukorhaan Z: Umbukwane
Ss: Lekakarane Le Letalalehodimo G: Blautrappe

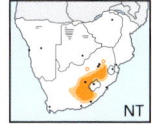

HELMETED GUINEAFOWL

Grasslands and bush. White-spotted dark body, blue neck, red helmet, and horn-coloured casque and bill. 53–58 cm

A: Gewone Tarentaal Z: Impangele Lehlathi
Ss: Kgaka Ya Lenaka Ts: Mhangela Nd: Intendele
Sh: Hanga N: ||nâxa |khenas H: Onganga G: Helmperlhuhn

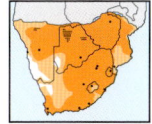

WESTERN BANDED SNAKE EAGLE

Riverine forests. Brownish-grey from head to lower breast, and yellow cere and legs.
55 cm

A: Enkelbandslangarend
Tw: Lejanoga La Moelediswev
N: daoxa≠are |ao!khās
G: Band-Schlangenadler

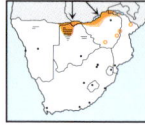

PALE CHANTING GOSHAWK

Semi-desert. Pale grey upperparts and chest, finely barred belly, white rump and secondaries, black primaries and tail, and orange-red cere and legs. 53–63 cm

A: Bleeksingvalk
Z: Uheshoculayo Wasehlane
N: !uri-||gawo |hai|aub
G: Silbersinghabicht

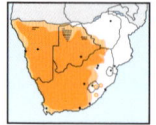

SOUTHERN BANDED SNAKE EAGLE

Riverine forests. Brownish-grey from head to upper breast, and yellow cere and legs.
60 cm

A: Dubbelbandslangarend
Z: Indlanyokempungu
G: Graubrust-Schlangenadler

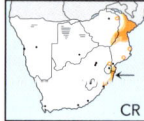

DARK CHANTING GOSHAWK

Woodland. Dark grey upperparts and breast, barred rump, black primaries and tail, finely barred underparts, and coral-pink cere and legs.
50–56 cm

A: Donkersingvalk
Z: Uheshoculayo Wasehlanze
Tw: Mmankokonono Wa Lefukakotswana
G: Graubürzel-Singhabicht

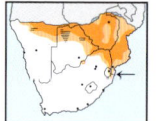

AFRICAN HARRIER-HAWK (GYMNOGENE)

Woodland. Grey upperparts and breast, black-tipped flight feathers, banded underparts, white-banded black tail, and yellow cere and legs. 60–66 cm

A: Kaalwangvalk
Z: Ijikanyawo
Ss: Seitlhwaeledi
N: !huni-ai hïsabes
G: Höhlenweihe

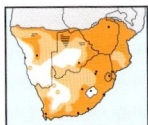

CASPIAN TERN

Inland waters, coastal lagoons and estuaries. Grey upperwings and back, white body, black cap, and large red bill. 52 cm

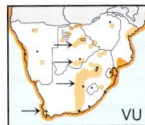

A: Reusesterretjie **Z:** Ubhaklakliyo **Ss:** Lepheulane Le Leholoholo **N:** !nau-am ||au!khōb **G:** Raubseeschwalbe

VERREAUX'S EAGLE-OWL

Woodland. All grey, paler underparts, black-edged facial disc, dark eyes and pink eyelids. 60–65 cm

A: Reuse-ooruil
Z: Ifubesi
Ss: Makgohlo
Sp: Lekota
Tw: Marawele
Ts: Nkuhunsi
Nd: Ifubesi
N: kai ≠uwib
G: Blassuhu

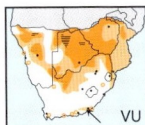

GREATER CRESTED (SWIFT) TERN

Coastal shores. Grey upperwings and back, white body, and a yellow bill. 50 cm

A: Geelbeksterretjie **Z:** Unolwandle **Ss:** Lepheulane La Molomosehla **N:** !huni-am ||au!khōb

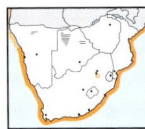

BLACK-CROWNED NIGHT HERON

Wetlands. Grey upperwings and tail, black crown and back, white body and yellow legs. 56 cm

A: Gewone Nagreier
Z: Usiba
Ss: Kokolofitwe Ya Bosiu
H: Etuva Routuku
G: Nachtreiher

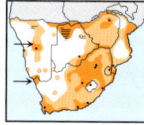

HADADA IBIS

Wetlands and gardens. Dull grey-brown with iridescent greenish-black wings. 76 cm

A: Hadeda
Z: Inkankane
X: Ing'ang'ane
Ss: Lengaangane
Sp: Lehaahaa
Tw: Tshababarwa
Ts: Man'An'Ani
N: |hai ǂkhani||khâbams
G: Hagedasch-Ibis

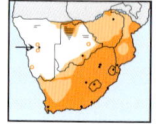

SOUTH AFRICAN SHELDUCK

Brackish waters. Rich rufous body and grey head; female has white face. 64 cm

A: Kopereend **Z:** Idadelibomvu **Ss:** Letata La Hlohoputswa **N:** ǂai|uri !kharas **G:** Graukopf-Rostgans

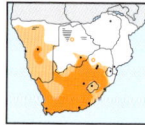

♀ ♂

GREY HERON

Wetlands. Grey wings and back, grey-white body, black band on head, and yellow bill and legs. 100 cm

A: Bloureier **Z:** Unokilonkojwayelekile **Tw:** Sengwepe **N:** |hai |gurikhoeseb **G:** Graureiher

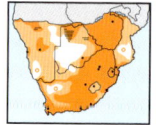

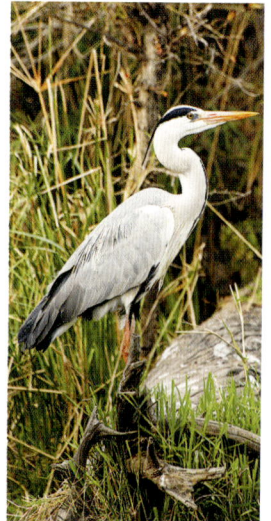

BLUE CRANE

Grasslands and vleis. Blue-grey with white crown, black wing tips and yellowish bill. 105 cm

A: Bloukraanvoël
Z: Indwe **X:** Indwe
Ss: Moholodi
Tw: Mogolodi
Sh: Ijorkwe
N: ≠hoa !goaharab (!)
G: Paradieskranich

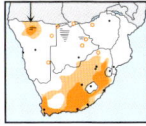

WATTLED CRANE

Grasslands and floodplains. Grey crown, back and wings, white head, neck, wattles and mantle, yellow bill, and red facial skin. 120 cm

A: Lelkraanvoël **Z:** Ubhamukwe **X:** Iqaqolo **Ss:** Motlathomo
N: !uri!ao !goaharab (!) **G:** Klunkerkranich

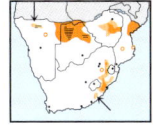

GREY CROWNED CRANE

Grasslands and marshes. Grey neck and body, yellow crest on black crown, and white facial patch. 105 cm

A: Mahem
Z: Unohemu
X: Ihem
Ss: Lehehemu
Tw: Leowang
Sh: Muhori
N: ǀhai≠amǃnâ !noab
G: Kronenkranich

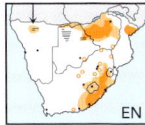

SECRETARYBIRD

Grasslands. Grey upperparts, black flight feathers, upper legs and tail tip, reddish-orange facial skin, and pink lower legs. 125–150 cm

A: Sekretarisvoël
Z: Intungunono
X: Ingxangxosi
Ss: Mmamolangwane
Tw: Tlhangwe
Sh: Hwata
N: turureb/duruǃkhobab
G: Sekretär

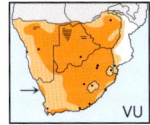

PURPLE HERON

Wetlands. Striped, rufous neck, and grey-brown wings. 89 cm

A: Rooireier **Z:** Unokhoboyi
Ss: Kokolofitwe Ya Molalafubedu **Ts:** Rikolwa
N: |awa-!ao |gurikhoeseb **G:** Purpurreiher

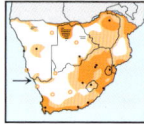

MARABOU STORK

Bushveld and wetlands. Dark grey wings, white underparts, massive bill, bare head and pinkish inflatable throat pouch. 152 cm

A: Maraboe **Z:** Inqelendlovu **X:** Usilwangula **Ss:** Ghube
Sh: Svorenyama **N:** aurairi **H:** Otjimbirinyama **G:** Marabu

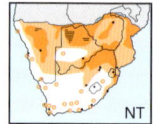

BLACK-HEADED HERON

Grasslands. Grey body, bill and legs, and black cap, hindneck and flight feathers. 97 cm

A: Swartkopreier
Z: Unokilonkolikhandamnyama
Ss: Kokolofitwe Ya Hlohontsho
N: ≠nū-dana |gurikhoeseb
G: Schwarzkopfreiher

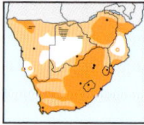

ad.

juv.

GOLIATH HERON

Inland waters. Grey upperwings, back, tail, lower neck and bill, and rufous head, neck and underparts. 140 cm

A: Reusereier
Z: Unozalizingwenya
Ss: Kokolofitwe E Kgolo
N: kai |gurikhoeseb
H: Etuva Romasa
G: Goliathreiher

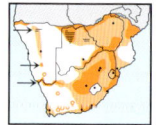

LESSER FLAMINGO (juv.)

Salt pans. Grey-brown body, head and neck, black wings and entirely dark bill. 102 cm

A: Kleinflamink
Z: Ukholwasomncane
Sp: Tlatšana
Tw: Lekukara
N: ≠khari ǀapaǀnūbeb
H: Kakueya Okaṯiṯi
G: Zwergflamingo

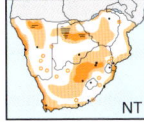

juv.

PINK-BACKED PELICAN

Inland waters. Grey and white with pinkish back; br. birds are paler; non-br. birds have grey wings. 135 cm

A: Kleinpelikaan **Z:** Ivubelincane
Ss: Leya Le Lenyenyane **N:** ≠khari ǀēdeharab
G: Rötelpelikan

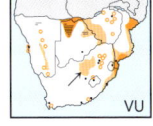

GREATER FLAMINGO (juv.)

Salt pans and soda lakes. Grey body, paler grey head and neck, black wings, black-tipped grey bill. 140 cm

A: Grootflamink
Z: Ukholwasomkhulu
Tw: Tladi
N: kai ǀapaǀnūbeb
H: Kakueya
G: Flamingo

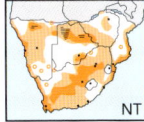

juv.

COMMON OSTRICH ♀

Bushveld and arid lands. Brown-grey plumage and long neck and legs; unmistakable. 2 m

A: Volstruis
Z: Intshe
X: Inciniba
Ss: Mpshe
Tw: Ntshe
Ts: Yinca
Sh: Mhou
N: ǀamib
H: Ombo
G: Strauß

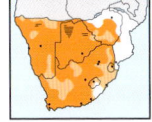

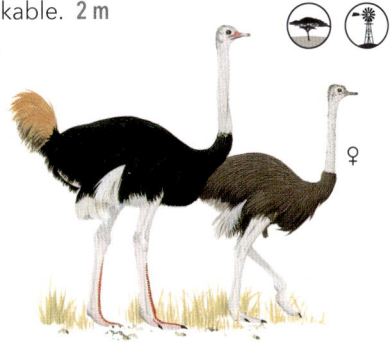

♀

WHITE PLUMAGE

Most white birds are waterbirds. There are also many white or partially white seabirds that do not fall within the scope of this book, but those that occur on inland waters and at the coast are included here.

White feathers are the result of an absence of colour pigments. While white colouring is the norm for many species, there are occasionally individual birds that are, due to albinism or leucism, uncommonly white for their species.

How does white plumage help a bird?

Camouflage: White coloration makes waterbirds less noticeable against a bright skyline.

Heat reflection: As white tends to reflect light and heat, it is possible that the pale plumage helps birds forage in the hot sun for much of the day.

ALBINISM AND LEUCISM

Leucism and albinism are two common conditions that result in abnormal white plumage, due to a lack of the colour pigment melanin. Since these conditions have similar characteristics, it can be difficult to distinguish between them.

In **albinism**, the enzyme tyrosinase, which is responsible for producing melanin, is absent. Birds with albinism are entirely white, with pink or red eyes. Albino birds are rare in the wild; their sensitivity to light and poor eyesight make them vulnerable, and they tend to die early on.

Leucism is thought to result from a genetic mutation that causes a partial or complete absence of pigmentation in all or parts of the bird's body. Birds with leucism may have completely white plumage or irregular patches of white. Eye colour is not affected by leucism.

A partial reduction of pigment can be as detrimental as complete albinism. Like albino birds, animals with leucism are easier to spot by predators and may not be recognised or accepted by other members of the species. Leucistic traits in birds may also cause feathers to weaken and, therefore, affect flight.

TRACTRAC CHAT

Arid plains. Southern race pale grey-brown above; Namibian race very pale brown, almost white above; both races white below with buff or white rump. 14–15 cm

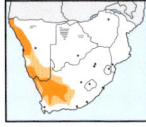

A: Woestynspekvreter **Z:** Umbexomhlophe **G:** Namibschmätzer

Namibian morph

southern morph

WATTLED STARLING

Open bushveld. Whitish with black tail; br. male has head ornamented with black and yellow. 21 cm

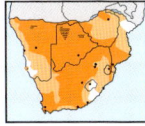

A: Lelspreeu **Z:** Impofazana **X:** Unowambu
Ss: Lehodi-Le-Mekadi **Sp:** Lefokori
Ts: Khwezu Elimhlope **G:** Lappenstar

br.♂

♀

BARE-CHEEKED BABBLER

Woodland. White underparts and head, brown upperparts and rufous nape. 24cm

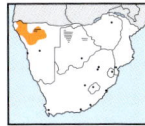

A: Kaalwangkatlagter **G:** Nacktohrdroßling

SOUTHERN PIED BABBLER

Woodland. White bird with black wings and tail, and orange eyes. 26 cm

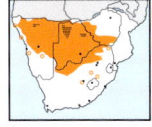

A: Witkatlagter
Z: Ihlekehlelimhlophe
H: Onḍera Otjiapa
G: Elsterdroßling

BLACK-WINGED KITE

Grasslands. White under-parts, grey upperparts, black wing tips and shoulder patches. 30 cm

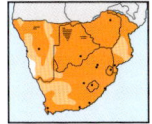

A: Blouvalk
Z: Udemezane
X: Isitshisane
Ss: Segootsane
Ts: Nwarikapanyana
N: ≠nū-‖gawo hīsabes
G: Gleitaar

HARTLAUB'S GULL

Coastal. White body, grey upperwings and back, and red bill and legs. 38 cm

A: Hartlaubmeeu **Z:** Unochweba WaseKapa
Ss: Mmamawatle Wa Bophirimela
Tw: Lenongwatle La Bophirima **N:** !khawaga ≠kharigaos
G: Hartlaubsmöwe

GREY-HEADED GULL

Wetlands. White with grey head, back and upperwings, and red bill and legs. 42 cm

A: Gryskopmeeu **Z:** Indewula
Ss: Mmamawatle Wa Hlohoputswa
Tw: Lenongwatle La Tlhogokotswana
N: |hai-dana ≠kharigaos **G:** Graukopfmöwe

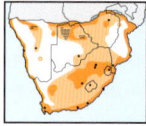

SQUACCO HERON (in flight)

Wetlands. White underparts are visible in flight; br. birds have pale red-brown upperparts; non-br. pale tawny brown. 43 cm

A: Ralreier **Z:** Umacuthomhlophe **Ss:** Kokolofitwe Ya Molomotalalehodimo **Tw:** Kokolohutwe Ya Molomotalalegodimo **N:** ≠hoa-am |gurikhoeseb **G:** Rallenreiher

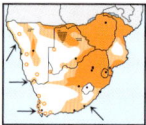

br.

non-br.

WESTERN CATTLE EGRET

Pastures and mixed grasslands. White plumage, with yellowish bill and legs; br. birds have buff on head, neck and back. 54 cm

A: Veereier **Z:** Ilanda **X:** Ilanda **Ss:** Leholotsiane Le Leholo
Tw: Modisakgomo **Ts:** Masemgahomu **Sh:** Kafudzamombe
N: kai |ēdeharab **H:** Etuva Rovinamuinyo **G:** Kuhreiher

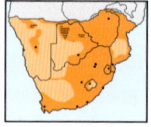

LITTLE EGRET

Wetlands. All-white plumage, black bill and legs, and yellow feet. 64 cm

A: Kleinwitreier **Z:** Ingeklencane
Ss: Leholotsiane Le Lenyenyane **Tw:** Moleane O Monnye
N: kai |apa|nūbeb **G:** Seidenreiher

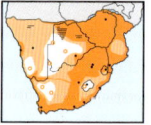

YELLOW-BILLED EGRET

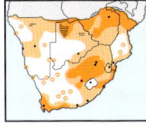

Wetlands. White plumage, yellow bill and upper legs, and black lower legs.
68 cm

A: Geelbekwitreier
Z: Umanyatheludaka
X: Unowambu
Ss: Leholotsiane La Molomosehla
Tw: Moleane Wa Molomosetlha
G: Mittelreiher

MARTIAL EAGLE (imm.)

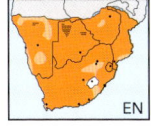

Woodland and bushveld. White underparts, brown upperparts and yellow feet.
78–83 cm

A: Breëkoparend
Z: Isihuhwa
Ss: Ntsu E Kgolo
Sp: Mmakgwana
Tw: Ntsu E Thamaga
Ts: Manole
N: !ari!khās
G: Kampfadler

imm.

GREAT EGRET

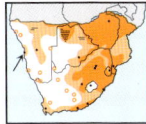

Wetlands. White plumage, black legs and feet, and yellow bill; br. ad. may have darker bill. 95 cm

A: Grootwitreier
Z: Ingeklenkulu
Ss: Leholotsiane Le Leholo
Tw: Moleane O Mogolo
Sh: Svorechena
N: kai gai-!noab
G: Silberreiher

AFRICAN SPOONBILL

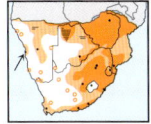

Wetlands. White plumage, red and grey spatulate bill, and red face and legs.
91 cm

A: Lepelaar
Z: Isixulamasele
Ss: Molomokgaba
Tw: Mmaleswana
N: ‖goabams
G: Afrikanischer Löffler

AFRICAN SACRED IBIS

Wetlands. White bird with black head, neck and decurved beak. 89 cm

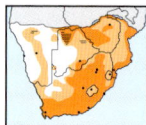

A: Skoorsteenveër
Z: Inkankanelunga
Ss: Lehalanyane
N: ≠khani‖khâbams
G: Heiliger Ibis

YELLOW-BILLED STORK

Inland waters. White bird with distinctive yellow bill and red face, and red legs. 97 cm

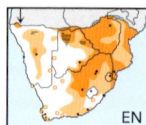

A: Nimmersat
Z: Unomlomophuzi
Ss: Mokotatsie Wa Molomosehla
Tw: Lenompoo
N: !huni-am oefari
G: Nimmersatt

CAPE GANNET

Coastal shores. Mostly white, with black tail and flight feathers, and a distinctive yellow wash on head and neck.
84–94 cm

A: Witmalgas
Z: Isicibamanzi
X: Umkholonjane
Ss: Seqwelo Sa Kapa
N: ǀui !handas
G: Kaptölpel

WHITE STORK

Grassveld and bushveld. Black and white with red bill and legs. 117 cm

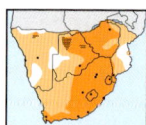

A: Witooievaar
Z: Unogolantethe
Ss: Mokotatsie O Mosweu
N: !uri oefari
G: Weißstorch

LESSER FLAMINGO

Salt pans. Pinkish-white, sometimes fairly white, with red wing feathers, bill and legs. 102 cm

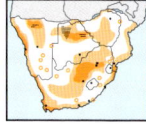

A: Kleinflamink
Z: Ukholwasomncane
Sp: Tlatšana
Tw: Lekukara
N: ≠khari |apa|nūbeb
H: Kakueya Okaṭiṭi
G: Zwergflamingo

GREATER FLAMINGO

Salt pans and soda lakes. White plumage, red-and-black wings, pink and black bill, and long pink legs. 140 cm

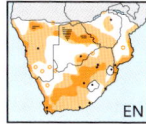

A: Grootflamink **Z:** Ukholwasomkhulu
Ss: Mmamolalana E Moholo **Tw:** Tladi **N:** kai |apa|nūbeb
G: Flamingo

PINK-BACKED PELICAN

Inland waters. Grey and white with a pinkish back; non-br. birds have grey wings; br. birds are paler. 135 cm

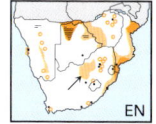

A: Kleinpelikaan **Z:** Ivubelincane
Ss: Leya Le Lenyenyane **Tw:** Leya Le Lennye
N: ≠khari |ēdeharab **G:** Rötelpelikan

GREAT WHITE PELICAN

Estuaries and lagoons. White with black flight feathers, yellowish bill and pink legs. 180 cm

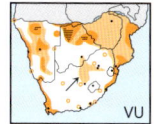

A: Witpelikaan
Z: Ivubelikhulu
Ss: Leya Le Leholo
Tw: Leya Le Legolo
N: kai |ēdeharab
G: Rosapelikan

BLUE PLUMAGE

Some of our most colourful birds owe their brilliance to blue plumage – often iridescent blue as seen, for example, in starlings, swallows and wood hoopoes, which appear metallic blue or green, depending on the light. Certain raptors may also appear blue-black in full sun.

What makes a bird appear blue or iridescent?

While most plumage colours are the result of pigments, this is not the case in blue and iridescent birds. These striking plumage colours are, in fact, a product of the interaction between light and the structure of the feathers.

Iridescence is produced in two ways: when light that passes through a thin layer of a substance called keratin is refracted on the surface of the feather barbules; or when light is refracted by minute granules of melanin that occur in a thin layer just below the surface of the feather barbules. The colour changes depending on the angle at which one views the bird. The feathers might appear dull at one moment, then iridescent the next. Flight feathers are usually not iridescent.

Non-iridescent blue is created by the scattering of light when it passes through minute air-filled cavities between the keratin and the feather barbules. The thickness of the keratin cortex determines the intensity of the blue reflected back, while the remaining light is absorbed by the feathers' underlying pigments. As a result, the colour does not change if the bird is viewed from a different angle. Rollers, such as the Lilac-breasted Roller, all exhibit brilliant blue wings, often described as electric blue. This is a true colour, which also occurs in some bee-eaters and the Blue Waxbill.

WIRE-TAILED SWALLOW

Rivers. Metallic blue upperparts, orange cap, white underparts, and long tail streamers. 13 cm

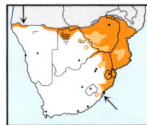

A: Draadstertswael
Z: Inkonjanesileside
G: Rotkappenschwalbe

WESTERN (COMMON) HOUSE MARTIN

Wetlands. Metallic blue upperparts, white rump and underparts, and shallowly forked tail. 14 cm

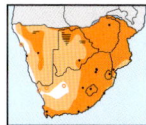

A: Huisswael
Z: Inhlolamvula
Ss: Lekabelane-Nkatatshweu
G: Mehlschwalbe

PEARL-BREASTED SWALLOW

Open woodland. Metallic blue upperparts, white underparts, and forked tail. 14 cm

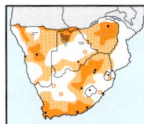

A: Pêrelborsswael
Z: Inkonjanencwaba
Ss: Lefokotsane-Kokotloputswa
G: Perlbrustschwalbe

WHITE-THROATED SWALLOW

Wetlands. Metallic blue upperparts, orange forehead, white underparts, black breast band, and forked tail. 17 cm

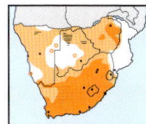

A: Witkeelswael
Z: Inkonjanemqalomhlophe
X: Unocel' Izapholo
G: Weißkehlschwalbe

BARN SWALLOW

Savanna bushveld. Metallic blue upperparts, orange forehead and chin, black throat and white under-parts, and forked tail. Forked tail. **18 cm**

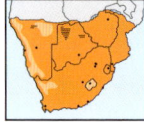

A: Europese Swael
Z: Inkonjane YaseYutobhu
Ss: Lepeolane
G: Rauchschwalbe

juv.

GREY-RUMPED SWALLOW

River banks and grassy slopes. Metallic blue upperparts, greyish cap and rump, and forked tail. **14 cm**

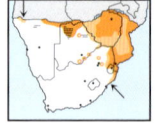

A: Gryskruisswael **Z:** Inkonjanemqolomlotha
G: Graubürzelschwalbe

SOUTH AFRICAN CLIFF SWALLOW

Bridges and towers. Metallic blue upperparts, orange forehead, white underparts, black breast band, and forked tail. **15 cm**

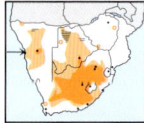

A: Familieswael
Z: Inkonjane Yamawa
Ss: Lefokotsane-La-Dilomo
G: Klippenschwalbe

LESSER STRIPED SWALLOW

Bushveld. Metallic blue upperparts, orange head and rump, heavily streaked white underparts, and forked tail. **16 cm**

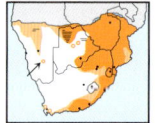

A: Kleinstreepswael
Z: Inkonjanecane
Ss: Lefokotsane-Mereto
G: Kleine Streifenschwalbe

GREATER STRIPED SWALLOW

Grassland. Metallic blue upperparts, orange head and rump, lightly streaked white underparts, and forked tail. 20 cm

A: Grootstreepswael
Z: Inkonjanenkulu
G: Große Streifenschwalbe

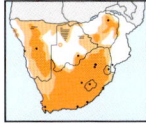

MOSQUE SWALLOW

Woodland. Metallic blue upperparts, white throat and upper breast, orange underparts, and forked tail. 23 cm

A: Moskeeswael **Z:** Inkonjane Yemiboshongo **G:** Senegalschwalbe

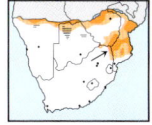

RED-BREASTED SWALLOW

Grasslands. Metallic blue upperparts, orange underparts, and forked tail. 24 cm

A: Rooiborsswael
Z: Inkonjanesifubabomvu
Ss: Lekabelane-Petakgubedu
G: Rotbauchschwalbe

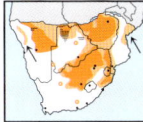

BLUE WAXBILL

Thornveld. Brown upperparts and blue underparts. 12–14 cm

A: Gewone Blousysie **Z:** Isicelankobe
Sp: Tšwee **Nd:** Umtinti **Sh:** Katsiitsii
G: Angola-Schmetterlingsfinke

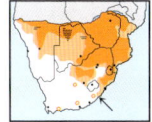

WHITE-BELLIED SUNBIRD

Woodland. Glossy blue-green upperparts and breast, white belly, and curved black bill. 11 cm

A: Witpenssuikerbekkie
Z: Incwincwemhlope
G: Weißbauch-Nektarvogel

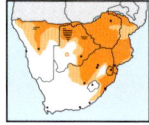

MALACHITE KINGFISHER

Ponds. Deep blue upperparts, orange-buff underparts, white ear-patch and throat, and red bill and feet. 14 cm

A: Kuifkopvisvanger
Z: Uzangozolo
Ss: Seinodi Sa Motlwenya
Sh: Kanyururahove
N: !amxadana ||audīb
G: Malachiteisvogel

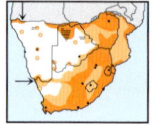

AFRICAN PYGMY KINGFISHER

Woodland. Deep blue upperparts, buff underparts, mauve cheeks, and red bill and feet. 13 cm

A: Dwergvisvanger
Z: Isikhilothi
Ss: Seinodi Se Senyenyane
N: ≠khari ||audīb
G: Natalzwergfischer

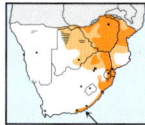

STRIPED KINGFISHER

Woodland. Blue back, tail and wings, black wing coverts, brown streaking on cap and white underparts, and dark brown-and-red bill. 18–19 cm

A: Gestreepte Visvanger
Z: Unongozolwane
Ss: Seinodi Sa Metjhato
Sp: Senwamorula Sa Mela
N: daoxa ||audīb
G: Streifenliest

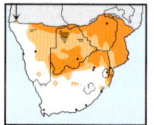

GREY-HEADED KINGFISHER

Mixed woodland. Royal blue back, tail and wings, black wing coverts, grey head and mantle, chestnut belly, and red bill. 20 cm

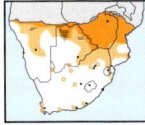

A: Gryskopvisvanger
Z: Isiphikelelesikhandampunga
Ss: Seinodi Sa Hlohoputswa
N: |hai-dana ||audīb
G: Graukopfliest

WOODLAND KINGFISHER

Woodland. Turquoise-blue upperparts, black wing coverts, white underparts, and red-and-black bill.
23–24 cm

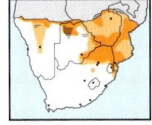

A: Bosveldvisvanger
Z: Imbuyelelo
Ss: Seinodi Sa Moru
Tw: Thathadikoma
N: hai|gom ||audīb
G: Senegalliest

HALF-COLLARED KINGFISHER

Rivers. Brilliant blue upperparts, white throat, buffy underparts, black bill and red legs. 20 cm

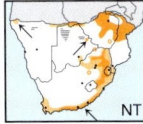

A: Blouvisvanger
Z: Isixula
Ss: Seinodi Se Setalalehodimo
N: ≠hoa ||audīb
G: Kobalteisvogel

BROWN-HOODED KINGFISHER

Woodland. Blue rump and tail, blue-and-black upper wings, brownish-streaked head and mantle, white underparts and red bill.
23–24 cm

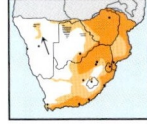

A: Bruinkopvisvanger
Z: Isiphikeleli
G: Braunkopfliest

MIOMBO BLUE-EARED STARLING

Miombo woodland. Glossy blue-green with purple flanks and yellow eyes.
20 cm

A: Klein-blouoorglansspreeu
Z: Ikhwezi LaseZimbabwe
G: Messingglanzstar

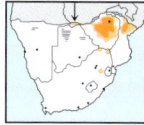

CAPE STARLING

Woodland and suburbia. Glossy blue-green with bluer head and yellow eyes.
23–25 cm

A: Kleinglansspreeu Z: Ikhwezi
X: Inyakrini Ss: Lehodi-Pilwane
Sw: Likhweti N: ||nuwub
G: Rotschulter-Glanzstar

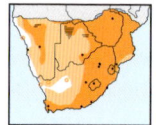

GREATER BLUE-EARED STARLING

Woodland Glossy blue head and breast, glossy green wings, purple-blue flanks and belly, and yellow eyes. 21–23 cm

A: Groot-blouoorglansspreeu
Z: Ikhwezi LaseNyakatho
G: Grünschwanz-Glanzstar

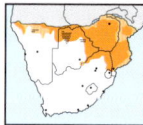

BLACK-BELLIED STARLING

Riparian and coastal woodland. Dull blue-green with black belly. 21 cm

A: Swartpensglansspreeu
Z: Ikhwezi Lasogwini
X: Intenenengu
G: Schwarzbauch-Glanzstar

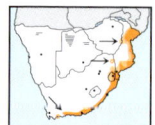

SHARP-TAILED STARLING

Woodland. Glossy blue-green with black ear-patch and red eyes. 26 cm

A: Spitsstertglansspreeu
G: Keilschwanz-Glanzstar

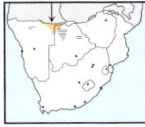

MEVES'S STARLING

Mopane woodland. Glossy purple-blue with dark eyes and long, graduated tail. 30–34 cm

A: Langstertglansspreeu **Z:** Ikhwezelimsilomude
N: ‖nuwub **G:** Meves-Glanzstar

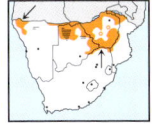

BURCHELL'S STARLING

Woodland. Glossy blue and purple with black mask and dark eyes. 30–34 cm

A: Grootglansspreeu
Z: Ikhwezelikhulu
Tw: Letleretlere Le Legolo
N: ‖nuwub
G: Riesenglanzstar

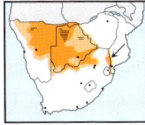

EUROPEAN BEE-EATER

Woodland. Blue forehead and underparts, chestnut, yellow and green upperparts, and yellow throat. 25–29 cm

A: Europese Byvreter
Z: Inkothanyosi
Ss: Thlapolome Ya Leboya
Tw: Seselamarumo Ya Bokone
Sh: Gamanyuchi
N: ǀapa nīb
G: Europäischer Bienenfresser

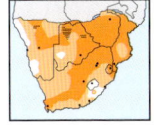

SWALLOW-TAILED BEE-EATER

Woodland. Blue collar, upper tail and belly, green upperparts, yellow throat, with forked tail. 20–22 cm

A: Swaelstertbyvreter
Z: Inkothesankonjane
Ss: Thlapolome Ya Setonolekabelane
Tw: Sabotlhoko
N: swawel-≠are nīb
H: Onḍera Yotjiongo
G: Schwalbenschwanzspint

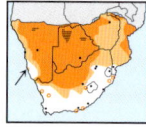

SOUTHERN CARMINE BEE-EATER

Rivers and bushveld. Carmine red with blue cap and underbelly. 33–38 cm

A: Rooiborsbyvreter
Z: Inkothaenkulu
Ss: Thlapolome Ya Sefubafubedu
Tw: Morokapula
N: ǀawa-ǀgā nīb
G: Scharlachspint

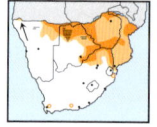

BLUE-CHEEKED BEE-EATER

Riverine woodland. Blue eyebrows, cheeks, rump and belly, green upperparts, yellow chin and chestnut throat. 27–33 cm

A: Blouwangbyvreter **Z:** Indlanyosi
Ss: Thlapolome Ya Leramatalalehodimmo
N: ≠hoa-ai nīb
G: Blauwangenspint

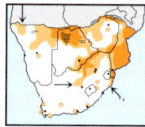

EUROPEAN ROLLER

Woodland. Pale blue head and underparts, brown back, and square tail. 30–31 cm

A: Europese Troupant
Z: Ifefeliluhlaza
Ss: Letleretlere Le Letalalehodimo
N: ǀapa kōkō-īas
G: Blauracke

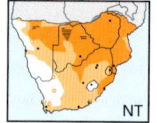

RACKET-TAILED ROLLER

Woodland. Pale blue underparts, brown back, and spatulate tail shafts. 36 cm

A: Knopsterttroupant
Z: Ifefenomsilasantshengula
Tw: Letlhakela
N: !guwu-≠are kōkō-îas
G: Spatelracke

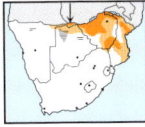

BROAD-BILLED ROLLER

Woodland. Pale blue vent and tail, deep blue wings, brown upperparts, purple breast and yellow bill. 27 cm

A: Geelbektroupant
Z: Ifefelibomvu
Sp: Lehlake
Tw: Lephakewa
N: ō-ō||nâ-es
G: Zimtroller

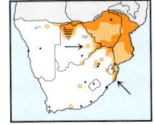

LILAC-BREASTED ROLLER

Woodland. Blue belly, wings and tail, and lilac breast. 36 cm

A: Gewone Troupant
Z: Ifefelihle
Ss: Letleretlere La Sefubaperese
Tw: Majeke
Nd: Itshegela
N: ≠hoa|awa-|gā kōkō-îas
H: Onḓera Wovanatje
G: Gabelracke

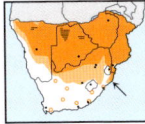

PURPLE ROLLER

Woodland. Deep blue tail and wings, brown upperparts, white-streaked maroon underparts. 36–40 cm

A: Groottroupant
Z: Ifefemidwa
Ss: Letleretlere Le Leholo
Tw: Letleretlere Le Legolo
N: ≠hoa|awa kōkō-îas
G: Strichelracke

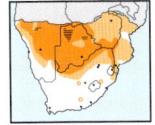

MEYER'S PARROT

Woodland. Brown upper-
parts with pale blue rump,
and green underparts.
23 cm

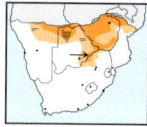

A: Bosveldpapegaai
Z: Isikhwenenesimahlombaphuzi
G: Goldbugpapagei

COMMON SCIMITARBILL

Woodland. Glossy dark
purple-blue with sharply
curved black bill.
24–28 cm

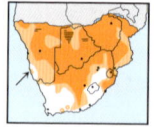

A: Swartbekkakelaar
Z: Unosungulo
Ss: Sebodu
Tw: Sebodu
N: ≠nū-am hai‖nūres
G: Sichelhopf

RÜPPELL'S PARROT ♀

Woodland. Dark brown with
blue rump, underbelly and
vent. 23 cm

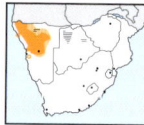

A: Bloupenspapegaai
Ss: Heka Ya Mpatalalehodimo
Sh: Hwenga
N: ≠hoa-!nā ‖giririb
G: Rüppellpapagei

♀

GREEN WOOD HOOPOE

Woodland. Glossy dark blue
with blue-and-green head,
curved red bill and long tail.
30–36 cm

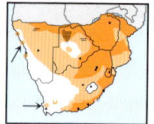

A: Rooibekkakelaar
Z: Inhlekabafazi
X: Umkulunga
Ss: Pekadifate E Tala
Sp: Senkgamogwete
Tw: Foofoo
Ts: Lokoloko
Sh: Zhwezhwezhwe
N: !am hai‖nūres
G: Steppenbaumhopf

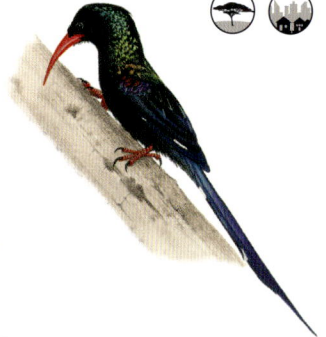

AFRICAN PARADISE FLYCATCHER

Woodland. Blue-black head and underparts, chestnut upperparts, and bright blue eye-ring and bill.
23 cm (br. male 41 cm)

A: Paradysvlieëvanger
Z: Inzwece
X: Ujejane
Ss: Kapantsi-Ya-Meru
Tw: Mothwapea **Nd:** Eve
Sh: Kateredemu
G: Paradiesschnäpper

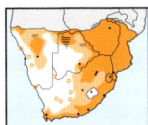

ALLEN'S GALLINULE

Wetlands. Green upperparts, blue head, frontal shield and underparts, and red bill and legs. 33 cm

A: Kleinkoningriethaan
Z: Unomhlangomncane
Ss: Mmamathebe E Monyenyane
N: ≠khari ≠āgaob
G: Afrikanisches Sultanshuhn

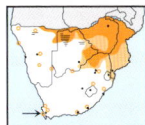

BLUE-BILLED TEAL

Shallow pans and dams. Small, brown-capped duck with blue-grey bill.
35 cm

A: Gevlekte Eend **Z:** Idadelincane
Ss: Sefudi Sa Molomo-Talalehodimo
H: Ombaka Yehi Rowakwena
G: Pünktchenente

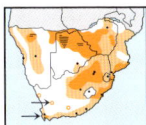

AFRICAN SWAMPHEN

Reed beds and marshes. Green upperparts, blue head and underparts, red frontal shield and bill, and pinkish legs. 46 cm

A: Grootkoningriethaan
Z: Inkukhuyomhlanga
Ss: Mmamathebe E Moholo
Tw: Mmamathebe Yo Mogolo
N: kai ≠āgaob
G: Purpurhuhn

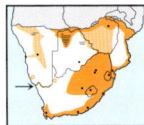

MACCOA DUCK ♂

Inland waters. Chestnut body, black head and bright blue bill. 46 cm

A: Bloubekeend **Z:** Idadelikhandamnyama
Ss: Letata La Molomo-Talalehodimo
N: ≠nüdana ≠naras **G:** Maccoa-Ente

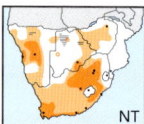

KNYSNA TURACO

Forest canopy. Green, with iridescent blue upper tail and wings, and red primary feathers visible in flight. 47 cm

A: Knysnaloerie **Z:** Igwalagwaleliluhlaza
X: Igolomi **Ss:** Kgologolo Ya Borwa **Sh:** Hurungira
G: Helmturako

PURPLE-CRESTED TURACO

Woodland. Purple-blue crest, iridescent blue wings and upper tail, green underparts with orange wash; red primary feathers visible in flight. 47 cm

A: Bloukuifloerie
Z: Igwalagwala lehlanze
Ss: Kgologolo Ya Motlwenyaperese
Tw: Kgologolo Ya Setlopophepole
G: Glanzhaubenturako

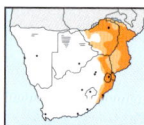

BLUE KORHAAN ♂

Grassveld. Grey-blue neck and body, and tawny brown upperwings. 50–58 cm

A: Bloukorhaan
Z: Umbukwane
Ss: Lekakarane Le Letalalehodimo
G: Blautrappe

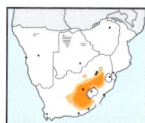

TRUMPETER HORNBILL

Riverine forests. Dark metallic blue-black upperparts and breast, white belly, and huge bill with casque. 58–65 cm

A: Gewone Boskraai
Z: Imemela
X: Ilithwa
Ss: Koro Ya Leramasweu
Tw: Koro Ya Lesamasweu
N: ǀawa-ai kôkôseb
G: Trumpeter-Hornvogel

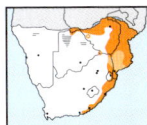

SOUTHERN BALD IBIS

Montane grassland. Glossy blue-black, with red cap, bill and legs. 79 cm

A: Kalkoenibis
Z: UmXwagele
Ss: Mokgotlo
G: Glattnackenrapp

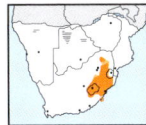

KNOB-BILLED DUCK

Wetlands. Glossy blue above, black-speckled white face and white underparts. 64–79 cm

A: Knobbeleend
Z: Unosimila
Ss: Letata La Kotjwana
Tw: Ranko
N: kai-am !kharas
G: Höckerente

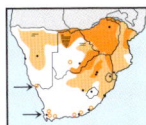

BLUE CRANE

Grasslands. Pale blue-grey, with white crown and black wing feathers. 105 cm

A: Bloukraanvoël
Z: Indwe
X: Indwe
Ss: Moholodi
N: ≠hoa !goaharab (!)
G: Paradieskranich

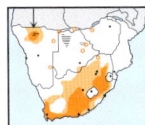

RED PLUMAGE

(including crimson and pink)

Red plumage in birds can be dominant or restricted to just a few conspicuous feathers. The colour is mostly caused by a pigment called carotenoid, which is also responsible for the yellow and orange colour seen in some birds' plumage. Birds obtain carotenoids from their diet.

How does red plumage serve a bird?

Courtship displays: A predominance of red makes a bird conspicuous. It is usually seen in the male of the species and often, but not always, during the breeding season only. The male Southern Red Bishop in breeding plumage displays with its feathers fluffed out, serving both to deflect attention from the incubating female and as a warning to other males to stay away.

Signalling: Birds with partially red plumage often have this colour on the head, breast, or both, as seen in the Black-collared Barbet. Since these are the parts of the bird presented to a rival, or to a mate, the colour may either serve as a warning signal or facilitate mate recognition. The red cap or forehead of many woodpeckers, like the Cardinal Woodpecker, is prominently displayed when the bird peers from its nest hole, probably to warn other woodpeckers that the territory is occupied.

WHY DO WOODPECKERS TAP?

Woodpeckers are well known for their habit of tapping audibly on trees with their sharp, chisel-like beaks, but the reason for this behaviour is not always understood. Aside from the actual excavation of nest holes, normal tapping has the function of disturbing insects beneath the bark or loosening the bark in search of wood beetle burrows. Tapping on hollow logs is also used by many woodpecker species as a means of territorial communication, a much-heard example of this being the far-carrying, rhythmic tapping of the **Bearded Woodpecker.**

Woodpeckers are equipped with a very long, sticky tongue (in the case of ant and termite feeders) or a **barbed tongue** (in birds that feed on wood beetle grubs). In the latter, the tongue, with its backward projecting barbs, is inserted deep into the burrow of the beetle grub until the prey is hooked and extracted.

RED-BILLED FIREFINCH

Woodland. Male has red head, underparts and upper–tail coverts, and brown wings; female is brown with red lores and upper tail. **10 cm**

A: Rooibekvuurvinkie **Z:** Inkashana
Ss: Mphubetswana-Lomofubedu **G:** Senegal-Amarant

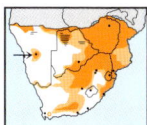

AFRICAN FIREFINCH

Woodland. Upperparts grey-brown, red face, underparts and rump, and blue-black bill. **11 cm**

A: Kaapse Vuurvinkie **Z:** Ubucubu **X:** Isicibilili
Sp: Mošalašopeng **Ts:** Xintsingiri **G:** Dunkelroter Amarant

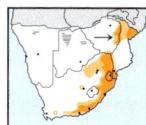

JAMESON'S FIREFINCH ♂

Woodland. Pinkish-red head, underparts and rump, brown upperparts with pinkish wash, and blue-black bill. **11 cm**

A: Jamesonvuurvinkie
Z: Insewane
G: Rosenamarant

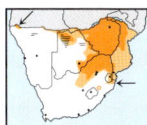

RED-THROATED TWINSPOT ♂

Dense bush. Red head (excluding crown), face and breast, and black underparts with white spots. **12.5 cm**

A: Rooikeelkolpensie
Z: Umagumejanobomvu
G: Rotkehl-Tropfenastrild

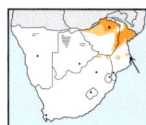

PINK-THROATED TWINSPOT ♂

Dense scrub. Pink face, breast and rump, cinnamon wings and back, black underparts with white spots. 12 cm

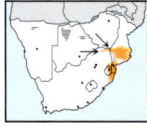

A: Rooskeelkolpensie
Z: Umagumejana
G: Perlastrild

ORANGE-WINGED PYTILIA ♂

Thickets. Red forehead, bill, throat, rump and upper tail, olive back, and orange-edged wings. 11 cm

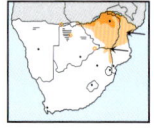

A: Oranjevlerkmelba
Z: Usantiyane WaseNyakatho
G: Wiener Astrild

GREEN TWINSPOT ♂

Forest fringes. Red face, green upperparts, and black underparts with white spots. 10 cm

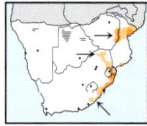

A: Groenkolpensie **Z:** Intiyaneluhlaza
G: Grüner Tropfenastrild

GREEN-WINGED PYTILIA ♂

Thickets. Red forehead, bill, throat and rump, and olive back and wings. 12–13 cm

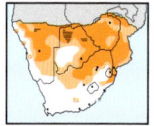

A: Gewone Melba
Z: Usantiyane
Sp: Kgakanagae
Ts: Xindzinghiri Mbandi
Sh: Zazo
N: |gîbes
G: Buntastrild

RED-HEADED QUELEA ♂

Damp grasslands and adjoining woodland. Red head, black bill and streaky brown body.
11.5 cm

A: Rooikopkwelea
Z: Ukhandabomvu
G: Rotkopfweber

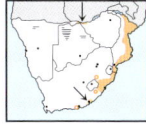

♂

RED-HEADED FINCH ♂

Thornveld. Red head, grey-brown upperparts, speckled underparts, and heavy bill.
13 cm

A: Rooikopvink **Z:** Ugazini **Ss:** Jeremane
G: Rotkopfamadine

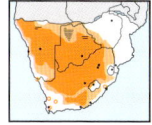

♂

RED-BILLED QUELEA ♂

Croplands. Red or pinkish bill, and streaky brown body; br. male has blackish face.
13 cm

A: Rooibekkwelea
Z: Isicibilili
G: Blutschnabelweber

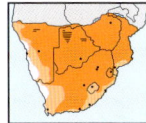

non-br. ♀

br. ♂

br. ♂

CUT-THROAT FINCH ♂

Woodland. Speckled brown, with broad red throat band, and white bill.
12 cm

A: Bandkeelvink
Z: Unongilonegazi
G: Bandfink

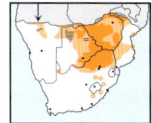

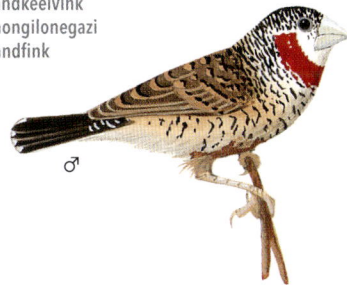

♂

ORANGE-BREASTED WAXBILL

Moist grasslands, reed beds and vleis. Yellow underparts with banded flanks, orange breast and vent, and red bill and rump. 8.5–9 cm

A: Rooiassie **Z:** Isabhonsi **X:** Impinzi
Ss: Borane-Mpatshehla **G:** Goldbrüstchen

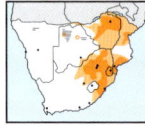

COMMON WAXBILL

Reed beds and moist grasslands. Red mask, bill and central belly, and brown-barred underparts.
13 cm

A: Rooibeksysie **Z:** Intiyanejwayelekile **X:** Intshiyane
Ss: Borane-Mpatsoku **G:** Wellenastrild

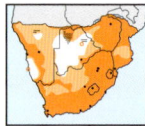

GREY WAXBILL

Woodland thickets. Mostly grey, with red eyes, rump and uppertail coverts, and black bill. 11 cm

A: Gryssysie **Z:** Ivuzigazi **Sp:** Rramphitlimphitli
Ve: Luṭimba **G:** Schwarzschwanz-Schönbürzel

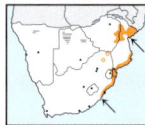

SWEE WAXBILL

Thick bush. Olive back, greyish underparts, red back and uppertail coverts, and red-and-black bill.
9–10 cm

A: Suidelike Swie
Z: UbuSukuswane
X: Utsoyi
Ss: Borane-Swaswi
G: Gelbbauchastrild

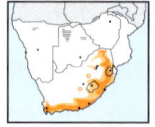

BLACK-FACED WAXBILL

Thornveld. Deep red rump and underparts, and black mask and bill.
12–13 cm

A: Swartwangsysie
Z: Intiyanelibusobumnyama
G: Elfenastrild

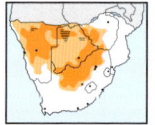

GREATER DOUBLE-COLLARED SUNBIRD ♂

Moist forest edges, kloofs and gardens. Glossy green head and mantle, wide red breast band, and greyish belly. 14 cm

A: Groot-rooibandsuikerbekkie
Z: Incuncu
Ss: Pinyane-Petakgubedu
G: Großer Halsband-Nektarvogel

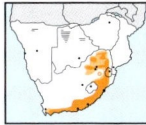

SCARLET-CHESTED SUNBIRD ♂

Woodland. Black with scarlet throat and breast, and green forehead. 15 cm

A: Rooiborssuikerbekkie **Z:** Usifubabomvu
H: Otjiondaosondu **G:** Rotbrust-Glanzköpfchen

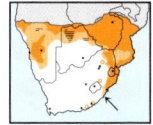

SOUTHERN DOUBLE-COLLARED SUNBIRD ♂

Woodlands, fynbos and gardens. Glossy green head and mantle, narrow red breast band, and greyish belly. 12.5 cm

A: Klein-rooibandsuikerbekkie
Z: Incuncwana
Ss: Pinyane-Petakgubetswana
G: Halsband-Nektarvogel

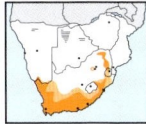

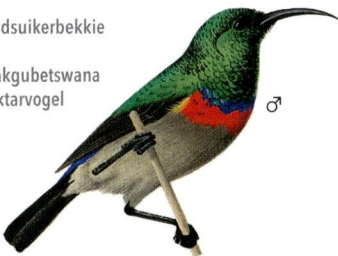

MARICO SUNBIRD ♂

Thornveld. Glossy green upperparts and upper breast, claret red breast band, and black belly. 13–14 cm

A: Maricosuikerbekkie
Z: Insonsi
G: Bindennektarvogel

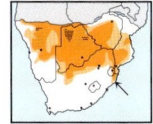

SOUTHERN RED BISHOP ♂

Reed beds and moist grasslands. Red upperparts, breast and vent, brown wings, and black face and underparts. 14 cm

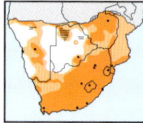

A: Rooivink **Z:** Ibomvana **X:** Intakomlilo **Ss:** Thaha-Kgube
G: Oryxweber

RED-HEADED WEAVER ♂

Woodland. Red head, mantle and breast, pink bill, and white belly. 15 cm

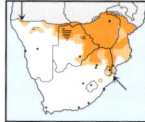

A: Rooikopwewer **Z:** Ukhandaklebhu
G: Scharlachweber

FAN-TAILED WIDOWBIRD (br. ♂)

Reed beds and marshy areas. Black, with red shoulder. 19 cm

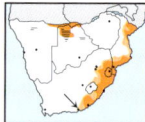

A: Kortstertflap **Z:** Umangube **X:** Isahomba
Ss: Molepe-Hetl afubedu **G:** Stummelwida

br. ♂

RED-COLLARED WIDOWBIRD (br. ♂)

Bushveld vleis. Black, with red collar and long tail; collar often difficult to see unless bird is perched.
15 cm (br. male 40 cm)

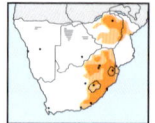

A: Rooikeelflap **Z:** Ujojo **X:** Ujojo **Ss:** Molepe-Lalafubedu
G: Schildwida

br. ♂

LONG-TAILED WIDOWBIRD (br. ♂)

Moist grasslands and valleys. Black, with conspicuous red shoulder and very long tail.
15–18 cm (br. male 60 cm)

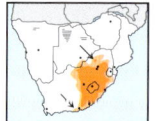

A: Langstertflap **Z:** Ibhaku **X:** Ujobela
Sp: Lekphaka **Ts:** Cilori **G:** Hahnschweifwida

br. ♂

non-br. ♂

♀

ROSY-FACED LOVEBIRD

Rocky gorges. Green body and wings, red forecrown, face and neck, and pale bill. 17–18 cm

A: Rooiwangparkiet
Ss: Hekana Ya Leramapinki
Tw: Hekana Ya Leramapinki
N: |awa-ai ||giririb
H: Onḓera Tjapolise
G: Rosenpapagei

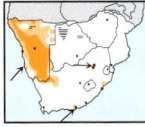

CARDINAL WOODPECKER ♂

Woodland. Red cap, brown forehead, and streaked black underparts. 14–16 cm

A: Kardinaalspeg
Z: Inqondaqonda
X: Isiqola
Ss: Kgatajwe Ya Metjhatoholo
Tw: Phaphadikota Ya Meeledigolo
Nd: Inqondoqonda
N: kai-an hai!gõ!gõseb
H: Ongongoramuti
G: Kardinalspecht

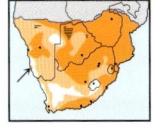

LILIAN'S LOVEBIRD

Woodland. Green body and wings, reddish forecrown, face and bill. 17–18 cm

A: Njassaparkiet
Ss: Hekana Ya Leramafubedu
Tw: Hekana Ya Lesamahubidu
G: Erdbeerköpfchen

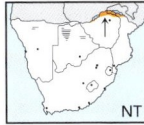

OLIVE WOODPECKER

Forests and woodland. Olive body, grey head and red rump; male has red cap. 18–20 cm

A: Gryskopspeg
Z: Isigqobhamithesiluhlaza
Ss: Kgatajwe Ya Hlohoputswa
Tw: Phaphadikota Ya Tlhogokotswana
N: |hai-dana hai!gõ!gõseb
G: Goldrückenspecht

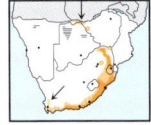

KNYSNA WOODPECKER

Coastal bush. Olive upperparts, and heavily spotted underparts; male has red cap and moustachial streak; female has black cap and red nape. **20 cm**

A: Knysnaspeg **Z:** Isigqobhamithi Saseningizimu
Ss: Kgatajwe Ya Moru **Tw:** Kokopa **G:** Natalspecht

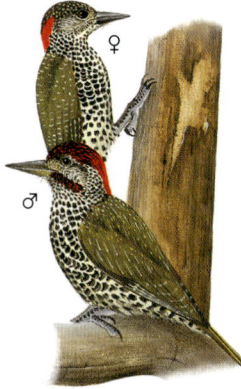

BEARDED WOODPECKER ♂

Woodland. Olive upperparts, banded grey underparts, red crown and black forehead. **23–25 cm**

A: Baardspeg
Z: Isigqonhamithintshebe
Ss: Kgatajwe Ya Ditedu
Sp: Phaphadikota Ya Lebedu
G: Namaspecht

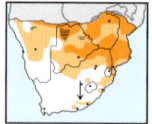

GOLDEN-TAILED WOODPECKER

Woodland. Olive upperparts, and black-streaked underparts; male has red cap and moustachial streak; female has red nape. **20–23 cm**

A: Goudstertspeg **Z:** iSibagwebe **Ss:** Kgatajwe Ya Setonokgauta
Tw: Kokonya **N:** !huni|uri-≠are hai!gõ!gõseb **H:** Ombetamiti
G: Goldschwanzspecht

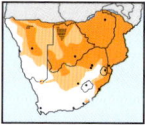

BENNETT'S WOODPECKER

Woodland. Olive upperparts, and lightly spotted underparts; male has red cap and moustachial streak; female has red nape, and brown face and throat. **22–24 cm**

A: Bennettspeg **Z:** Isigqobhamithesimadevabomvu
Ss: Kgatajwe Ya Mmetsosweu **Sp:** Phaphadikota Ya Mogološweu
Tw: Kokomere **N:** !uri-dom hai!gõ!gõseb **G:** Bennettspecht

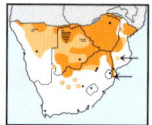

GROUND WOODPECKER

Rocky outcrops. Olive-grey upperparts, red-streaked underparts, red rump, grey head, and pale eyes. 26 cm

A: Grondspeg **Z:** UmNqangqandolo **X:** Umnqangq andola
Ss: Mohetle **Sp:** Llapaleome **Tw:** Mohetle **G:** Erdspecht

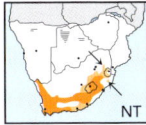

GORGEOUS BUSHSHRIKE

Mixed bush thickets. Red chin and throat, bold black breast band, and yellow belly. 20 cm

A: Konkoit
Z: Ingongoni
G: Vierfarbenwürger

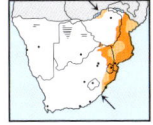

CRIMSON-BREASTED SHRIKE

Thornveld. Black upperparts with white wing stripe, and crimson underparts. 22–23 cm

A: Rooiborslaksman
Z: Ibhobhonelisisesibomvu
Sp: Palamafsika
Tw: Kgaragoba
Nd: Ibilibomvu
N: |naorab
H: Orowa
G: Rotbauchwürger

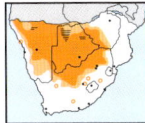

BLACK-COLLARED BARBET

Woodland. Red crown, cheeks, throat and breast, black collar, and yellowish belly. 19–20 cm

A: Rooikophoutkapper
Z: Isiqonqotho
Ss: Kopaope
Sp: Serokolo
Tw: Kopaope
N: |awa-ai kurib toas
G: Halsband-Bartvogel

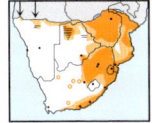

CRESTED BARBET

Woodland. Black upperparts and crest, red rump, and red speckles on yellow head and breast. 23 cm

A: Kuifkophoutkapper
Z: Usiqhovana
Ss: Mmadiwatjhe
Sp: Mphago
Tw: Sekokonyane
Sh: Chizuvaguru
N: !amxadana kurib toas
G: Haubenbartvogel

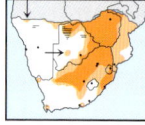

RETZ'S HELMETSHRIKE

Woodland and riverine and coastal forest. Black, with red bill, eye-rings and legs, and white vent. 22 cm

A: Swarthelmlaksman
Z: Impevelimehlabomvu
G: Dreifarb-Brillenwürger

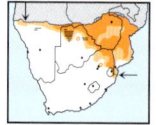

RED-BILLED OXPECKER

Woodland and areas with game or cattle. Brown body, red bill and eyes, and yellow eye-ring. 20–22 cm

A: Rooibekrenostervoël
Z: Ihlalanyathi
Ss: Kalla-Tjepa
Sp: Tšhomi
Ts: Ndzandza
G: Rotschnabel-Madenhacker

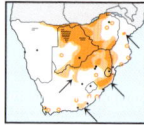

RED-BILLED BUFFALO WEAVER

Woodland. Blackish, with stout red bill. 24 cm

A: Buffelwewer
Z: Usoqhawomnyama
G: Büffelweber

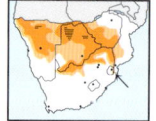

SPECKLED PIGEON

Woodlands, cliffs and building ledges. Deep reddish wings with white spots, grey underparts, and red facial skin and legs. 33 cm

A: Kransduif **Z:** Ivukuthu **Ss:** Lehoboi **Sp:** Leebarupi
Tw: Leebarope **N:** !garo≠nabis **G:** Guineataube

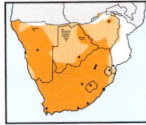

RING-NECKED DOVE

Diverse habitats. Pale grey with pinkish wash, black collar and bill, and dark red legs. 28 cm

A: Gewone Tortelduif **Z:** Usamdokwe
X: Untamnyama

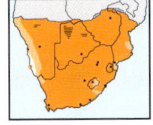

EMERALD-SPOTTED WOOD DOVE

Woodland. Pinkish breast, emerald green spots on wings, and rufous flight feathers.   20 cm

A: Groenvlekduifie **Z:** Isikhombazane-sehlanze
G: Bronzeflecktaube

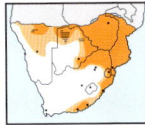

MOURNING COLLARED DOVE

Riverine woodland. Grey head, black hindcollar, pinkish breast, and yellow eyes. 30 cm

A: Rooioogtortelduif **Z:** Ihobhelililayo **Ss:** Mokuru Wa Leihlosehla
Tw: Mokuru Wa Leitlhosetlha **N:** !huni-mû ≠nais **G:** Brillentaube

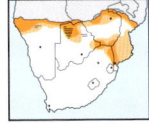

LAUGHING DOVE

Diverse habitats. Pinkish head, cinnamon blotched back, blue-grey wings, cinnamon breast with black flecks, and dark pink legs. 25 cm

A: Rooiborsduifie **Z:** UKhonzane **X:** Icelekwane **Ss:** Mofubetswana
Sp: Mphephane **Tw:** Lephoi **Ts:** Serhu **Sh:** Mhetura
N: |apa!ao≠nais **H:** Ohanda **G:** Senegaltaube

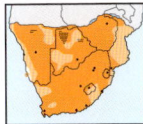

RED-EYED DOVE

Woodland. Pinkish head and breast, broad black hindcollar, and red eyes. 33–36 cm

A: Grootringduif
Z: Ihobhelimehlabombu
G: Halbmondtaube

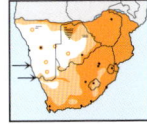

RED-FACED MOUSEBIRD

Woodland and suburbia. Greyish upperparts, buffy underparts, red facial mask and legs, and long tail. 32–34 cm

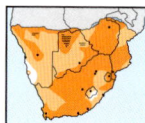

A: Rooiwangmuisvoël **Z:** UmTshivovo **X:** Intshili **Ss:** Letsiababa **Sp:** Letswiababa **Ts:** Ncivovo **Sh:** Swenya **N:** |awa-ai |khenni **G:** Rotzügel-Mausvogel

SOUTHERN CARMINE BEE-EATER

Riverine bush. Carmine-red body and wings, and curved black bill. 33–38 cm

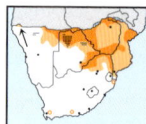

A: Rooiborsbyvreter **Z:** Inkothaenkulu **Ss:** Thlapolome Ya Sefubafubedu **Tw:** Morokapula **Ts:** Nkonyana Leyi Kulu **N:** |awa-|gã nĩb **G:** Scharlachspint

GREEN WOOD HOOPOE

Woodland and gardens. Glossy blue-green body, red legs and curved bill, and long tail. 30–36 cm

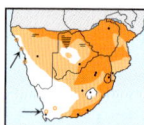

A: Rooibekkakelaar **Z:** Inhlekabafazi **X:** Umkulunga **Ss:** Pekadifate E Tala **Sp:** Senkgamogwete **Tw:** Foofoo **Ts:** Lokoloko **Sh:** Zhwezhwezhwe **N:** !am hai||nüres **G:** Steppenbaumhopf

WHITE-FRONTED BEE-EATER

Riverine woodland. Green upperparts, cinnamon nape and breast, red throat, white forehead and chin, blue vent and belly. 22–24 cm

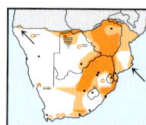

A: Rooikeelbyvreter **Z:** Inkotha **Ss:** Thlapolome Ya Phatlasweu **Tw:** Seselamarumo Sa Phatlasweu **N:** !uri-!ũ nĩb **G:** Weißstirnspint

NARINA TROGON

Dense forests and woodland thickets. Glossy green upperparts and head, red belly, and greenish-yellow bill. 29–34 cm

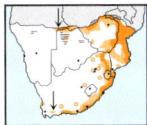

A: Bosloerie Z: Umjenenengu X: Intshatshongo Ss: Tsoko
Sp: Tsoko Tw: Tsoko N: hainoeab G: Narina-Trogon

RED-NECKED SPURFOWL

Coastal bush. Red facial and throat skin, bill and legs; plumage variable, may have white on head. 32–44 cm

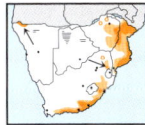

A: Rooikeelfisant
Z: Isikhwehlesimqalabomvu
X: Inkwali
Ss: Kgwale Ya Mmetsofubedu
Tw: Lesogo La Mometsohubidu
Ts: N'warimakokwe Sh: Nhindiro
N: ǀawadom ≠nanas
G: Rotkehlfrankolin

AFRICAN RAIL

Reed beds. Rufous upper-parts, grey head and underparts, and red bill and legs. 36 cm

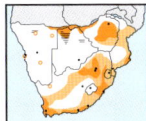

A: Grootriethaan Z: Isizinzi Ss: Mopakapaka
Ts: Nwatsekutseku N: kai ≠ā-anib G: Kapralle

SWAINSON'S SPURFOWL

Open grass woodlands. Dark brown body, red facial and throat skin, black-tipped red bill, and dark legs. 34–39 cm

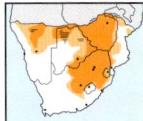

A: Bosveldfisant
Z: Inkwali
H: Ongwari Yovihua Vyo Mokuti
Ss: Kgwale Ya Leotontsho
Sp: Lehoho La Leotoso
Tw: Rakodukhubidu
Ts: Nghwari Ya Xidhaka
N: ≠nūǀnū ≠nanas
G: Swainsonfrankolin

RED-BILLED SPURFOWL

Dry woodland. Dark brown body, red bill and legs, and yellow eye-ring.
30–38 cm

A: Rooibekfisant
Z: Isikhwehlesimlomobomvu
Ss: Kgwale Ya Molomofubedu
Tw: Letšankgarane
N: ǀawa-am ǂnanas
H: Ongwari
G: Rotschnabelfrankolin

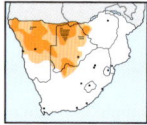

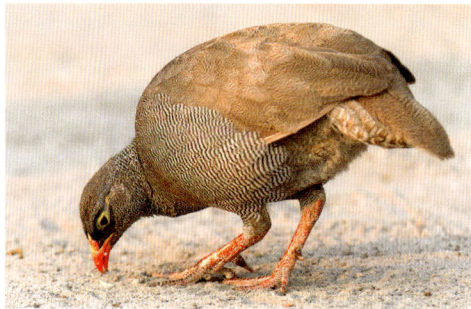

KNYSNA TURACO

Forest canopy. Green head and body, white crest, and red flight feathers. 47 cm

A: Knysnaloerie
Z: Igwalagwaleliluhlaza
X: Igolomi
Ss: Kgologolo Ya Borwa
Ts: Tlulutlulu
Nd: Umguwe
Sh: Hurungira
G: Helmturako

NATAL SPURFOWL

Koppies and river banks. Brown upperparts, speckled underparts, red-and-yellow bill, and red legs.
30–38 cm

A: Natalse Fisant
Z: Unomemeza
X: Isakhwehle
Ss: Kgwale Ya Molomolamunu
Tw: Segweba
Ts: Nghwari Ma Ntshengwhayi
Nd: Mkwari
G: Natalfrankolin

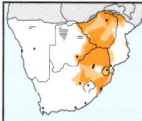

PURPLE-CRESTED TURACO

Riverine woodland. Purple crest and wings, green head, neck and chest, red eye-ring and flight feathers.
47 cm

A: Bloukuifloerie
Z: Igwalagwala lehlanze
Ss: Kgologolo Ya Motlwenyaperese
Tw: Kgologolo Ya Setlopophepole
G: Glanzhaubenturako

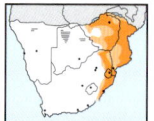

RED-BILLED TEAL

Open fresh water. Mottled brown plumage, brown cap, and red bill. 48 cm

A: Rooibekeend Z: Idadelimlomobomvu
Ss: Sefudi Sa Molomofubedu
Tw: Sehudi Sa Molomohubidu N: ǀawa-am ǂnaras
H: Ombaka Yoheya G: Rotschnabelente

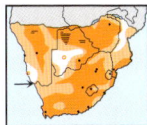

CAPE TEAL

Brackish pans. Dark brown upperparts, pale head and underparts with dark brown speckling, and pink bill. 46 cm

A: Teeleend Z: Unosikhutha Ss: Sefudi Sa Molomopinki
Tw: Sehudi Sa Molomopinki N: ǀawara-am ǂnaras
H: Ombaka YaKapa G: Kapente

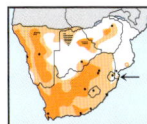

AFRICAN FINFOOT

River edges. Brown and white barred plumage, and red bill and legs. 63 cm

A: Watertrapper Z: Igwedlamanzi
Ss: Sehatametsi Tw: Segatametsi N: ǁgamdāb
G: Afrikanische Binsenralle

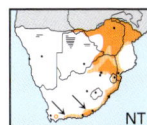

SOUTHERN RED-BILLED HORNBILL

Woodland. Black and white, with speckled upperparts, and prominent red bill. 42–50 cm

A: Rooibekneushoringvoël
Z: UmKholwane
Ss: Korwe Ya Molomofubedu
Ts: Manon'wana
N: ǀawa-am kōkōseb
H: Etoko Rotjinjotjiserandu
G: Mopanetoko

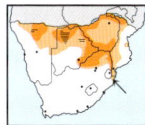

CROWNED HORNBILL

Lowland forests. Dark brown upperparts, white underparts, and prominent red bill with yellow base. 50–57 cm

A: Gekroonde Neushoringvoël
Z: UmKhololwane
X: Umkholwane
Ss: Korwe Ya Moqhaka
Tw: Kgoropo Kg Serokwa
Ts: Nkorhonyarhi
N: gao-aoǀgapa kōkōseb
H: Etoko Rotjinkorone
G: Kronentoko

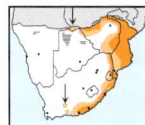

MONTEIRO'S HORNBILL

Arid woodland. Dark upper-parts, head and breast, white underparts, and red bill with white base.
54–58 cm

A: Monteironeushoringvoël
Tw: Korwe Ya Lefukasweu
N: !uri-||gawo kôkôseb
G: Monteirotoko

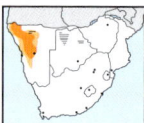

BATELEUR

Game reserves and open woodlands. Black, with tawny wings, red bill, facial skin and legs, and short tail.
55–70 cm

A: Berghaan **Z:** Ingqungqulu
X: Ingqanga **Ss:** Petleke
Sp: Kgwadira **Ts:** Ximhungwe
Nd: Ingqungqulu **Sh:** Chapungu
N: !nuwu-≠are !khãs **G:** Gaukler

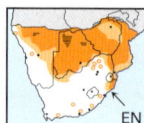

SOUTHERN GROUND HORNBILL

Woodland. Black, with red skin on face and throat; white in wings visible in flight.
90 cm

A: Bromvoël **Z:** Insigizi
X: Intsikizi **Ss:** Lekgotutu
Tw: Lehututu **Ts:** Nghututu
Nd: Insingizi **Sh:** Dendera
N: !hükôkôseb **H:** Epumutu
G: Hornrabe

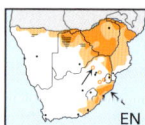

SOUTHERN BALD IBIS

Agricultural land and dry grasslands. Glossy blue-black, with red cap, bill and legs.
71 cm

A: Kalkoenibis
Z: UmXwagele
Ss: Mokgotlo
G: Glattnackenrapp

WHITE STORK

Open grass bushveld. Black and white, with red bill and legs.
117 cm

A: Witooievaar
Z: Unogolantethe
Ss: Mokotatsie O Mosweu
N: !uri oefari
G: Weißstorch

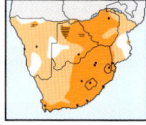

LESSER FLAMINGO

Salt pans and lagoons. Pinkish-white, sometimes fairly white, with red wing feathers, bill and legs.
102 cm

A: Kleinflamink
Z: Ukholwasomncane
Ss: Mmamolalana E Monyenyane
Sp: Tlatšana
Tw: Lekukara
N: ≠khari ǀapaǀnũbeb
H: Kakueya Okaṱiṯi
G: Zwergflamingo

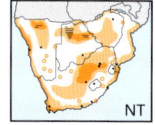

SADDLE-BILLED STORK

Freshwater bodies. Black-and-white plumage, and red-and-black bill with yellow saddle. 145 cm

A: Saalbekooievaar **Z:** Umadolabomvu
Ss: Molombwe **Ts:** Ngwamhlanga
N: !aroda-am oefari
H: Endongo Otjikaviriro
G: Sattelstorch

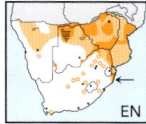

GREATER FLAMINGO

Salt pans and lagoons. White plumage, red-and-black wings, pink and black bill, and long, pink legs.
140 cm

A: Grootflamink **Z:** Ukholwasomkhulu
Ss: Mmamolalana E Moholo **Sp:** Tladi
Tw: Tladi **Ts:** Ximinta Ntsengele **N:** kai ǀapaǀnũbeb
H: Kakueya **G:** Flamingo

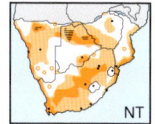

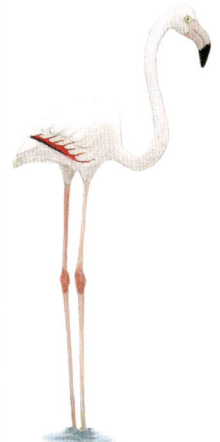

First impression
ORANGE PLUMAGE

This bright colouring usually occurs on the forehead or breast, where it can easily be seen by other birds.

Orange coloration is used for various signalling functions in birds, from species recognition to courtship, and even mate-bonding rituals.

The role of colour in the rearing of chicks

Recognition: Colour can also function as a recognition feature when birds feed their young, as chicks will not take food from the wrong-coloured bill. For example, experiments have shown that Western Cattle Egret nestlings will only accept food presented by the orange bill of the parent.

Feeding stimulus: The Cape Longclaw has a bright orange-red throat with a black border that mimics the orange-red interior of its nestlings' mouths. When the parent bird comes to the nest with food, the chicks, on seeing the brightly coloured throat, are stimulated to open their gapes to receive the food. The parent, in turn, on seeing the chicks' bright gapes, is stimulated to deliver the meal.

THE CERE AND LORES

The **cere** is a swollen fleshy area at the base of the upper mandible of some birds, such as birds of prey, parrots and pigeons. In pigeons, such as the **Rock Dove**, it appears as two fleshy swellings above the nostrils. The colour of the cere varies according to species, and may be grey, yellow (as in many birds of prey), orange or red. The exact function of the cere is unknown.

The **lore** is a bare patch of skin between the base of the bill and the eye, on each side of a bird's head. In many birds of prey the lores are featherless, and the skin may be red, yellow or grey. Lores probably help maintain cleanliness, especially in those raptors that feed on messy food items such as carcasses. In the **African Harrier-Hawk (Gymnogene)**, the entire face and front section of the head is bare, while in many vultures the entire head and much of the neck is featherless.

ORANGE-BREASTED WAXBILL

Reed beds. Red bill and mask, yellow underparts with banded flanks, orange breast and vent.
8.5–9 cm

A: Rooiassie
Z: Isabhonsi
X: Impinzi
Ss: Borane-Mpatshehla
G: Goldbrüstchen

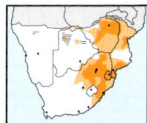

LONG-BILLED CROMBEC

Bushveld. Grey upperparts, buff-orange underparts, and tailless appearance.
10–12 cm

A: Bosveldstompstert
Z: Inkashana
Ss: Poponaka
Sp: Kurutle
Tw: Sepone
Ts: Nqcunu
G: Langschnabel-Sylvietta

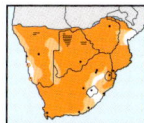

GREY PENDULINE TIT

Woodland. Dark greyish upperparts, buff forehead, face, belly and vent, and pale grey breast.
8–9 cm

A: Gryskapokvoël
Z: Iklosi
X: Unogushana
G: KWeißtirnbeutelmeise

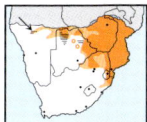

ORANGE-BREASTED SUNBIRD ♂

Fynbos. Glossy green head and throat, purple breast band, and orange breast fading to yellow at vent.
15 cm

A: Oranjeborssuikerbekkie
Z: Incwincwi YaseKapa
G: Goldbrust-Nektarvogel

AFRICAN PYGMY KINGFISHER

Woodland. Deep blue upperparts, orange-buff underparts, orange face, mauve cheeks, and red bill and feet. 13 cm

A: Dwergvisvanger
Z: Isikhilothi
Sp: Tsirro Ye Nnyane
Tw: Setshwaraditlhapi Se Sennye
N: ≠khari ‖audĩb
G: Natalzwergfischer

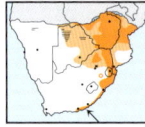

WIRE-TAILED SWALLOW

Lowveld rivers. Orange cap, blue upperparts, white underparts, and fine tail streamers. 13 cm

A: Draadstertswael
Z: Inkonjanesileside
G: Rotkappenschwalbe

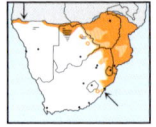

MALACHITE KINGFISHER

Ponds and rivers. Deep blue upperparts, orange-buff underparts, orange face, and red bill and feet. 14 cm

A: Kuifkopvisvanger
Z: Uzangozolo
Ss: Seinodi Sa Motlwenya
Ts: Thungununu
Nd: Intangaza
Sh: Kanyururahove
G: Malachiteisvogel

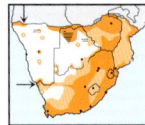

SOUTH AFRICAN CLIFF SWALLOW

Bridges and towers. Brownish cap, dull metallic blue upperparts, orange rump, breast and vent, dark speckling on throat and breast, white belly, and square tail. 15 cm

A: Familieswael
Z: Inkonjane Yamawa
Ss: Lefokotsane-La-Dilomo
G: Klippenschwalbe

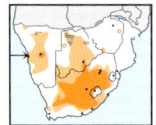

LESSER STRIPED SWALLOW

Lowveld. Orange cap, ear coverts and rump, white underparts heavily streaked with black, and forked tail. 16 cm

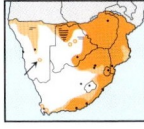

A: Kleinstreepswael
Z: Inkonjanecane
Ss: Lefokotsane-Mereto
G: Kleine Streifenschwalbe

GREATER STRIPED SWALLOW

Highveld. Orange cap and rump, whitish underparts lightly streaked with black, and forked tail. 20 cm

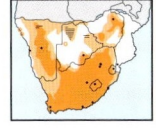

A: Grootstreepswael
Z: Inkonjanenkulu
G: Große Streifenschwalbe

BARN SWALLOW

Aerial. Metallic blue upperparts, orange forehead and chin, black throat, white underparts, and forked tail. 18 cm

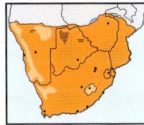

A: Europese Swael
Z: Inkonjane YaseYutobhu
Ss: Lepeolane
G: Rauchschwalbe

juv

MOSQUE SWALLOW

Woodland. Metallic blue upperparts, deep orange underparts, white throat, upper breast and underwings, and forked tail. 23 cm

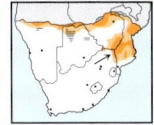

A: Moskeeswael
Z: Inkonjane Yemibhoshongo
G: Senegalschwalbe

RED-BREASTED SWALLOW

Grass savanna. Metallic blue upperparts, deep orange underparts, and forked tail. 24 cm

A: Rooiborsswael
Z: Inkonjanesifubabomvu
Ss: Lekabelane-Petakgubedu
G: Rotbauchschwalbe

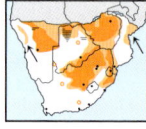

CAPE ROBIN-CHAT

Forest fringes and gardens. Grey upperparts, orange breast, vent, rump and tail fringes, grey-buff belly, and white eyebrows. 18 cm

A: Gewone Janfrederik
Z: Ugaga
X: Ugaga
Ss: Sethwenamoru
G: Kaprötel

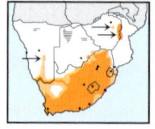

WHITE-THROATED ROBIN-CHAT

Thickets. Grey, black and white upperparts, white throat and breast, and orange wash on belly and flanks. 16–18 cm

A: Witkeeljanfrederik
Z: Umbhekle
Sp: Lekonko
G: Weißkehlrötel

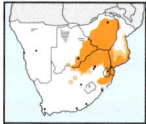

RED-CAPPED ROBIN-CHAT

Forests. Orange head, tail and underparts, brownish crown, and silver-grey wings. 18–20 cm

A: Nataljanfrederik
Z: Unonkositini
G: Natalrötel

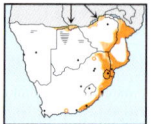

WHITE-BROWED ROBIN-CHAT

Thickets. Grey wings, orange underparts, and white eyebrows on black hood. 19–20 cm

A: Heuglinjanfrederik **Z:** Unomtshingo
Sp: Monotobidi **Tw:** Mmaleseka
G: Weißbrauenrötel

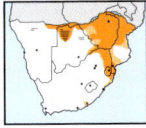

MOCKING CLIFF CHAT ♂

Rocky regions and suburbia. Black upperparts, and chestnut-orange belly and rump. 20–23 cm

A: Dassievoël
Z: Isikhwelemaweni
Ss: Sethwena-Nketsisane
Sp: Leseka
G: Rotbauchschmätzer

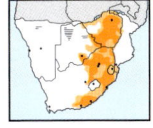

CHORISTER ROBIN-CHAT

Forests. Dark grey wings and upper tail, orange underparts, and black hood. 20 cm

A: Lawaaimakerjanfrederik
Z: Umananda
X: Ugagasisi
Sp: Tšhakga
G: Lärmrötel

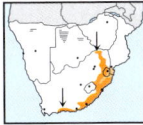

ROCKRUNNER

Rocky and bushy hillsides. Heavily streaked head and mantle, white throat and breast, and buffy orange back, belly and vent. 17 cm

A: Rotsvoël
G: Klippensänger

OLIVE BUSHSHRIKE
(buff form)

Forest thickets. Olive upperparts, buff-yellow breast, and grey cap. 17 cm

A: Olyfboslaksman **Z:** Umabhashinhlayelohlaza
G: Olivwürger

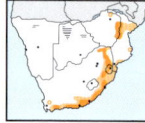

BLACK-FRONTED BUSHSHRIKE ♂

Forests. Olive-green upperparts, rich orange breast, yellow vent, grey cap and black mask. 19 cm

A: Swartoogboslaksman **Z:** Inkovebusobumnyama
G: Schwarzstirn-Buschwürger

ORANGE-BREASTED BUSHSHRIKE ♂

Bushveld. Olive-green upperparts, yellow underparts with orange breast, and grey cap and mantle. 18–19 cm

A: Oranjeborsboslaksman
Z: Umabhashinhlayela
G: Orangewürger

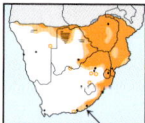

GREY-HEADED BUSHSHRIKE

Riverine forests. Olive-green upperparts, yellow underparts, orange breast, grey head, orange-yellow eyes, and heavy black bill. 25–27 cm

A: Spookvoël
Z: Usipoki
X: Umbankro
G: Graukopfwürger

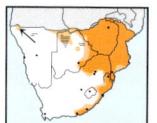

CAPE LONGCLAW

Grasslands. Grey-brown upperparts, yellow underparts, and orange throat with black border. 20 cm

A: Oranjekeelkalkoentjie
Z: Inqomfi
X: Inqilo
Ss: Lethwele
G: Kapgroßsporn

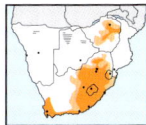

HALF-COLLARED KINGFISHER

Wooded streams and rivers. Blue upperparts, orange wash on belly and vent, white throat, black bill, and red legs. 20 cm

A: Blouvisvanger
Z: Isixula
Ss: Seinodi Se Setalalehodimo
Ts: Xitserere
G: Kobalteisvogel

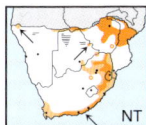

SHORT-TOED ROCK THRUSH ♂

Rocky hills. Grey upperparts and throat, dull orange underparts, and white cap. 18 cm

A: Korttoonkliplyster
Z: Inhlaletshenekhandalimhlophe
G: Kurzzehenrötel

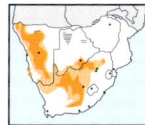

MIOMBO ROCK THRUSH ♂

Miombo woodland. Mottled grey head and upperparts, dull orange breast fading to white belly. 18 cm

A: Angolakliplyster **G:** Miomborötel

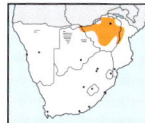

SENTINEL ROCK THRUSH ♂

Rocky hills. Blue-grey upperparts and breast, and orange underparts. 21 cm

A: Langtoonkliplyster **Z:** Ikhwelemarsheni
X: Umganto **Ss:** Thume-Kokotloputswa
G: Langzehenrötel

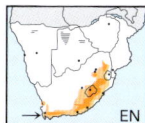

CAPE ROCK THRUSH ♂

Cliffs. Brownish back, dull orange underparts, and grey head. **21 cm**

A: Kaapse Kliplyster **Z:** Isihlalamatsheni
X: Unomaweni
Ss: Thume-Hlohoputswa
G: Klippenrötel

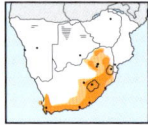

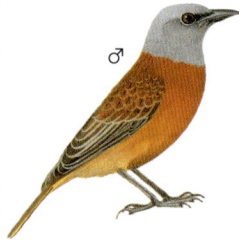

KURRICHANE THRUSH

Woodland. Greyish upperparts, orange bill, eye-ring, flanks and legs, white belly, and black moustachial streaks. **22 cm**

A: Rooibeklyster **Z:** Insansane **Ss:** Setsipitsipi-Koduphatshwa **G:** Rotschnabeldrossel

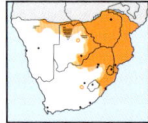

ORANGE GROUND THRUSH

Evergreen forests. Brown back, white wingbars, and rich orange throat and breast. **23 cm**

A: Oranjelyster **Z:** Inswinswi **G:** Gurneys Grunddrossel

OLIVE THRUSH

Montane forests and gardens. Dark olive-brown upperparts, speckled throat, orange belly, pale vent, and orange-yellow bill and legs. **24 cm**

A: Olyflyster
Z: UmuNswili
X: Umswi
Ss: Setsipitsipi-Sa-Bokone
G: Kapdrossel

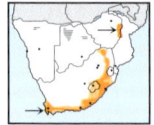

KAROO THRUSH

Highveld and scrubland. Dark grey-brown with orange belly, and orange-yellow bill and legs. **24 cm**

A: Geelbeklyster
Z: UmuNswomduba
Ss: Setsipitsipi-Sa-Moru
G: Karrudrossel

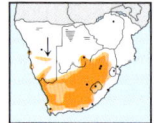

DRAKENSBERG ROCKJUMPER ♂

Rocky grasslands. Grey upperparts, and orange rump, uppertail coverts and underparts.
21 cm

A: Oranjeborsberglyster
Z: Unogxumetsheni
Ss: Modisadipela
G: Natal-Felsenspringer

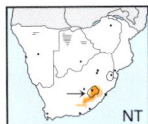

AFRICAN PYGMY GOOSE

Wetlands with floating vegetation. Dark green upperparts, orange-buff underparts, and orange bill.
33 cm

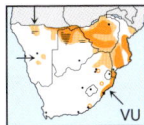

A: Dwerggans **Z:** Ivevenyane **Ss:** Lefalwana **Sp:** Lefalwana
Tw: Sehutsana **Ts:** Xisekwana
N: ≠khari !kharas **G:** Afrikanische Zwerggans

CAPE ROCKJUMPER

Rocky hillsides. Male has black-and-white upperparts and throat and chestnut underparts; female has grey streaked upperparts, orange-brown underparts, and streaked breast.
25 cm

A: Kaapse Berglyster
Z: Unogxumetsheni WaseKapa
G: Kap-Felsenspringer

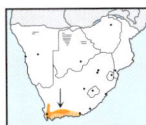

MACCOA DUCK ♂

Inland waters. Chestnut body, black head, bright blue bill, and stiff tail. 46 cm

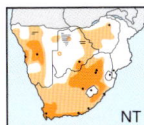

A: Bloubekeend **Z:** Idadelikhandamnyama
Ss: Letata La Molomo-Talalehodimo
N: ≠nũdana ≠naras
G: Maccoa-Ente

YELLOW PLUMAGE

Of all the bright colours seen in birds, yellow is probably the most common. In this chapter, only true yellow, a colour likely to make a lasting impression on an observer, is included. Waterbirds that are identifiable by their yellow bills are included, but not the many birds of prey that have yellow ceres and legs, since these cannot be regarded as specific identification features.

In most birds with yellow plumage, it is their underparts that carry this colour, many being yellow from chin to tail.

The role of colour in camouflage and sexual dimorphism

Countershading: It is common to see birds with darker upperparts and paler underparts. This colouring can help camouflage a bird and is called countershading. In sunlight, a uniformly coloured bird will look paler above, while its underparts will be shaded and appear darker. However, a bird that is green above and yellow below will appear to be the same colour all over, since its yellow underparts will take on a greenish appearance in the shade, helping the bird blend into the background.

Sexual dimorphism: When breeding, Yellow-crowned Bishop and Southern Masked Weaver males have conspicuous plumage, which they use in displays and territorial defence. The females, however, remain comparatively dull, as they need to be inconspicuous and not attract the attention of predators while incubating their eggs and raising their young.

FEATHER MAINTENANCE

Because a bird's feathers are so important, they are given regular care and maintenance by preening. A bird will clean and rearrange dirty or disarranged feathers by pulling them through its bill, and will scratch with its feet to loosen dust, old feather particles and parasitic mites. In order to keep feathers strong, flexible and waterproof, birds apply a preen oil to their plumage. The bird gathers the oil by rubbing its bill or head against a gland on its rump, near the base of the tail, and distributes the oil over the feather surfaces, especially the flight feathers.

SOUTHERN YELLOW WHITE-EYE

Woodland and gardens. Yellow-green upperparts, and yellow underparts, and distinctive white eye-ring. 10.5 cm

A: Geelglasogie
Z: Umehlwanophuzi
G: Senegalbrillenvogel

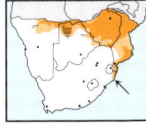

ORANGE RIVER WHITE-EYE

Arid woodland and gardens. Yellow-green upperparts, yellow throat and vent, and cinnamon flanks, and distinctive white eye-ring. 12 cm

A: Gariepglasogie
Z: Umehlwane weSangqu
Sp: Setsiololo
G: Oranjebrillenvogel

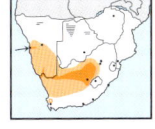

CAPE WHITE-EYE

Woodland and gardens. Yellow-green upperparts, and variable underparts, from grey to yellow, and distinctive white eye-ring. 12 cm

A: Kaapse Glasogie
Z: Umbicini
Ss: Setona-Mahlwana
Sp: Lentsiana
G: Oranjebrillenvogel

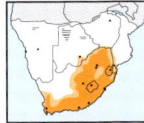

ORANGE-BREASTED WAXBILL

Reed beds. Grey upperparts, yellow underparts with banded flanks, and red bill and rump. 8.5–9 cm

A: Rooiassie **Z:** Isabhonsi
X: Impinzi
Ss: Borane-Mpatshehla
G: Goldbrüstchen

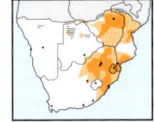

♂

♀

COLLARED SUNBIRD

Riverine woodland. Glossy green upperparts and head, and yellow underparts; male has green throat. 10 cm

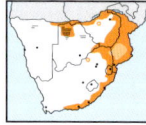

A: Kortbeksuikerbekkie
Z: Intonso
X: Inqathane
G: Waldnektarvogel

CAPE PENDULINE TIT

Acacia woodland and fynbos. Brownish-grey upperparts, blackish forehead, yellow underparts, and white throat. 9–10 cm

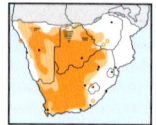

A: Kaapse Kapokvoël
Z: Iklosi Lasehlane
Ss: Leswarelela
Sp: Kgororwane
G: Weißstirn-Beutelmeise

VARIABLE SUNBIRD ♂

Riverine forests and bush. Glossy blue-green head and mantle, purple breast, and yellow belly. 11 cm

A: Geelpenssuikerbekkie
Z: Incwincwembalabala
G: Gelbbauch-Nektarvogel

WHITE-STARRED ROBIN

Coastal and montane mistbelt forests. Dark olive upperparts, grey head, and yellow underparts. 15–16 cm

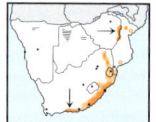

A: Witkoljanfrederik
Z: Usonkanyezi
G: Sternrötel

LIVINGSTONE'S FLYCATCHER

Riverine forest. Green upperparts, grey head, lemon breast, and orange tail. 12 cm

A: Rooistertvlieëvanger
Z: Igwalagwala Logu
G: Elfenschnäpper

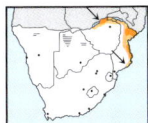

BAR-THROATED APALIS
(northern race)

Wooded kloofs, and forests. Olive-grey upperparts, white throat, black breast band, and yellow breast. 12–13 cm

A: Bandkeelkleinjantjie
Z: Umabilwane
X: Ugxakhweni
Ss: Pilipili-Mpasehla
G: Halsband-Feinsänger

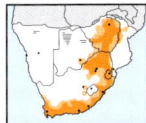

YELLOW-BREASTED APALIS

Bushveld and forest fringes. Olive upperparts, white throat and belly, and yellow breast; some males have a small black bar below breast. 10–12 cm

A: Geelborskleinjantjie
Z: Umankolophuzi
X: Umhlantonono
G: Gelbbrust-Feinsänger

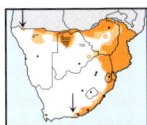

YELLOW-THROATED WOODLAND WARBLER

Evergreen forest and forest canopy. Olive upperparts, chestnut cap, yellow eyebrows and breast, and white belly. 11 cm

A: Geelkeelsanger
Z: Umqalaphuzi
X: Umbese
G: Rotkopf-Laubsänger

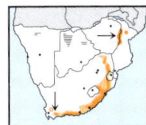

WILLOW WARBLER

Diverse woodland habitats. Olive upperparts, pale yellow eyebrows and underparts, and notched tail.
12 cm

A: Hofsanger
Z: Isicagogwane
Ss: Pidipidi-Sa-Mabelete
G: Fitis

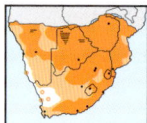

AFRICAN (DARK-CAPPED) YELLOW WARBLER

Reed banks and forest fringes. Olive-brown upperparts, yellow underparts, and yellow-edged wing feathers and tail.
14–15 cm

A: Geelsanger
Z: Ujamelumhlangophuzi
G: Natalspötter

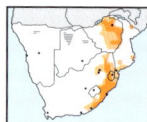

ICTERINE WARBLER

Acacia thornveld. Brown upperparts, yellow underparts, and yellow-edged wing feathers.
14–15 cm

A: Spotsanger
Z: Usikhothapela
Sp: Rametlae
G: Gelbspötter

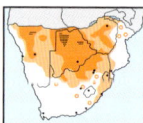

YELLOW-BELLIED EREMOMELA

Acacia and broad-leaved woodland. Grey-brown upperparts, pale grey breast, with a variable yellow belly.
9–10 cm

A: Geelpensbossanger **Z:** Imbuzanephuzi
G: Gelbbauch-Eremomela

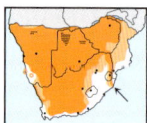

DRAKENSBERG PRINIA

Forest fringes and marshy scrub. Brown upperparts, yellowish eyebrows and lightly streaked underparts, and long tail. **14 cm**

A: Drakensberglangstertjie
Z: Ujenga Wokhahlamba
X: Injwiza
G: Gelbbauchprinie

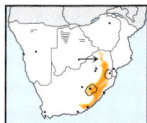

LESSER MASKED WEAVER

Reed beds, thornveld and riverine forests. Yellow, with greenish back, and pale yellow eyes; br. male has black mask and bill. **14 cm**

A: Kleingeelvink
Z: Ihlokohlokwana
G: Cabanisweber

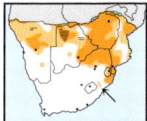

SOUTHERN MASKED WEAVER

Wetlands and gardens. Br. male yellow with black mask and bill, and red eyes; non-br. male and female greener above, with yellow wash on breast, and whitish belly. **15 cm**

A: Swartkeelgeelvink **Z:** Umzwigili **Ss:** Letoloptje

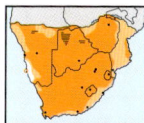

br. ♂ ♀

SOUTHERN BROWN-THROATED WEAVER

Riverine reed beds and adjacent forests. Male yellow with brown bib, and black bill; female greener above, with white belly, and horn-coloured bill. **15 cm**

A: Bruinkeelwewer **Z:** Igeleshelimqalonsundu **G:** Braunkehlweber

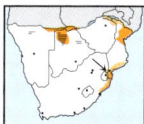

br. ♂ br. ♀

SPECTACLED WEAVER

Riverine and thornveld forests. Yellow, with greenish wings, orange wash on head, pale eyes, black eye-stripe and bill; male has black bib. **15–16 cm**

A: Brilwewer **Z:** Uzibukwana **X:** Ikreza **Ss:** Letoloptje-Mmaloborele
G: Brillenweber

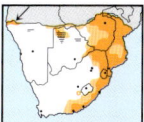

♂ ♀

RED-HEADED WEAVER ♀

Broad-leaved woodland. Grey back with yellow-edged wing feathers, yellowish head and breast, orange-pink bill, and white belly. **15 cm**

A: Rooikopwewer **Z:** Ukhandaklebhu
G: Scharlachweber

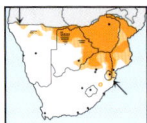

♀

DARK-BACKED WEAVER

Dense riverine and valley forests. Dark brown upper–parts, yellow underparts, and pale bill and legs. **16 cm**

A: Bosmusikant **Z:** Idonsi **G:** Waldweber

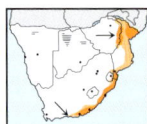

southern morph

EASTERN GOLDEN (YELLOW) WEAVER

Reed beds, lagoons and adjacent wetland bush. All yellow, with red eyes and dark bill. **16 cm**

A: Geelwewer **Z:** Igelesha Logu **X:** Isihlahlane

br. ♂

br. ♀

VILLAGE WEAVER

Reeds, thorn trees and mixed woodland. Br. male yellow, with dark wings, yellow-speckled mantle, and black mask (or head); non-br. male and female olive-greyish above, with yellow throat and breast, and whitish belly. **17 cm**

A: Bontrugwewer
Z: Ihlokohloko Lomuzi
Ss: Letoloptje-Le-Kokotlokgwatsana
G: Textor

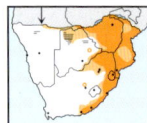

br. ♂

non-br. ♀

CAPE WEAVER

Waterside woodland and gardens. Male yellow, darker above, orange wash on head and throat, and pale eyes; female paler, with yellow wash on head and breast, dark eyes, and white belly. **16–18 cm**

A: Kaapse Wewer
Z: Ihlokohlokelikhulu
Ss: Talane
G: Kapweber

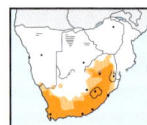

♀

♂

HOLUB'S (AFRICAN) GOLDEN WEAVER

Reed beds, marshes and gardens. Greenish upperparts, yellow underparts, black bill, and pale eyes; male with orange throat in northwest.
18 cm

A: Goudwewer
Z: Igelesha Lehlathi
G: Großer Goldweber

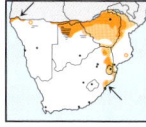

br. ♂
br. ♀

YELLOW BISHOP (br. ♂)

Vleis and moist grasslands. Black, with yellow rump and shoulder.
15 cm

A: Kaapse Flap
Z: Umambathilanga
X: Amabalengwe
Ss: Thaha-Thekatshehla
G: Samtweber

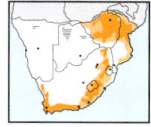

br. ♂

YELLOW-CROWNED BISHOP (br. ♂)

Reed beds and marshy grasslands. Yellow crown, nape and back, black underparts and bill, and pink legs.
12 cm

A: Goudgeelvink
Z: Intakanyosi
Ss: Thaha-Tshehla
Sp: Rramakgatho
G: Tahaweber

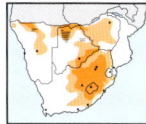

br. ♂

WHITE-WINGED WIDOWBIRD (br. ♂)

Damp grasslands, mixed bushveld and cultivated land. Black, with yellow and white shoulder, and pale grey bill.
19 cm

A: Witvlerkflap
Z: Intakemaphikamhlophe
G: Spiegelwida

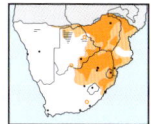

br. ♂

YELLOW-MANTLED WIDOWBIRD (br. ♂)

Marshes and moist grasslands. Black, with yellow mantle and shoulder. 22 cm

A: Geelrugflap
G: Gelbschulterwida

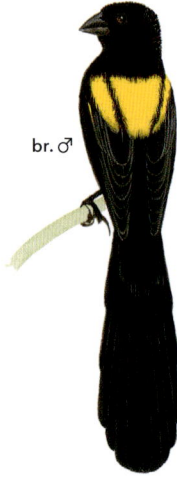
br. ♂

LEMON-BREASTED CANARY ♂

Bush and grasslands. Dull greenish upperparts, yellow breast and rump, and white belly. 10 cm

A: Geelborskanarie
Z: Umalaleni
G: Gelbbrustgirlitz

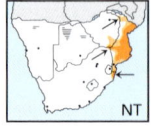
NT

♂

CUCKOO-FINCH ♂

Vleis and adjacent grasslands. Yellow, with dark wings, tail, bill and legs. 12–13 cm

A: Koekoekvink
Z: Unondindwa
G: Kuckucksweber

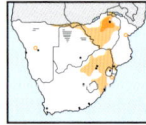

♂

BLACK-THROATED CANARY

Grassy woodland. Greyish upperparts, pale underparts, yellow rump, and black throat. 11–12 cm

A: Bergkanarie
Z: Unogilomnyama
Ss: Tswere-Koduntsho
G: Angolagirlitz

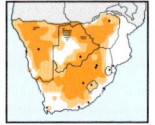

YELLOW-FRONTED CANARY

Open woodlands, forest fringes and gardens. Greenish upperparts, grey crown and nape, and yellow eyebrows, cheeks and underparts.
12 cm

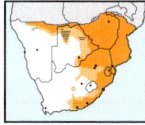

A: Geeloogkanarie
Z: Umbhalanomadevu
X: Unyileyo
Ss: Tswere-Ihlotshehla
Sp: Thaganyane
Sh: Nzvirihi
G: Mossambikgirlitz

YELLOW CANARY ♂

Dry bush and karoo and coastal scrub. Yellow eyebrows, cheeks and underparts, and pale to dark olive upperparts.
13–14 cm

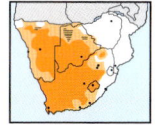

A: Geelkanarie
Z: Umbhalanophuzi
Ss: Tswere-Tshehla
G: Gelbbauchgirlitz

♂

FOREST CANARY

Montane and timber forests and adjacent fringes. Yellow, with heavy streaking.
13 cm

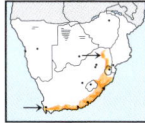

A: Gestreepte Kanarie
Z: Umbhalane Wehlathi
G: Schwarzkinngirlitz

CAPE CANARY

Mountain slopes and montane grasslands. Streaky yellow-green plumage, grey nape and mantle, and yellow eyebrows.
13–14 cm

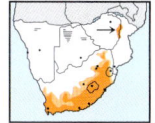

A: Kaapse Kanarie
Z: UmZwilili
X: Umlonji
Ss: Tswere-Lotaputswa
Sp: Tale
G: Gelbscheitelgirlitz

BRIMSTONE CANARY

Woodland, forest edges, fynbos and suburbia. Green upperparts, yellow underparts; male darker above, with green on breast; female paler above, entirely yellow below. 14–15 cm

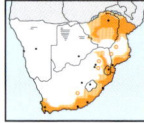

A: Dikbekkanarie
Z: Umbhalanomkhulu
X: Indweza Eluhlaza
Ss: Tswere-Hlohokgolo
G: Schwefelgirlitz

southern morph

northern morph

DRAKENSBERG SISKIN ♂

Mountain slopes. Dark brown upperparts, streaky head, and greenish-yellow underparts. 13 cm

A: Bergpietjiekanarie
Z: Umbhalane Wokhahlamba
Ss: Swaswi
G: Drakensberggirlitz

♂

WHITE-THROATED CANARY

Karoo thicket and coastal scrub. Greyish, with yellow rump, and heavy bill.
14–15 cm

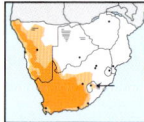

A: Witkeelkanarie
Z: Umbhalanongilemhlophe
Ss: Tswere-Kodutshwana
G: Weißkehlgirlitz

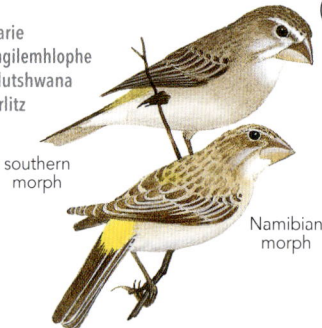

southern morph

Namibian morph

CAPE SISKIN

Montane scrub. Brown upperparts, and yellow rump and underparts; female has light streaking on throat.
13 cm

A: Kaapse Pietjiekanarie **Z:** Umbhalane WaseKapa
G: Kapgirlitz

♀

♂

CABANIS'S BUNTING

Miombo woodland. Brown back with white-edged shoulder feathers, black head with white streaks, and yellow underparts. 15 cm

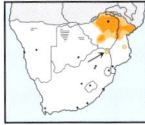

A: Geelstreepkoppie
G: Cabanisammer

YELLOW-RUMPED TINKERBIRD

Coastal and montane forests. Black upperparts, white facial stripes and throat, and yellow wing edges, rump and belly. 10 cm

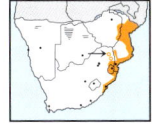

A: Swartblestinker
Z: Isipopop
Ss: Modisatsatsi Wa Phatlantsho
Tw: Toutou Ya

GOLDEN-BREASTED BUNTING

Mixed woodland. Black-and-white streaked head, brown mantle, white shoulder patch, yellow underparts, orange breast, and white belly and vent. 16 cm

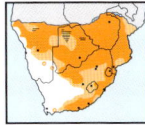

A: Rooirugstreepkoppie
Z: Usokhandamidwombalabala
X: Intsasa
Ss: Mmaborokwane-Petatshehla
G: Gelbbauchammer

RED-FRONTED TINKERBIRD

Lowland forests and wooded river banks. Black-and-white upperparts with yellow wing patch, red forehead, and pale yellow underparts. 10.5 cm

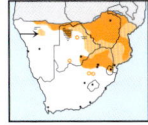

A: Rooiblestinker
Z: Unkovuka
X: Unogandilanga
Ss: Modisatsatsi Wa Phatlafubedu
Sp: Tetengwa Ya Phatlahwibidu
G: Feuerstirn-Bartvogel

YELLOW-FRONTED TINKERBIRD

Woodland. Black-and-white upperparts, yellow forehead and pale yellow underparts. **12 cm**

A: Geelblestinker
Z: Unkovuka WaseNyakatho
Ss: Modisatsatsi Wa Phatslasehla
Tw: Mothudi
Sh: Chivangazuva
G: Gelbstirn-Bartvogel

WESTERN YELLOW WAGTAIL

Wetland edges. Green-grey upperparts and yellow underparts; variable head coloration. **18 cm**

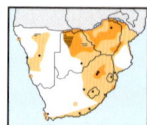

A: Geelkwikkie
Z: Umvemvophuzi
G: Schafstelze

LITTLE BEE-EATER

Open woodland and river banks. Green upperparts, rufous underparts, yellow throat and black throat patch. **17 cm**

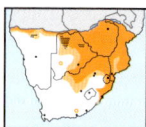

A: Kleinbyvreter
Z: Inkothana
Ss: Thlapolome E Nnyenyane
Tw: Seselamarumo Se Sennye
N: ≠khari nib
G: Zwergspint

ORANGE-BREASTED BUSHSHRIKE

Mixed woodland, bush and thickets. Olive upperparts, grey cap and mantle, yellow eyebrows and underparts, orange breast. **18–19 cm**

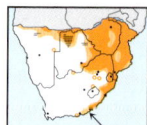

A: Oranjeborsboslaksman **Z:** Umabhashinhlayela
G: Orangewürger

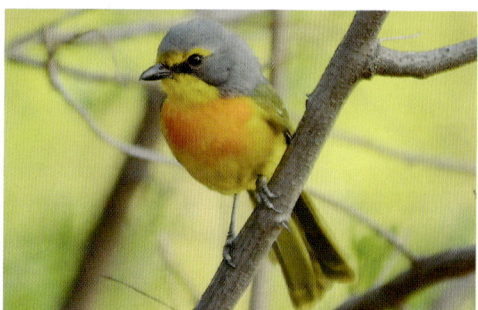

ACACIA PIED BARBET

Dry woodland. Black upperparts, yellow-edged wing and tail feathers, white underparts, yellow eyebrows and red forehead. **17–18 cm**

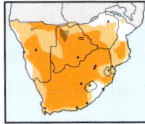

A: Bonthoutkapper
Z: Unomunga
Ss: Serokolo
Sp: Kokonya
Tw: Tlholabaeng
Ts: Xitsemahangoni
N: |hõ kurib toas
H: Ombonde
G: Rotstirn-Bartvogel

EASTERN NICATOR

Dense bushveld thickets. Greenish upperparts, yellow-edged wing feathers and tail, and yellow underbelly, vent and thighs.
23 cm

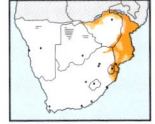

A: Geelvleknikator
Z: Umalusinkomo
G: Bülbülwürger

CRESTED BARBET

Woodland and gardens. Black upperparts and crest, yellow head and underparts with red speckles. **23 cm**

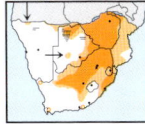

A: Kuifkophoutkapper
Z: Isiqhvana
Ss: Mmadiwatjhe
Sp: Mphago
Tw: Sekokonyane
Sh: Chizuvaguru
N: !amxadana kurib toas
G: Haubenbartvogel

AFRICAN GOLDEN ORIOLE ♂

Woodland and riverine forests. Yellow, with black mask, primaries and central tail feathers; female is greener. **24 cm**

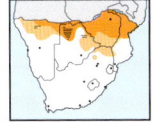

A: Afrikaanse Wielewaal
Z: Impofana YaseAfrika
G: Schwarzohrpirol

♂

EURASIAN GOLDEN ORIOLE ♂

Mixed woodland. Yellow, with black wings, tail feathers and lores.
24 cm

A: Europese Wielewaal
Z: Impofana
Ss: Lehlokoloko-La-Mose
G: Europäischer Pirol

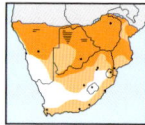

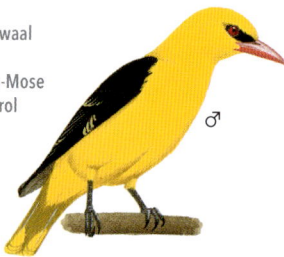

YELLOW-BELLIED GREENBUL

Riverine forests. Olive-brown upperparts and yellow underparts. 20–23 cm

A: Geelborswillie
Z: iBhada
G: Gelbbrustbülbül

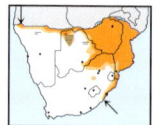

BLACK-HEADED ORIOLE

Woodland and riverine forests. Yellow, with black head, throat and primaries, and green upper tail. 25 cm

A: Swartkopwielewaal
Z: Usibo
X: Umkro
Ss: Lehlokoloko-Hlohontsho
Sp: Khulong
Ts: Khitsha Homu
Sh: Gotowa
G: Maskenpirol

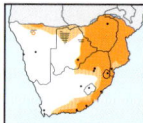

CAPE LONGCLAW

Short moist grassland. Grey-brown upperparts, yellow eyebrows and underparts, and orange throat with black gorget.
20 cm

A: Oranjekeelkalkoentjie
Z: Inqomfi
X: Inqilo
Ss: Lethwele
G: Kapgroßsporn

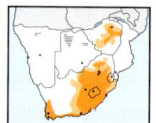

YELLOW-THROATED LONGCLAW

Open woodland. Grey-brown upperparts, yellow eyebrows, throat and underparts, and black gorget. 20 cm

A: Geelkeelkalkoentjie **Z:** Itoyiya **G:** Gelbkehlpieper

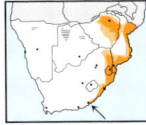

GORGEOUS BUSHSHRIKE

Dense bush. Olive upperparts, red chin and throat, black gorget, and yellow belly. 20 cm

A: Konkoit **Z:** iNgongoni **G:** Vierfarbenwürger

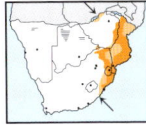

GREY-HEADED BUSHSHRIKE

Woodland and riverine bush. Olive-green upperparts, yellow underparts, orange breast, grey head, orange-yellow eyes, and heavy black bill. 25–27 cm

A: Spookvoël **Z:** Usipoki **X:** Umbankro **G:** Graukopfwürger

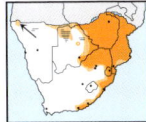

BLACK CUCKOOSHRIKE ♀

Broad-leaved woodland and coastal bush. Dull olive-brown upperparts, yellow-edged wing and tail feathers, and black-banded white underparts. 22 cm

A: Swartkatakoeroe
Z: Inhlangu
X: Usasa
Ss: Rankwetsidi
G: Kuckuckswürger

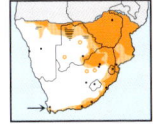

AFRICAN EMERALD CUCKOO ♂

Evergreen and riverine forests. Bright green upper-parts, throat and breast, and yellow belly. 20 cm

A: Mooimeisie
Z: Ubantwanyana
Ss: Ntetekeng Ya Mpasehla
Tw: Tlhotlhamedupe Ya Mpasetlha
N: !huni!nā hōhōseb
G: Smaragdkuckuck

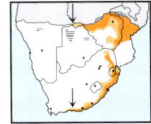

BOKMAKIERIE

Bush and urban areas. Grey crown and mantle, olive upperparts, yellow underparts and black gorget. 23 cm

A: Bokmakierie **Z:** iNkovu **X:** Ingqwangi
Ss: Ptjemptjete **Sp:** Mpherwane **G:** Bokmakiri

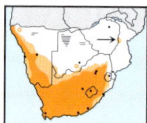

SWALLOW-TAILED BEE-EATER

Dry woodland. Green upperparts and upper breast, yellow throat, and forked tail. 20–22 cm

A: Swaelstertbyvreter **Z:** Inkothesankonjane
Ss: Thlapolome Ya Setonolekabelane **Tw:** Sabotlhoko
N: swawel-≠are nïb **H:** Onḍera Yotjiongo
G: Schwalbenschwanzspint

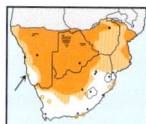

EUROPEAN BEE-EATER

Woodland. Chestnut, yellow and green upperparts, yellow throat, and blue forehead and underparts. 25–29 cm

A: Europese Byvreter **Z:** Inkothanyosi
Ss: Thlapolome Ya Leboya **Tw:** Seselamarumo Ya Bokone
Sh: Gamanyuchi **N:** ǀapa nïb **G:** Europäischer Bienenfresser

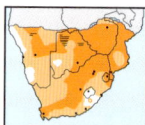

AFRICAN RED-EYED BULBUL

Woodland and gardens. Dark brown, with tufted black head, red eye-ring and yellow vent. 21 cm

A: Rooioogtiptol
Z: Iphothwelimehlabomvu
Ss: Hlakahlothwana-Ihlofubedu
G: Maskenbülbül

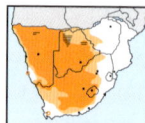

CAPE BULBUL

Coastal bush and scrub. Dark brown, with tufted head, white eye-ring and yellow vent. 21 cm

A: Kaapse Tiptol
Z: Iphothwelimehlamhlophe
Sp: Lekolo
G: Kapbülbül

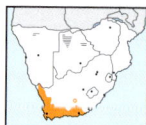

DARK-CAPPED BULBUL

Woodland and gardens. Dark brown, with tufted head, and yellow vent.
20–22 cm

A: Swartoogtiptol
Z: Iphothwe
X: Ikhwebula
Ss: Hlakahlothwana-Ihlotsho
Sp: Rankgwetshe
Ts: Mabyitana
Sh: Gwenhure
G: Graubülbül

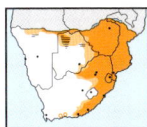

RÜPPELL'S PARROT ♀

Arid woodland. Dark brown, with yellow shoulders and underwing coverts, and blue rump, underbelly and vent.
23 cm

A: Bloupenspapegaai
Ss: Heka Ya Mpatalalehodimo
Sh: Hwenga
N: ≠hoa-!nä ‖giririb
G: Rüppellpapagei

MEYER'S PARROT

Broad-leaved and riverine woodland. Brown upperparts, yellow forehead and shoulders, and green belly and rump.
23 cm

A: Bosveldpapegaai
Z: Isikhwenenesimahlombaphuzi
Tw: Heka Ya Phatlasetlha
N: !huni-!ü ‖giririb
G: Goldbugpapagei

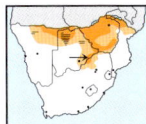

YELLOW-BILLED DUCK

Dams and rivers. Speckled dark brown body, and yellow bill. 53–58 cm

A: Geelbekeend
Z: Idadelimlomophuzi
Ss: Letata La Molomosehla
Sp: Lepelebele
Tw: Sehudi Sa Molomosetlha
G: Gelbschnabelente

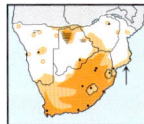

GREEN PLUMAGE

Green coloration in birds ranges from bright greens to dull olive. Very few waterbirds have green plumage, an exception being the African Pygmy Goose, which lives among floating water lily leaves and has green upperparts. Some dabbling ducks have an iridescent green patch on the upperwings called a speculum.

Green plumage is the result of pigments called porphyrins, which also have ultraviolet characteristics that only birds can see.

How does green plumage serve a bird?

Camouflage: Green plumage serves as cryptic coloration, allowing the bird to blend into its predominantly green habitat. Bright green lovebirds, for example, are very difficult to detect when they are settled in a leafy tree canopy or are feeding in fresh green grass, unless they move.

Courtship displays and territorial dominance: A duck's speculum probably functions as a species-specific visual stimulant or 'advertisement', which the male uses to establish its status within a flock. This is done frequently, with the male standing erect and flapping its wings, thereby displaying the colourful speculae.

WHAT MAKES A TURACO GREEN?

Turacos, such as the **Knysna Turaco**, have two unique porphyrin pigments: **turacoverdin**, responsible for green, and **turacin**, responsible for red. These pigments contain copper, which the turacos are able to ingest and metabolise. The copper is derived from the berries and buds that the turacos eat, and it can take up to 18 months to accumulate enough of the mineral in order to saturate the birds' pigment cells.

SOUTHERN DOUBLE-COLLARED SUNBIRD ♂

Woodlands, fynbos and gardens. Glossy green head and mantle, narrow blue and red breast bands, and greyish belly.
12.5 cm

A: Klein-rooibandsuikerbekkie
Z: Incuncwana
Ss: Pinyane-Petakgubetswana
G: Halsband-Nektarvogel

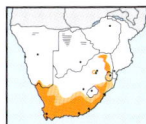

GREATER DOUBLE-COLLARED SUNBIRD ♂

Moist forest edges, kloofs and gardens. Glossy green head and mantle, narrow blue and wide red breast bands, and greyish belly.
14 cm

A: Groot-rooibandsuikerbekkie
Z: Incuncu
Ss: Pinyane-Petakgubedu
G: Großer Halsband-Nektarvogel

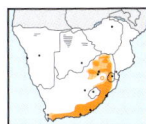

MARICO SUNBIRD ♂

Thornveld. Glossy green upperparts, head and upper breast, purple and red breast bands, and black belly.
13–14 cm

A: Maricosuikerbekkie **Z:** Insonsi **G:** Bindennektarvogel

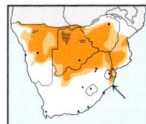

COLLARED SUNBIRD

Riverine forests, woodlands and gardens. Glossy green upperparts and head, and yellow underparts; male has green throat. 11 cm

A: Kortbeksuikerbekkie **Z:** Intonso **X:** Inqathane
G: Waldnektarvogel

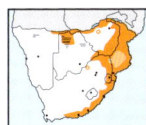

VARIABLE SUNBIRD ♂

Broad-leaved woodland. Glossy blue-green head and mantle, purple breast, and yellow belly. 11 cm

A: Geelpenssuikerbekkie **Z:** Incwincwembalabala
G: Gelbbauch-Nektarvogel

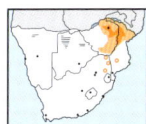

MALACHITE SUNBIRD ♂

Fynbos and mountain scrub. Glossy green with a long tail.
male 25 cm, female 13 cm

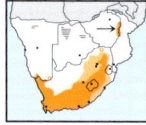

A: Jangroentjie **Z:** Uhlazazana
X: Ingcungcu Eluhlaza
Ss: Tale-Tale
Sp: Tšhekgere
G: Kleine Malachitnektarvogel

non-br.♂

br.♂

♀

WHITE-BELLIED SUNBIRD ♂

Woodland. Glossy blue-green upperparts, head and breast, purple breast band and white belly. 11 cm

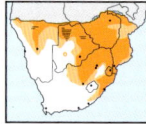

A: Witpenssuikerbekkie **Z:** Incwincwemhlope
G: Weißbauch-Nektarvogel

♂

OLIVE SUNBIRD

Lowland forests. Dull, dark olive upperparts and paler yellowish-olive underparts.
13–15 cm

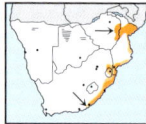

A: Olyfsuikerbekkie **Z:** Incwincweluhlaza
Sp: Taletale **G:** Olivnektarvogel

GREEN-BACKED CAMAROPTERA

Woodland thickets, forest fringes, gardens. Dull olive upperparts and white underparts; tail usually raised.
12 cm

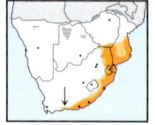

A: Groenrugkwêkwêvoël
Z: Ibhoyi
G: Grünmantel-Bogenflügel

GREEN TWINSPOT

Forest fringes. Green upperparts and white-spotted underparts; male has red face; female has yellowish face. 10 cm

A: Groenkolpensie **Z:** Intiyaneluhlaza **G:** Grüner Tropfenastrild

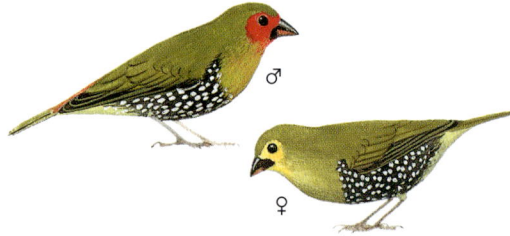

♂

♀

RUDD'S APALIS

Coastal bush. Olive upperparts, grey cap, white underparts and black breast band. 10.5–12 cm

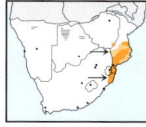

A: Ruddkleinjantjie **Z:** Umankole **G:** Rudds Feinsänger

SWEE WAXBILL

Forest fringes. Dark olive back and wings, grey cap, red lower bill, rump and uppertail covers, and greyish underparts; male has a black face. 9–10 cm

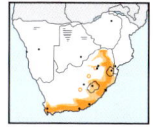

A: Suidelike Swie
Z: UbuSukuswane
X: Utsoyi
Ss: Borane-Swaswi
G: Gelbbauchastrild

YELLOW-BREASTED APALIS

Forest fringes, woodland. Olive upperparts, white belly, and yellow breast; some males have a small black bar below breast. 10–12.5 cm

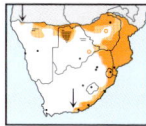

A: Geelborskleinjantjie
Z: Umankolophuzi
X: Umhlantonono
G: Gelbbrust-Feinsänger

GREEN-WINGED PYTILIA

Thorn thickets. Yellow-green back and wings, grey head, banded underparts, and red bill, rump and upper tail; male has red forehead and throat. 12–13 cm

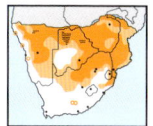

A: Gewone Melba **Z:** Usantiyane **Sp:** Kgakanagae
Ts: Xindzinghiri Mbandi **Sh:** Zazo **N:** |gîbes **G:** Buntastrild

CAPE WHITE-EYE

Woodland and urban areas. Yellow-green upperparts, white eye-rings, and variable underparts, from grey to yellow. 12 cm

A: Kaapse Glasogie **Z:** Umbicini **Ss:** Setona-Mahlwana
Sp: Lentsiana **G:** Kapbrillenvogel

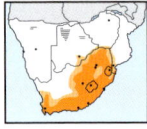

DIEDERIK CUCKOO

Woodland and urban areas. Green upperparts with white wing spots, and white underparts with barred flanks; male has red eyes; female has coppery mantle. 18.5 cm

A: Diederikkie **Z:** Unononekhanda **Ss:** Ntetekeng Ya Leihlofubedu **Tw:** Tlhotlhamedupe Ya Leitlhohubidu
Ts: Mandzamandza **N:** ǀawamû hôhôseb **G:** Diderikkuckuck

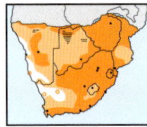

KLAAS'S CUCKOO

Woodland. Plain green upperparts and white underparts; male has dark eyes; female duller, with barred flanks. 17 cm

A: Meitjie **Z:** Umazalashiye **Ss:** Ntetekeng Ya Mpasweu **Tw:** Tlhotlhamedupe Ya Mpasweu **N:** !uri!nā hôhôseb
G: Klaaskuckuck

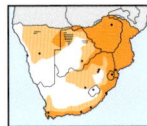

ROSY-FACED LOVEBIRD

Rocky gorges. Green body and wings, blue rump, rosy face, and pale bill. 17–18 cm

A: Rooiwangparkiet
Ss: Hekana Ya Leramapinki
Tw: Hekana Ya Leramapinki
N: ǀawa-ai ǁgiririb
H: Onḓera Tjapolise
G: Rosenpapagei

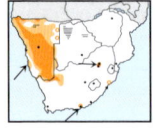

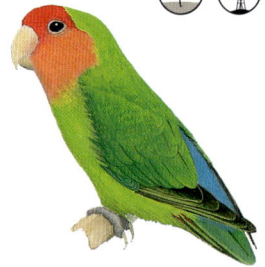

LILIAN'S LOVEBIRD

Woodland. Green body and wings, reddish face and bill. 17–18 cm

A: Njassaparkiet
Ss: Hekana Ya Leramafubedu
Tw: Hekana Ya Lesamahubidu
G: Erdbeerköpfchen

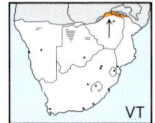

LITTLE BEE-EATER

Woodland. Green upperparts, rufous underparts, yellow throat and black throat patch.
17 cm

A: Kleinbyvreter
Z: Inkothana
Ss: Thlapolome E Nnyenyane
Tw: Seselamarumo Se Sennye
N: ≠khari nīb
G: Zwergspint

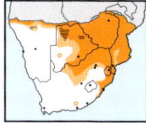

OLIVE WOODPECKER

Forests and woodland. Olive body, grey head and red rump; male has red cap.
18–20 cm

A: Gryskopspeg **Z:** Isigqobhamithesiluhlaza
Ss: Kgatajwe Ya Hlohoputswa **N:** |hai-dana hai!gō!gōseb
G: Goldrückenspecht

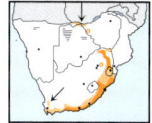

♂

♀

OLIVE BUSHSHRIKE

Forests. Olive upperparts, grey or olive head, and buff or yellow breast; male has black mask. 17 cm

A: Olyfboslaksman **Z:** Umabhashinhlayelohlaza
G: Olivwürger

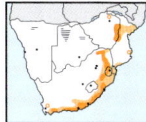

♂   ♀

cinnamon morph

olive-green morph

♂

SWALLOW-TAILED BEE-EATER

Woodlands. Green upperparts and upper breast, yellow throat, and blue throat band, belly and forked tail.
20–22 cm

A: Swaelstertbyvreter
Z: Inkothesankonjane
Ss: Thlapolome Ya Setonolekabelane
Tw: Sabotlhoko
N: swawel-≠are nīb
H: Onḓera Yotjiongo
G: Schwalbenschwanzspint

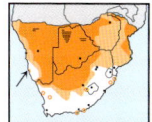

BLUE-CHEEKED BEE-EATER

Riverine woodland. Green upperparts, pale blue eyebrows, cheeks and belly, yellow chin and rufous throat.
27–33 cm

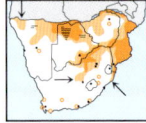

A: Blouwangbyvreter
Z: Indlanyosi
Tw: Seselamarumo Sa Lesamatalalegodimo
N: ≠hoa-ai nïb
G: Blauwangenspint

AFRICAN EMERALD CUCKOO ♂

Forest canopy. Bright green upperparts, throat and breast, and yellow belly.
20 cm

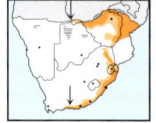

A: Mooimeisie **Z:** Ubantwanyana
Ss: Ntetekeng Ya Mpasehla
Tw: Tlhotlhamedupe Ya Mpasetlha
N: !huni!nā hōhōseb
G: Smaragdkuckuck

WHITE-FRONTED BEE-EATER

Riverine woodland. Green upperparts, cinnamon nape and breast, white forehead and chin, blue vent and belly.
22–24 cm

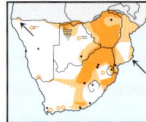

A: Rooikeelbyvreter
Z: Inkotha
G: Weißstirnspint

SOMBRE GREENBUL

Forest fringes. Birds in the south, dull olive with whitish eyes; beyond Zambezi, brighter green upperparts and yellow-green underparts.
19–24 cm

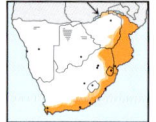

A: Gewone Willie **Z:** Iwili **X:** Inkwili **G:** Kap-Grünbülbül

southern morph

northern morph

COMMON STARLING

Suburbia. Green-black with a purple sheen on upper breast and mantle.
20–22 cm

A: Europese Spreeu **Z:** Ikhwinsi LaseYurobhu
Ss: Lehodi-Papapa **G:** Star

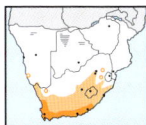

CAPE STARLING

Woodland and suburbia. Glossy blue-green, with bluer head, and yellow eyes.
23–25 cm

A: Kleinglansspreeu **Z:** Ikhwezi
X: Inyakrini **Ss:** Lehodi-Pilwane **N:** ||nuwub
G: Rotschulter-Glanzstar

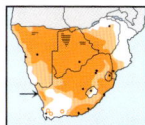

MIOMBO BLUE-EARED STARLING

Miombo woodland. Glossy blue-green, with purple flanks and yellow eyes. 20 cm

A: Klein-blouoorglansspreeu **Z:** Ikhwezi LaseZimbabwe
G: Messingglanzstar

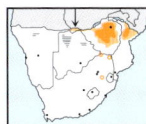

BLACK-BELLIED STARLING

Riparian and coastal woodland. Blue-green, with blackish belly, and yellow eyes; duller than other starlings. 21 cm

A: Swartpensglansspreeu **Z:** Ikhwezi Lasogwini
X: Intenenengu **G:** Schwarzbauch-Glanzstar

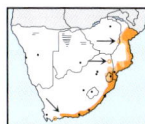

GREATER BLUE-EARED STARLING

Woodland. Glossy blue head and breast, glossy green wings, purple belly and flanks, and yellow eyes. 21–23 cm

A: Groot-blouoorglansspreeu **Z:** Ikhwezi LaseNyakatho
G: Grünschwanz-Glanzstar

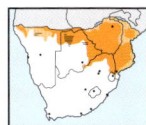

SHARP-TAILED STARLING

Woodlands. Glossy blue-green, with a wedge-shaped tail; male has red eyes; female has orange eyes.
26 cm

A: Spitsstertglansspreeu **G:** Keilschwanz-Glanzstar

BURCHELL'S STARLING

Woodland. Glossy blue-green and purple, with black mask and dark eyes. 30–34 cm

A: Grootglansspreeu **Z:** Ikhwezelikhulu
Tw: Letleretlere Le Legolo **Ts:** Vhevhe Nkomo **N:** ||nuwub
G: Riesenglanzstar

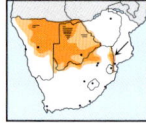

MEVES'S STARLING

Mopane woodland. Glossy blue-green and purple, with dark eyes and long, graduated tail. 30–34 cm

A: Langstertglansspreeu
Z: Ikhwezelimsilomude
N: ||nuwub
G: Meves-Glanzstar

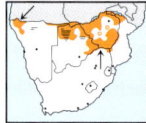

BROWN-HEADED PARROT

Woodland. Pale green body, dark green wings, and brown head. 23 cm

A: Bruinkoppapegaai **Z:** Isikhwenenesikhandansundu
Tw: Heka Ya Tlhogorokwa **Ts:** Yhokwe
G: Braunkopfpapagei

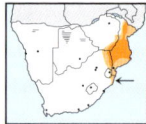

MEYER'S PARROT

Woodland. Brown upperparts, green belly and rump, and yellow shoulders. 23 cm

A: Bosveldpapegaai
Z: Isikhwenenesimahlombaphuzi
Tw: Heka Ya Phatlasetlha
N: !huni-!ũ ||giririb
G: Goldbugpapagei

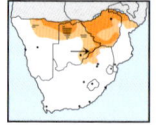

CAPE PARROT

Evergreen and riverine forests. Green body and wings, yellow-brown (or grey) head and neck, and orange-red forehead and shoulders. 35 cm

A: Woudpapegaai
Z: Isikhwenene
X: Isikhwenene
Ss: Heka Ya Moru
G: Kappapagei

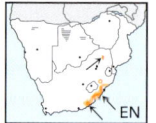

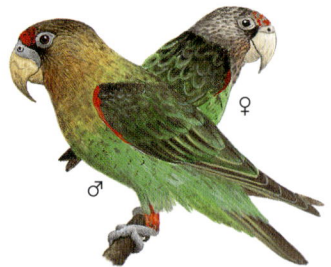

NARINA TROGON

Dense woodland and thicket. Glossy green upperparts and head, red belly, and greenish-yellow bill; male has green face and throat; female has rufous face and throat. 29–34 cm

A: Bosloerie
Z: Umjenenengu
X: Intshatshongo
Ss: Tsoko
N: hainoeab
G: Narina-Trogon

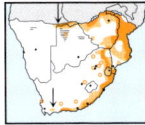

GREEN MALKOHA

Lowland forests. Greenish wings and long tail, grey-green underparts, and distinctive yellow bill. 33 cm

A: Groenvleiloerie Z: Umcwicwicwi

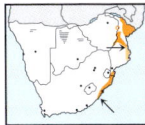

AFRICAN GREEN PIGEON

Riverine woodland. Predominantly green; eyes whitish; bill red and white; legs red; thighs yellow. 30 cm

A: Papegaaiduif Z: Ijubantondo
X: Intendekwane Sp: Legwalepa
Tw: Leeba La Motshaba Sh: Huriti
N: ≠nairas H: Onguti Otjihape
G: Rotnasen-Grüntaube

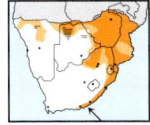

EMERALD-SPOTTED WOOD DOVE

Woodland. Fawn upperparts, rufous flight feathers, glossy green wing spots, and black bars on the back. 20 cm

A: Groenvlekduifie Z: Isikhombazane-sehlanze
G: Bronzeflecktaube

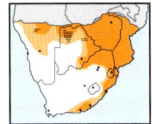

ROCK DOVE (Feral Pigeon)

Urban areas. Variable coloration; many individuals have glossy green neck feathers. 33 cm

A: Tuinduif
Z: Ijuba Ledolobha
G: Haustaube

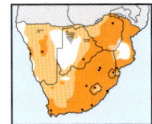

AFRICAN PYGMY GOOSE

Lily pans. Dark green upperparts, orange-beige underparts, and short, yellow bill. **33 cm**

A: Dwerggans **Z:** Ivevenyane
Ss: Lefalwana **Tw:** Sehutsana
N: ≠khari !kharas
G: Afrikanische Zwerggans

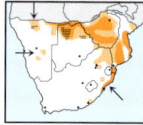

KNYSNA TURACO

Forest canopy. Green head, nape and underparts, white crest, glossy blue wings and tail, and red flight feathers. **47 cm**

A: Knysnaloerie **Z:** Igwalagwaleliluhlaza **X:** Igolomi
Ss: Kgologolo Ya Borwa **Nd:** Umguwe
Sh: Hurungira **G:** Helmturako

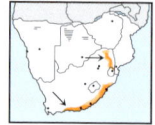

PURPLE-CRESTED TURACO

Woodland. Purple crest and wings, green head, neck and chest, black bill, and red flight feathers. **47 cm**

A: Bloukuifloerie **Z:** Igwalagwala lehlanze
Ss: Kgologolo Ya Motlwenyaperese **G:** Glanzhaubenturako

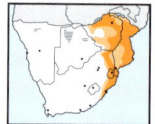

ROSE-RINGED PARAKEET

Urban areas. Apple-green, with red bill, pale eyes, and long tail. **40 cm**

A: Ringnekparkiet
Z: Unocu
Ss: Hekana Ya Setonolelele
G: Halsbandsittich

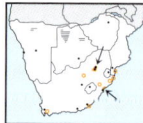

AFRICAN SWAMPHEN

Reed beds and marshes. Blue head and underparts, green back, wings and tail, red bill and frontal shield, and pink legs. **46 cm**

A: Grootkoningriethaan **Z:** Inkukhuyomhlanga
Ss: Mmamathebe E Moholo **N:** kai ≠āgaob **G:** Purpurhuhn

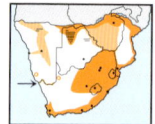

CAPE TEAL (in flight)

Salty and fresh water bodies. Pale, speckled body, and pink bill; upperwings show white secondaries with green central panel.
46 cm

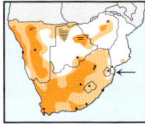

A: Teeleend **Z:** Unosikhutha
Ss: Sefudi Sa Molomopinki
H: Ombaka YaKapa
G: Kapente

YELLOW-BILLED DUCK (in flight)

Dams, pans and open water. Speckled body, and yellow bill; in flight, upperwings show green secondaries bordered with white. 53–58 cm

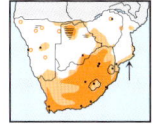

A: Geelbekeend **Z:** Idadelimlomophuzi **Sp:** Lepelebele
Tw: Sehudi Sa Molomosetlha **N:** !huni-am ≠naras
G: Gelbschnabelente

CAPE SHOVELER (in flight)

Shallow inland and tidal waters and lagoons. Speckled body, and black bill; in flight, upperwings show green secondaries separated from blue forewings by a white line.
53 cm

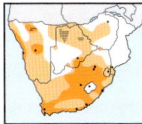

A: Kaapse Slopeend
Z: Unofosholo
Ss: Letatakgaba La
N: ||goa-am ≠naras
G: Kaplöffelente

SPUR-WINGED GOOSE

Large inland waters and croplands. Blackish upperparts with green sheen, white underparts, and pink bill and legs. 102 cm

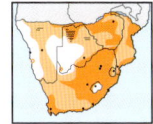

A: Wildemakou
Z: Ihhoye
X: Ihoye
Ss: Letshikgwi
Sp: Moselamotlaka
Tw: Letsukwe
Ts: Sekwanyarhi
N: ||khũ||gawo !kharas
G: Sporngans

PURPLE PLUMAGE
(including lilac and violet)

Purple, lilac and violet are some of the most beautiful colours to observe in our feathered friends. This coloration in birds is created by a combination of pigments called porphyrins, as well as iridescent feather structures.

How does violet plumage serve a bird?
These colours may appear to be purely decorative, but they feature strongly in courtship and are seen differently through the eyes of a bird.

Ultraviolet vision
Research has determined quite recently that many, if not all, birds can see the ultraviolet spectrum, something that is not normally visible to the human eye. The bird's ultraviolet vision may render colours such as purple more brilliant than the human eye can perceive.

Ultraviolet feathers
Many birds have ultraviolet feathers, which humans cannot see. Bustards and korhaans, for example, have ultraviolet breast feathers that are shown during the breeding season, when males puff out their chest while displaying to a female. To the human eye, this may appear to be a simple display of white feathers. However, this display appears far more radiant and eye-catching to a female bird.

SUNBIRDS

Sunbirds are the small, brightly iridescent birds with slender, decurved beaks that feed mostly on flower nectar. Their bill is adapted to probe into tubular flowers such as those of aloes and ericas. There are many misconceptions about sunbirds, resulting in the local usage of such misleading names as **honey-sucker** and **sugarbird,** the latter name properly referring to the unrelated genus Promerops, the **Cape Sugarbird** and **Gurney's Sugarbird.**

People often assume that sunbirds are a type of African hummingbird, whereas nothing could be further from the truth. **Hummingbirds** are found only in the Americas; Africa is the home of sunbirds. Their appearance, food and feeding habits are similar, but the two families are completely unrelated. **Hummingbirds** feed while hovering, with wingbeats of over 4,000 per minute in some species, and they can even fly backwards, whereas **sunbirds** are able to hover only very briefly and must settle to feed.

WESTERN VIOLET-BACKED SUNBIRD ♂

Broad-leaved woodland. Violet upperparts and chin, and white underparts.
12.5–14 cm

A: Blousuikerbekkie
Sp: Tswitswana
G: Violettmantel-Nektarvogel

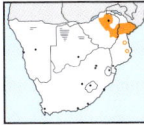

♂

MARICO SUNBIRD ♂

Thornveld. Glossy green upperparts, head and breast, purple and red bands on lower breast, and black belly.
13–14 cm

A: Maricosuikerbekkie
Z: Insonsi
G: Bindennektarvogel

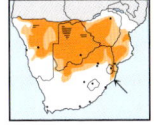

♂

AMETHYST SUNBIRD ♂

Woodland. Iridescent purple throat and shoulder patches. 15 cm

A: Swartsuikerbekkie
Z: Insusha
G: Amethyst-Glanzköpfchen

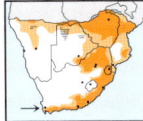

♂

VARIABLE SUNBIRD ♂

Broad-leaved woodland. Green head and upperparts, purple breast, and yellow belly. 11 cm

A: Geelpenssuikerbekkie
Z: Incwincwembalabala
G: Gelbbauch-Nektarvogel

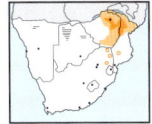

♂

PINK-THROATED TWINSPOT ♂

Dense scrub. Pink face, breast and rump, cinnamon wings and back, and white-spotted black belly and vent. 12 cm

A: Rooskeelkolpensie
Z: Umagumejana
G: Perlastrild

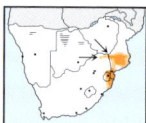

VIOLET-BACKED STARLING ♂

Broad-leaved woodland. Iridescent purple upperparts and breast, which may appear coppery, and white underparts. 18–19 cm

A: Witborsspreeu
Z: Ikhwezelimacwebi
Tw: Reole
Ts: Xinwavulombe
N: ≠nū-am hai‖nūres
G: Amethystglanzstar

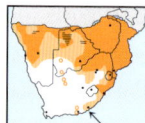

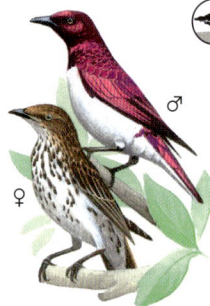

VIOLET-EARED WAXBILL

Dry thornveld. Violet ear coverts and cheeks, red bill, brown upperparts and blue rump; male has dark chestnut underparts; female has buffy underparts. 13–15 cm

A: Koningblousysie
Z: Intiyanelimbalabala
Sp: Lete
Tw: Raletsoku
G: Granatastrild

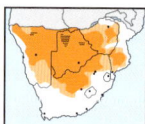

CAPE STARLING

Woodland and suburbia. Glossy blue-green with bluer head, and yellow eyes. 23–25 cm

A: Kleinglansspreeu
Z: Ikhwezi
X: Inyakrini
Ss: Lehodi-Pilwane
Sw: Likhweti
N: ‖nuwub
G: Rotschulter-Glanzstar

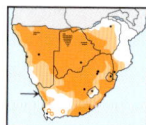

MIOMBO BLUE-EARED STARLING

Woodland. Glossy blue-green with magenta belly, and yellow eyes.
20 cm

A: Klein-blouoorglansspreeu
Z: Ikhwezi LaseZimbabwe
G: Messingglanzstar

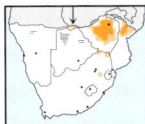

MEVES'S STARLING

Mopane woodland. Glossy blue-green with purple in mantle and upper tail.
30–34 cm

A: Langstertglansspreeu
Z: Ikhwezelimsilomude
N: ǁnuwub
G: Meves-Glanzstar

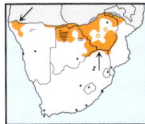

GREATER BLUE-EARED STARLING

Woodland. Glossy blue head and breast, glossy green wings, purple flanks and belly, and yellow eyes.
21–23 cm

A: Groot-blouoorglansspreeu
Z: IkhwezilaseNyakatho
G: Grünschwanz-Glanzstar

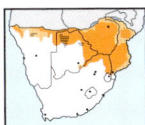

BURCHELL'S STARLING

Woodland. Glossy blue with purple in wings, upper tail and thighs.
30–34 cm

A: Grootglansspreeu
Z: Ikhwezelikhulu
Tw: Letleretlere Le Legolo
N: ǁnuwub
G: Riesenglanzstar

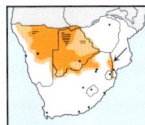

PURPLE ROLLER

Woodland. Brownish upperparts, multi-coloured wings, and purple shoulder patches and undertail coverts. 36–40 cm

A: Groottroupant **Z:** Ifefemidwa
Ss: Letleretlere Le Leholo
Ts: Vhevhe Nkomo
N: ≠hoa|awa kōkō-îas
G: Strichelracke

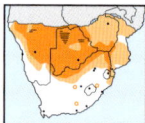

LILAC-BREASTED ROLLER

Bushveld. Lilac breast, and blue underparts and flight feathers. 36 cm

A: Gewone Troupant **Z:** Ifefelihle
Ss: Letleretlere La Sefubaperese
Tw: Majeke **Nd:** Itshegela
N: ≠hoa|awa-|gā kōkō-îas
H: Onḏera Wovanatje
G: Gabelracke

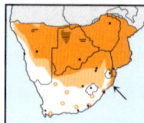

COMMON SCIMITARBILL

Woodland. Deep purple head, mantle and wings. 24–28 cm

A: Swartbekkakelaar **Z:** Unosungulo
Sp: Kuela **Tw:** Sebodu **Sh:** Shokosha
N: ≠nū-am hai||nūres **G:** Sichelhopf

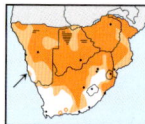

BROAD-BILLED ROLLER

Woodland. Cinnamon upperparts, purple underparts, and blue in wings and tail. 27 cm

A: Geelbektroupant
Z: Ifefelibomvu
Sp: Lehlake
Tw: Lephakewa
N: ō-ō||nâ-es
G: Zimtroller

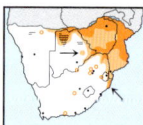

AFRICAN OLIVE PIGEON

Forests and plantations. Dark purple-brown with grey head, purple-grey neck, and bright yellow eye-rings, bill and legs bright. 36–40 cm

A: Geelbekbosduif **Z:** Ivukuthu-lehlathi **X:** Izuba
Ss: Leebamphapane **Ts:** Ngalakana **G:** Oliventaube

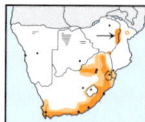

ROCK DOVE (Feral Pigeon)

Urban areas. Variable plumage; many have glossy purple neck feathers. 33 cm

A: Tuinduif
Z: Ijuba Ledolobha
G: Haustaube

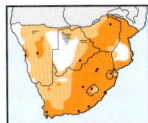

ALLEN'S GALLINULE

Wetlands. Green upperparts, blue head, frontal shield and underparts, and red bill and legs. 33 cm

A: Kleinkoningriethaan **Z:** Unomhlangomncane
Ss: Mmamathebe E Monyenyane **N:** ≠khari≠āgaob
G: Afrikanisches Sultanshuhn

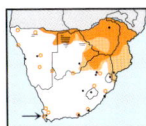

AFRICAN SWAMPHEN

Reed beds and marshes. Green upperparts, blue head, purple-blue underparts, and red frontal shield and bill. 46 cm

A: Grootkoningriethaan **Z:** Inkukhuyomhlanga
Tw: Mmamathebe **N:** kai ≠āgaob **G:** Purpurhuhn

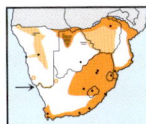

PURPLE-CRESTED TURACO

Riverine woodland. Purple crest, shiny green head, and red eye-ring and flight feathers. 47 cm

A: Bloukuifloerie
Z: Igwalagwala lehlanze
Ss: Kgologolo Ya Motlwenyaperese
G: Glanzhaubenturako

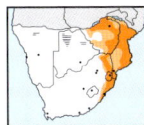

KNYSNA TURACO

Forest canopy. Green body, red flight feathers, and iridescent blue-purple on wings and upper tail. 47 cm

A: Knysnaloerie
Z: Igwalagwaleliluhlaza
X: Igolomi
Sp: Kgologolo ya Borwa
Ts: Tlulutlulu
G: Helmturako

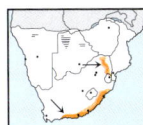

RUFOUS PLUMAGE

Rufous is a distinctive reddish-brown or reddish-orange colour that is fairly common in birds, for example, the Rock Kestrel and Burchell's Coucal. The colour rufous in birds' plumage is a combination of all the colour pigments (melanin, carotenoids and porphyrins), as well as structural colours.

How does rufous plumage serve a bird?

Camouflage and signalling: Rufous plumage can serve a number of functions. It can offer camouflage in environments with many earth tones, such as forests or grasslands. It may also play a role in attracting mates or establishing dominance, as the colour can be quite striking and captivating.

KESTRELS

Kestrels are a group of small falcons. They share certain characteristics with their larger cousins in that they have pointed wings and build no nest of their own. They hunt mostly ground-dwelling prey such as small rodents, reptiles and small birds, as well as flying insects caught on the wing. The summer-visiting **Lesser Kestrel** and **Amur** and **Red-footed falcons** are gregarious and hunt in flocks over grasslands, catching aerial prey, especially grasshoppers and flying termites. Resident kestrels hunt from a roadside post, making short aerial forays to catch their prey on the ground before returning with it to feed on their perch. The flight of the kestrel is graceful, with much hovering. Kestrels and falcons have greatly increased their feeding and breeding ranges in southern Africa through the increase in the number of human-made roadside perches, especially electricity pylons (towers). These are used by crows and other birds of prey to build their nests, which in acts of colonisation, are then used by the falcons and kestrels.

RED-BACKED MANNIKIN

Dune forests and bushveld. Black head and breast, rufous upperparts, and white bill and underparts.
9.5-10 cm

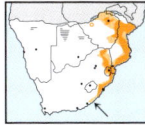

A: Rooirugfret **Z:** Amadojeyanabomvu
G: Glanzelsterchen

AFRICAN STONECHAT

Vleis and moist grasslands. Mainly black upperparts, white rump and half-collar, and rufous underparts.
14 cm

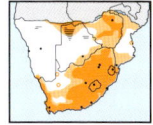

A: Gewone Bontrokkie **Z:** Isichegu **X:** Inchaphe **Ss:** Tlhatsinyane
Sp: Thisa **Sh:** Mujesi **G:** Schwarzkehlchen

♀

♂

BLACK-HEADED CANARY

Arid scrub. Rufous upperparts; male has black head, breast and belly; female has greyish head, breast and belly. 12-15 cm

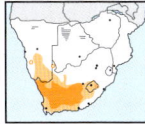

A: Swartkopkanarie, Bontkopkanarie
Z: Umbhalanokhandelimnyama
Ss: Tswere-Hlohontsho
G: Alariogirlitz

♀

♂

CHESTNUT WEAVER (br. ♂)

Arid thornveld. Chestnut body and black head.
15 cm

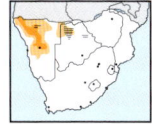

A: Bruinwewer
Z: Ihlokohlokelibubende
G: Maronenweber

br. ♂

BLACK-FACED WAXBILL

Thornveld and thickets. Deep red rump and underparts, and black mask and bill. 12–13 cm

A: Swartwangsysie
Z: Intiyanelibusobumnyama
G: Elfenastrild

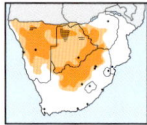

CINNAMON-BREASTED BUNTING

Rocky koppies. Cinnamon-brown with black-and-white streaked head (blacker in male). 13–14 cm

A: Klipstreepkoppie
Z: Usokhandamidwa Wamatshe
X: Undenjenje
Ss: Motweditwedi
Tw: Kwabebe
Sh: Mvemvere
G: Bergammer

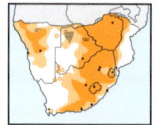

VIOLET-EARED WAXBILL

Dry thornveld. Violet ear coverts and cheeks, rufous upperparts and blue rump; male has dark chestnut underparts; female has buffy underparts. 15 cm

A: Koningblousysie
Z: Intiyanelimbalabala
Sp: Lete
Tw: Raletsoku
G: Granatastrild

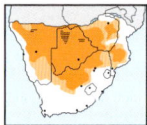

CAPE BUNTING

Arid areas. Black-and-white streaked head, rufous upperparts and grey-brown-washed underparts. 16 cm

A: Rooivlerkstreepkoppie
Z: Usokhandamidwonsundu
Ss: Mmaborokwane-Nyaopedi
G: Kapammer

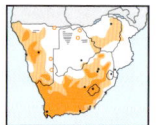

CHESTNUT-BACKED SPARROW-LARK

Grassy plains. Chestnut back and wings; male has black head and body, and white ear-patch and bill; female has chestnut head and streaked underparts. 12-13 cm

A: Rooiruglewerik
Z: Intakajolwane
Ss: Mmadiberwane-Nkatakgunong
G: Weißwangenlerche

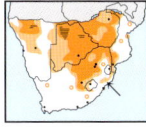

HOUSE SPARROW ♂

Urban areas and farms. Grey crown, Chestnut back and wings, small white wingbar, and black bib. 14 cm

A: Huismossie
Z: Ujolwane Wekhaya
G: Haussperling

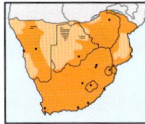

CAPE SPARROW

Farmlands and suburbia. Chestnut back, rump and wings, and white wingbar; male has black-and-white head and breast; female has grey-and-white head and breast. 15 cm

A: Gewone Mossie **Z:** Undlunkulu **X:** Unondlwane
Ss: Serobele-Hlohophatshwa **Sp:** Lemphorokgohlo La Kapa
H: Oyatuhere RwaKapa **G :** Kapsperling

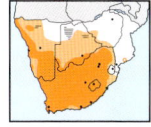

SOUTHERN GREY-HEADED SPARROW

Woodland and gardens. Grey head, chestnut upperparts, small white wingbar, and stout black or horn-coloured bill. 15-16 cm

A: Gryskopmossie **Z:** Ujolwanokhandaphunga
G: Graukopfsperling

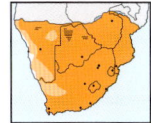

GREAT SPARROW

Dry thornveld. Grey crown, chestnut nape, back and wings, small white wingbar; male has conspicuous black bib. 15-16 cm

A: Grootmossie **Z:** Ujolwanomkhulu
Ss: Serobele-Se-Seholo **G:** Rostsperling

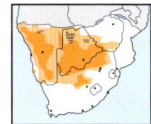

CAPE BATIS

Forest fringes. Grey cap, black mask, rufous wingbar; male has black chest; female has rufous throat and breast band.
12-13 cm

A: Kaapse Bosbontrokkie
Z: Udokotela
Ss: Swamahlaku-Sa-Kapa
G: Kapschnäpper

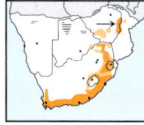

BRUBRU

Woodland. Black-and-white wingbar, rufous flanks and white underparts.
15 cm

A: Bontroklaksman
Z: Usacingo
G: Brubru

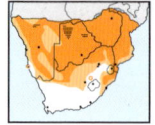

CHINSPOT BATIS ♀

Woodland. Black and white with grey cap and yellow eyes; female with rufous breast and chin-spot.
12-13 cm

A: Witliesbosbontrokkie
Z: Incwaba
X: Unondyola
Ss: Swamahlaku-Sa-Bokone
G: Weißflankenschnäpper

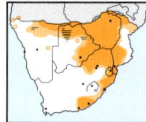

CINNAMON-BREASTED WARBLER

Dry, rocky bushveld. Dark brown upperparts, and rufous lower breast and vent.
13-14 cm

A: Kaneelborssanger
Z: Ujamelidwalobomvu
G: Zimtbrustsänger

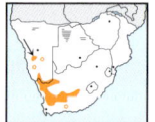

RUFOUS-EARED WARBLER ♂

Rocky scrub veld. Rufous mask and ear coverts, black breast band, white underparts; erect tail. **14 cm**

A: Rooioorlangstertjie
Z: Ujenga Wehlane
G: Rotbackensänger

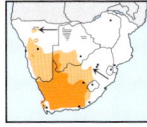

WHITE-BROWED SCRUB ROBIN

Scrub. Rufous rump and uppertail coverts, well-streaked breast, and white wing-markings. **15 cm**

A: Gestreepte Wipstert
Z: Ugaganomidwa
G: Weißbrauen-Heckensänger

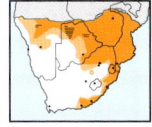

CHESTNUT-VENTED WARBLER (Tit-Babbler)

Thornveld thickets. Mostly dark grey, with chestnut vent, and spotted breast. **15 cm**

A: Bosveldtjeriktik
Z: Ihlekehleke
Ss: Pharalanku-Tonofubedu
G: Meisensänger

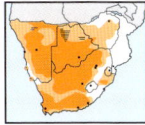

KALAHARI SCRUB ROBIN

Thornveld scrub. Rufous upperparts, greyish cap and pale underparts. **16–17 cm**

A: Kalahariwipstert
Z: Ugagana LwaseNtshonalanga
G: Kalahariheckensänger

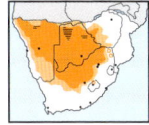

RED-CHESTED FLUFFTAIL ♂

Marshlands. Chestnut head, nape and upper breast, and black body with white streaks. 15–17 cm

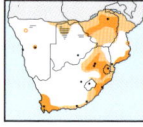

A: Rooiborsvleikuiken Z: Ubhavuzilobomvana
Ss: Tsuanelehlaka Ya Sefubafubedu
G: Rotbrust-Zwergralle

PINK-BILLED LARK

Short grasslands. South-eastern race has rich rufous plumage, and pink bill and legs. 12 cm

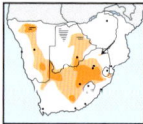

A: Pienkbeklewerik
Z: Unongqwashi
Ss: Tswibididi
G: Rotschnabellerche

SPIKE-HEELED LARK

Grasslands and scrub. SE race has rufous colouring overall and short tail. 15–16 cm

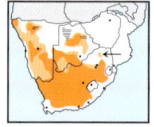

A: Vlaktelewerik Z: Isanqunzi
X: Ingqembe Ss: Tsirwane-Mekwebe G: Zirplerche

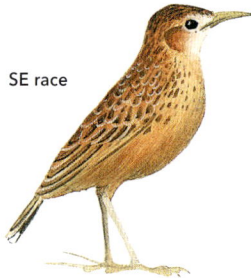

SE race

LARGE-BILLED LARK

Scrub and grassy croplands. Heavily streaked, dark brown upperparts, and pale underparts. 18 cm

A: Dikbeklewerik Z: Ungqwashomlomomkhulu
G: Dickschnabellerche

RUFOUS-NAPED LARK

Open grassland with bushes. Eastern race has rufous crest and wings; western race has rufous on wings only. 18–19 cm

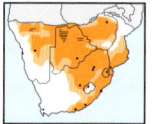

A: Rooineklewerik Z: Untilontilo X: Iqabathule Ss: Tsirwane-Pheotsoku Sp: Pulaekhudile Sh: Tsotso G: Rotnackenlerche

ROCKRUNNER

Rocky and bushy hillsides. Heavily streaked head and mantle, white throat and breast, and rufous back, belly and vent.
17 cm

A: Rotsvoël
G: Klippensänger

RED-BACKED SHRIKE

Woodland. Grey cap, nape and rump, rufous mantle and back, and white underparts.
18 cm

A: Rooiruglaksman
Z: Umathithibala
X: Ihlolo
Ss: Tshemedi-Kgunong
G: Neuntöter

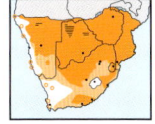

RED-THROATED WRYNECK

Woodland and gardens. Speckled brown-and-black upperparts, rufous throat, and creamish-white upper breast. 18 cm

A: Draaihals
Z: Unongilobomvu **Ss:** Molalareteleha
Tw: Molalamenoga **Sh:** Ndereka
G: Rotkehl-Wendehals

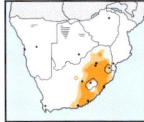

CAPE GRASSBIRD

Long grass and bracken hillsides. Dark brown, streaked back, and rufous cap and straggly tail feathers.
19–23 cm

A: Grasvoël
Z: Unontshiloza
X: Udwetya
G: Kap-Grassänger

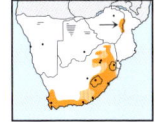

PYGMY FALCON ♀

Dry acacia veld. Grey upperparts, rufous mantle, white underparts, and red eye-ring, cere and legs.
19.5 cm

A: Dwergvalk
Z: Uklebenyana
Ss: Phakwana
Sp: Sepekwana
N: ≠khari ǀaub
H: Orukoze Okaṯiṯi
G: Zwergfalke

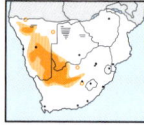

MIOMBO ROCK THRUSH

Miombo woodland. Grey head and upperparts with black flecks, dull orange-rufous breast, and pale white belly.
18 cm

A: Angolakliplyster
G: Miomborötel

SHORT-TOED ROCK THRUSH ♂

Rocky hills. Grey upperparts and throat, dull orange underparts, and white cap.
18 cm

A: Korttoonkliplyster
Z: Inhlaletshenekhandalimhlophe
G: Kurzzehenrötel

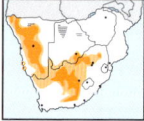

COLLARED PALM THRUSH

Palm savanna. Rufous upperparts and vent, black collar, cream throat, and grey flanks.
19 cm

A: Palmmôrelyster
Z: Umunswi Wasemalaleni
G: Morgenrötel

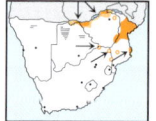

SENTINEL ROCK THRUSH ♂

Rocky hills and grasslands. Grey head, mantle and breast, and rufous underparts. 21 cm

A: Langtoonkliplyster
Z: Ikhwelemarsheni
G: Langzehenrötel

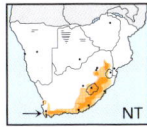

BROWN-CROWNED TCHAGRA

Thornveld thickets. Grey-brown crown and mantle, black border to crown, and chestnut wings. 19 cm

A: Rooivlerktjagra **Z:** Isikhwayimba **G:** Damaratschagra

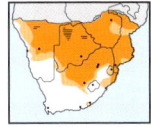

SOUTHERN TCHAGRA

Coastal bush and thickets. Brown crown and mantle, rufous wings, and heavy bill. 21 cm

A: Grysborstjagra **Z:** Ushowe **G:** Kaptschagra

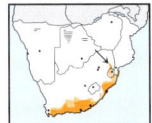

CAPE ROCK THRUSH

Rocky slopes and cliffs. Rufous underparts, rump and tail; male has rufous mantle, and grey head and neck; female is speckled brown above. 21 cm

A: Kaapse Kliplyster
Z: Isihlalamatsheni
X: Unomaweni
Ss: Thume-Hlohoputswa
G: Klippenrötel

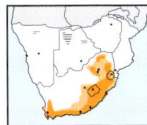

BLACK-CROWNED TCHAGRA

Mixed woodland thickets. Black crown, beige mantle, and rufous wings. 21–23 cm

A: Swartkroontjagra **Z:** UmNguphane **X:** Imbombo
Sp: Mmamapena **Ts:** Mghubhana Lowu Kulu
Sh: Nyamburo **G:** Senegaltschagra

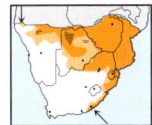

LITTLE GREBE

Inland waters. Chestnut sides to head and neck, and distinctive creamy patch at base of bill.
20 cm

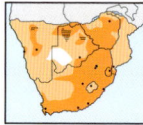

A: Kleindobbertjie **Z:** Imvukwane **X:** Unolwilwilwi
Ss: Thoboloko E Nnyenyane
Tw: Senwedi Se Sennye
N: ≠khari dûb
G: Zwergtaucher

MOCKING CLIFF CHAT ♀

Rocky regions and suburbia. Grey-black upperparts and head, and dark rufous underparts.
20–23 cm

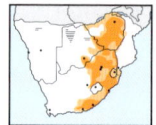

A: Dassievoël
Z: Isikhwelemaweni
Ss: Sethwena-Nketsisane
Sp: Leseka
G: Rotbauchschmätzer

GREY-HEADED KINGFISHER

Mixed open woodland. Grey head, breast and mantle, chestnut belly, and red bill.
20 cm

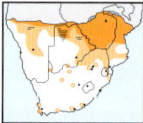

A: Gryskopvisvanger
Z: Isiphikelelesikhandampunga
Ss: Seinodi Sa Hlohoputswa
Tw: Seinwedi Sa Tlhogokotswana
G: Graukopfliest

RUDDY TURNSTONE (br.)

Shorelines. Chestnut upperparts, black-and-white head, neck and breast, and white underparts. 22 cm

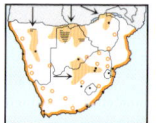

A: Steenloper **Z:** Umaphendulamatshe
Ss: Lekitinyane **N:** |ui!gûb **G:** Steinwälzer

AFRICAN PARADISE FLYCATCHER

Woodland canopy. Blue-black head and underparts, rufous upperparts and tail, and bright blue eye-ring and bill. 23 cm (br. male 41 cm)

A: Paradysvlieëvanger
Z: Inzwece **X:** Ujejane
Ss: Kapantsi-Ya-Meru
Tw: Mothwapea
Ts: Xiavava
Nd: Eve **Sh:** Kateredemu
G: Paradiesschnäpper

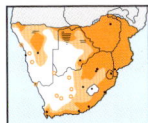

♀
♂

BURCHELL'S COURSER

Sparsely grassed areas. Chestnut, with grey nape, and white belly and legs. 23 cm

A: Bloukopdrawwertjie
Z: Unobulongwe
X: Ingegane
Ss: Mokopjwane Wa Bophirima
N: ≠hoa-gao-ao|gapa !naeb
G: Rostrennvogel

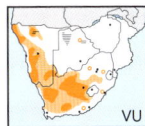

VU

TEMMINCK'S COURSER

Sparsely grassed and recently burnt areas. Rufous cap and lower breast, and white underbelly and legs. 20 cm

A: Trekdrawwertjie
Z: Unobulongwana
Ss: Mokopjwane Wa Leboya
N: |awa-gao-ao|gapa !naeb
G: Temminckrennvogel

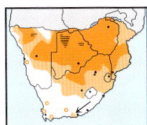

BURCHELL'S SANDGROUSE

Semi-arid areas. White-spotted rufous underparts; male has grey face; female has yellowish face. 25 cm

A: Gevlekte Sandpatrys
Z: Unogwadulogqabhagqabha
Ss: Kokwi Ya Leramatalalehodimo
Tw: Legorwagorwana
N: ≠hoa-ai !nabaris
G: Fleckenflughuhn

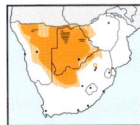

♀
♂

CAPE ROCKJUMPER

Rocky hillsides. Male has black-and-white upperparts and throat, and rufous breast and rump; female has speckled upperparts and rufous underparts with streaked breast.
25 cm

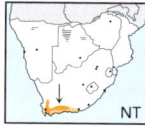

A: Kaapse Berglyster
Z: Unogxumetsheni WaseKapa
G: Kap-Felsenspringer

LEMON DOVE

Forest floor. Rufous, with greenish wings, and white forehead and chin.
25–30 cm

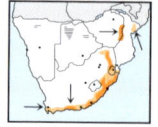

A: Kaneelduifie
Z: Isagqukwe
X: Isagqukhwe
Ss: Leeba La Molalatala
Sh: Mhuputi
G: Zimttaube

GURNEY'S SUGARBIRD

Mountain slopes with proteas and aloes. Rufous breast and cap, yellow vent, and long tail. 25–29 cm

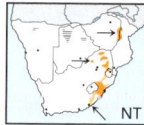

A: Rooiborssuikervoël
Z: Unosiqalaba
Ss: Mmanotswane
G: Gurneys Honigfresser

AFRICAN HOOPOE

Woodland and suburbia. Rufous crest, head and body, and black-and-white wings.
27 cm

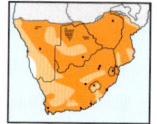

A: Hoephoep
Z: UmZolozolo
Ss: Pupupu
Sp: Kukuku
Ts: Phuphuphu
Nd: Uzinigweni
Sh: Mhupupu
N: ||nüres
G: Wiedehopf

GREATER PAINTED-SNIPE ♀

Pond fringes. Rufous face, nape and breast, olive back, white central crown, eye-stripe, shoulders and belly, and yellow legs.
28–32 cm

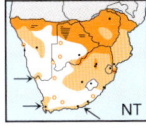

A: Goudsnip
Z: Umakhwaneni
Ss: Kwekwe Ya Kgauta
N: !huni|uri ||haigôa-ams
G: Goldschnepfe

SPECKLED PIGEON

Woodlands, cliffs and building ledges. Rufous wings with white spots, grey underparts, and red facial skin and legs.
33 cm

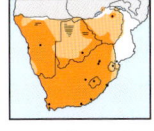

A: Kransduif **Z:** Ivukuthu
Ss: Lehoboi **Tw:** Leebarope
N: !garo≠nabis
G: Guineataube

CRESTED FRANCOLIN

Mixed woodland, forest fringes and thickets. Rufous-brown upperparts, black-and-white facial marks, well-spotted breast, and red legs. 32 cm

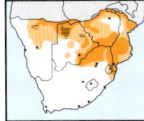

A: Bospatrys
Z: Isikhwehlesiqhova
Ss: Lesogo
Tw: Lekweekwane
Ts: Nghwari
Sh: Hwerekwere
N: !amxadana !nowos
H: Ongwari Ozondomba
G: Schopffrankolin

PURPLE ROLLER

Woodland. Brownish upperparts, multi-coloured wings, and white-streaked rufous underparts.
36–40 cm

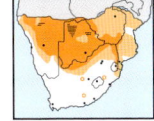

A: Groottroupant
Z: Ifefemidwa
Ss: Letleretlere Le Leholo
Tw: Letleretlere Le Legolo
Ts: Vhevhe Nkomo
N: ≠hoa|awa kōkō-îas
G: Strichelracke

LESSER KESTREL ♂

Open bushveld and grasslands. Rufous body; male has grey head, back, greater coverts and tail. 28–30 cm

A: Kleinrooivalk
Z: Umathethebanomncane
Ss: Seotsanyana Se Senyenyane
Tw: Phakalane E Nnye
N: ≠khari ǀawa ǀaub
G: Rötelfalke

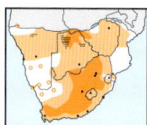

GREATER KESTREL

Open thornveld and semi-arid grasslands. Entirely rufous upperparts and body, and white under-wings and undertail. 36 cm

A: Grootrooivalk
Z: Umathethebanomkhulu
Ss: Seotsanyana Se Seholo
Tw: Phakalane E Kgolo
N: kai ǀawa ǀaub
H: Orukoze Orunene
G: Steppenfalke

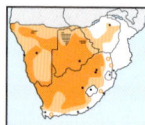

ROCK KESTREL

Hills and grasslands. Rufous body, grey head and tail; male has black tip on tail; female has barred tail. 30–33 cm

A: Kransvalk
Z: Umathethebana Wamadwala
X: Uthebethebana
Tw: Phakwe Ya Lefika
N: ǁhoa ǀaub
G: Turmfalke

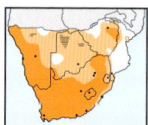

LITTLE SPARROWHAWK

Wooded savanna and riverine forests. Dark grey upperparts, rufous-banded underparts, and two white spots on tail. 23–25 cm

A: Kleinsperwer
Z: Uheshanyana
Ss: Fiolo E Nnyenyane
N: ≠khari aniǃkhāb
G: Zwergsperber

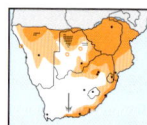

RUFOUS-BREASTED SPARROWHAWK

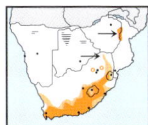

Open woodland. Dark grey upperparts, rufous underparts, and yellow eyes and legs. 33–40 cm

A: Rooiborssperwer
Z: Uheshanobomvu
X: Ukhetshe Womlambo
Ss: Fiolo Ya Sefubafubedu
G: Rotbauchsperber

AFRICAN CUCKOO-HAWK

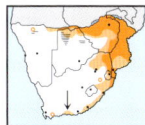

Mixed woodland. Grey head and barred tail, and rufous barring on breast, belly and underwing coverts. 40 cm

A: Koekoekvalk
Z: Usomthende
Ss: Fiolo-lehopoho
Tw: Segodi-Tlhotlhamedupe
N: hō-hōse hīsabes
G: Kuckucksweih

OVAMBO SPARROWHAWK (imm.)

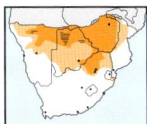

Woodland. Rufous morph has rufous head and body, yellow cere, and orange legs. 33–40 cm

A: Ovambosperwer
Z: Uheshosaklebe
Ss: Fiolo Ya Ovambo
Tw: Segodi Sa Ovambo
N: ǀhai-daoxa aniǃkhāb
H: Orukoze Yovambo
G: Ovambosperber

imm.

RED-FOOTED FALCON

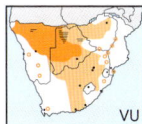

Open semi-arid grassland. Female has rufous head and underparts and grey upperwings; male grey with rufous vent. 29–30 cm

A: Westelike Rooipootvalk
Z: Uklebonyawobomvu
Ss: Phakwe Ya Leotofubedu
N: huri ǀawa-≠ai ǀaub
G: Rotfußfalke

♀   ♂

AMUR FALCON ♂

Open grassland and croplands. Grey, with rufous vent, white underwings, and red cere and legs. 28–30 cm

A: Oostelike Rooipootvalk **Z:** Oklebeklebe
Ss: Phakwe Ya Leotolamunu **Tw:** Phakwe Ya Lenao-orenji
N: ai≠oa ǀawa-≠ai ǀaub **G:** Amur-Rotfußfalke

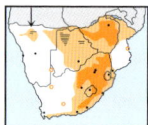

RED-NECKED FALCON

Kalahari thornveld. Grey, barred body, and rufous cap and nape. 36 cm

A: Rooinekvalk **Z:** Uklebontamobomvu
Tw: Phakwe Ya Molalahubidu **N:** ǀawa-ǀharo ǀaub
H: Orukoze Rosengu Serandu **G:** Rothalsfalke

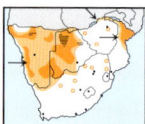

LANNER FALCON

Cliffs and open woodland. Grey upperparts, rufous crown, and buffy white underparts. 40–45 cm

A: Edelvalk **Z:** Uklebemawa **G:** Lannerfalke

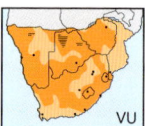

SHIKRA

Woodland. Plain grey upperparts, rufous-banded underparts. 30–34 cm

A: Gebande Sperwer
Z: Uheshomidwayidwa
Ss: Fiolo Ya Motjhato
Tw: Segodi Sa Moeledi
N: daoxa aniǃkhāb
G: Shikra

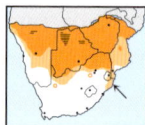

EURASIAN HOBBY

Light woodland. Dark upperparts, streaked under-parts, and rufous vent and leggings. 30–35 cm

A: Europese Boomvalk
Z: Uklebosankonjane
Ss: Phakwe Ya Leboya
Tw: Phakwe Ya Bokone
N: ǀapa haiǀaub
G: Baumfalke

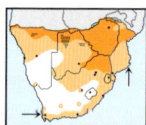

AUGUR BUZZARD

Well-wooded, rocky outcrops. Dark upperparts, white underparts, and rufous tail; female has black head; seldom flaps.
44–53 cm

A: Witborsjakkalsvoël
Tw: Ntswana Ya Sehubasweu
Sh: Nyamudzura
N: !uri-ǀgā anitsēbeb
G: Augurbussard

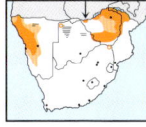

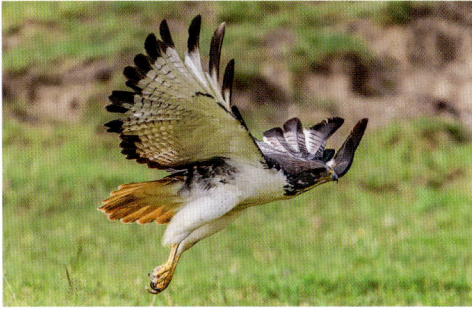

SENEGAL COUCAL

Dense thickets. Rufous wings, black cap and tail, and white underparts. 41 cm

A: Senegalvleiloerie
Z: Ufukwe WaseNyakatho
Sp: Mpue Ya Sekgwa
Tw: Letuutuu La Sekgwa
G: Senegal-Spornkuckuck

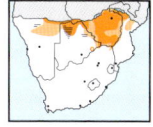

JACKAL BUZZARD

Forested mountains. Dark grey, with rufous breast and tail, and distinctive black-and-white underwings.
44–53 cm

A: Rooiborsjakkalsvoël
Z: Inhlandlokazi
Ss: Kgajwane Ya Sefubafubedu
Tw: Ntswana Ya Sehubahubidu
G: Felsenbussard

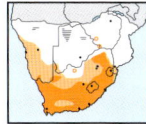

BURCHELL'S COUCAL

Moist thickets and gardens. Rufous wings, black cap and tail, faint barring on uppertail coverts, and white underparts. 44 cm

A: Gewone Vleiloerie
Z: Ufukwe
X: Ubikhwe
Ss: Lefututu La Botjhabela
Sp: Mpue Ya Bohlabela
Tw: Letuutuu La Botlhaba
G: Tiputip

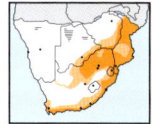

WHITE-BROWED COUCAL

Thickets. Rufous mantle and wings, blackish crown, white streaking from head to mantle, and white eyebrows.
44 cm

A: Gestreepte Vleiloerie
Tw: Mogofa
N: !uridaoxa |hīsabes
G: Weißbrauen-Spornkuckuck

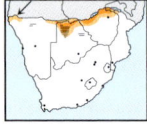

AFRICAN JACANA

Waterbodies with floating vegetation. Rufous body, black-and-white head, and long legs and toes.
40 cm

A: Grootlangtoon
Z: Unondwayizomkhulu
Ss: Mohatsakwena E Moholo
Tw: Mogatsakwena Yo Mogolo
Nd: Utolo
N: kai gāxü|khunus
H: Onimwe Mire
G: Blaustirn-Blatthühnchen

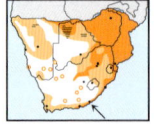

COPPERY-TAILED COUCAL

Reed beds. Rufous wings, darker on nape, and coppery black cap and tail.
44–50 cm

A: Grootvleiloerie
Tw: Letuutuu Le Legolo
N: kai |hīsabes
G: Angola-Mönchskuckuck

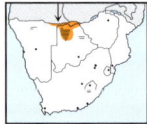

GIANT KINGFISHER

Inland waters. Black and white, with large black bill; male has rufous breast; female has rufous belly.
43–46 cm

A: Reusevisvanger
Z: Isivuba
X: Uxomoyi
Ss: Seinodi Se Seholo
Tw: Mmatlhapi Se Mogolo
Ts: N'wancakini
Sh: Teveteve
N: kai ||audīb
G: Riesenfischer

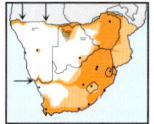

♂

♀

MACCOA DUCK ♂

Inland waters. Chestnut body, black head and bright blue bill and stiff tail. **46 cm**

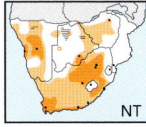

A: Bloubekeend
Ss: Letata La Molomo-Talalehodimo
Z: Idadelikhandamnyama
N: ≠nüdana ≠naras
G: Maccoa-Ente

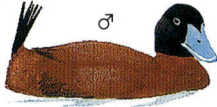

FULVOUS WHISTLING DUCK

Inland freshwater pans and dams. Rufous head and body, dark brown back and wings, and white flank feathers. **46 cm**

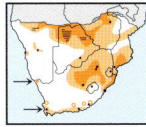

A: Fluiteend **Z:** Inzwinzwinzebomvu **Ss:** Lewewe La Melodi
N: ≠namxa ≠naras **G:** Gelbe Baumente

WHITE-FACED WHISTLING DUCK

Large dams and pans, and estuaries. Black head, white face, and rufous neck and upper breast. **48 cm**

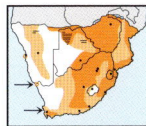

A: Nonnetjie-eend **Z:** UmaBhomfushane **Ss:** Lewewe La Leramasweu
Sp: Lewewe La Sehubašweu **Ts:** Xiyahkokeni **N:** !uri-ai ≠naras
H: Ombaka Yomurungu Omuvapa **G:** Witwenente

SOUTH AFRICAN SHELDUCK

Brackish waters. Rich rufous body and grey head; female has white face. **64 cm**

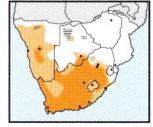

A: Kopereend **Z:** Idadelibomvu
Ss: Letata La Hlohoputswa **N:** ≠aiɬuri !kharas
Tw: Pidipidi Ya Tlhogokotswana **G:** Graukopf-Rostgans

EGYPTIAN GOOSE

Inland waters, lagoons and croplands. Rufous neck and upper body, pale underparts, and pink legs. **71 cm**

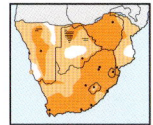

A: Kolgans **Z:** Ilongwe **X:** Ilowe **Ss:** Lefalwa
Tw: Leharathata **Ts:** Sekwamhala **N:** !khaiɬgā !kharas
H: Ombaka YaEgipte **G:** Nilgans

WHITE-BACKED NIGHT HERON

Inland rivers and dams. Rufous neck and mantle, black cap, and yellow facial skin and legs. 53 cm

A: Witrugnagreier **Z:** UmaCuthobomvu
Ss: Kokolofitwe Ya Mokokotlosweu **Tw:** Kokolohutwe Ya Mokotlasweu
G: Weißrücken-Nachtreiher

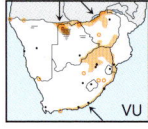

RUFOUS-BELLIED HERON

Inland waters. Dark body, with rich rufous belly and wings, and yellow bill and legs. 58 cm

A: Rooipensreier **Z:** UmaCuthomnyama
Ss: Kokolofitwe Ya Mpafubedu **Tw:** Kokolofitwe Ya Mpahubidu
G: Rotbauchreiher

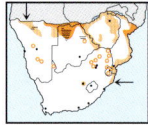

PURPLE HERON

Sheltered reed bed and water edges. Striped, rufous neck, and grey-brown wings. 89 cm

A: Rooireier **Z:** Unokhoboyi **Ts:** Rikolwa
Ss: Kokolofitwe Ya Molalafubedu **N:** |awa-!ao |gurikhoeseb
G: Purpurreiher

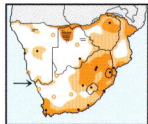

GOLIATH HERON

Inland waters. Grey upperwings, back, tail, lower neck and bill, and rufous head, neck and underparts.
140 cm

A: Reusereier **Z:** Unozalizingwenya
Ss: Kokolofitwe E Kgolo **Ts:** Ntsaviya
H: Etuva Romasa **G:** Goliathreiher

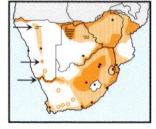

AFRICAN DARTER

Inland waters. Crown and body very dark brown; front of neck rufous in male, sandy in female.
79 cm

A: Slanghalsvoël **Z:** Inyoninyoka **X:** Ivuzi
Ss: Timeletsane **Ts:** Gororo **Sh:** Chigwikwi
N: |ao|haros **G:** Schlangenhalsvogel

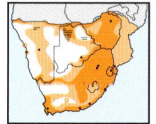

PEL'S FISHING OWL

Bushveld with large slow-flowing rivers. Rufous upperparts, cinnamon underparts, and black eyes. 63–65 cm

A: Visuil
Z: Isikhovanhlanzi
Sp: Leribišihlapi
Tw: Mongamolapo
N: ||au≠uwib
G: Bindenfischeule

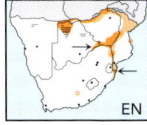

CROWNED EAGLE

Well-wooded forests. Black and white, with rufous underwings visible in flight. 80–90 cm

A: Kroonarend
Z: Isihuhwa
Ss: Makgwana
Sp: Makgwana
Tw: Makgwana
G: Kronenadler

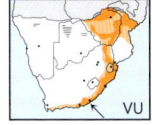

AFRICAN FISH EAGLE

Dams, lagoons and rivers. White head, mantle and breast, rufous body, and dark wings. 63–73 cm

A: Visarend **Z:** Inkwazi
X: Inkwaza
Ss: Ntsuhlapi
Sp: Ntšhuhlapi
Tw: Audi
Ts: Nghunghwa
Ve: Khuwadzi
Sw: Inkwazi
Nd: Iwunkwe
N: huri-am!ari!khās
H: Orukoze Yomahundju
G: Schreiseeadler

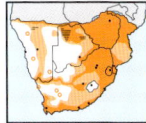

BEARDED VULTURE

High-altitude montane cliffs. Rufous body, dark brown wings and tail, black mask and beard, and white face. 110 cm

A: Baardaasvoël
Z: Ugaganontshebe
Ss: Seodi
G: Bartgeier

First impression

DARK BROWN PLUMAGE

Brown is probably the most common plumage colour. Many people tend to describe brown birds as 'greyish', which can make it harder to identify a brown bird that has flown away. This chapter covers only medium brown to dark brown birds, but with the acknowledgement that they may appear dark grey or blackish to some birders.

Brown birds come in all shapes and sizes, from the numerous 'little brown jobs' (LBJs), which are mostly brownish all over, to most birds of prey, many plovers, francolins and other terrestrial birds, which may be partially or entirely brown.

How does dark brown plumage serve a bird?

Camouflage: Brown plumage is useful for camouflage for terrestrial birds, such as the Natal Spurfowl, and those that live in the shadowy interiors of dense thickets, like the many LBJs.

THE FEEDING QUIRKS OF BIRDS OF PREY

Feeding behaviour: The most interesting feeding behaviour among birds of prey is observed in the **Bearded Vulture**, which is partial to bones and bone marrow. When a bone is too large to be swallowed, the vulture will clasp it in its feet, ascend to a good height and drop the bone onto the rocks below to break it. The bird usually has a favourite dropping area, and it may need to drop large bones several times in order to shatter them.

   Strange diet! The **Palm-nut Vulture** will eat a variety of fruit and small animals, as well as stranded fish and carrion. However, its name is derived from its habit of feeding on the fruits of raffia palms, and it is usually found in the vicinity of these trees.

   Insect-eating eagles: Another large bird that has an odd diet is the **Steppe Eagle**, a summer visitor from Eastern Europe and Asia, which is related to the resident **Tawny Eagle**, but is somewhat larger. In Europe it feeds on a variety of larger prey, but while in Africa, this eagles feeds on termite alates, commonly called 'flying ants'. To collect them, the eagles congregate at the point where the termites emerge. They are seldom alone: **Tawny Eagles**, **Lesser Spotted Eagles**, **Wahlberg's Eagles** and even **Bateleurs** will join in the feast.

TAWNY-FLANKED PRINIA

Riverine vegetation and gardens. Dark brown upperparts and eye-stripe, white eyebrows and under-parts, and tawny rump, flanks and vent. **10–15 cm**

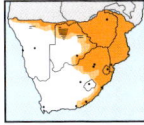

A: Bruinsylangstertjie
Z: Ujenga
X: Ungcuze
Sp: Nanaswi
Tw: Phenenku
Ts: Matsinyani
Ss: Seqeshe-Ropetshehla
G: Rahmbrustprinie

KAROO PRINIA

Dense fynbos and karoo undergrowth. Dark brown upperparts, pale yellow eyebrows and underparts, and black streaks on breast and flanks. **14 cm**

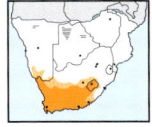

A: Karoolangstertjie
Z: Ujenga WaseKapa
X: Ijiza
Ss: Seqeshe-Meretwana
G: Gelbbauchprinie

BLACK-CHESTED PRINIA

Dry scrub and thornveld. Dark brown upperparts, white underparts and black breast band; non-br. has yellow underparts. **13–15 cm**

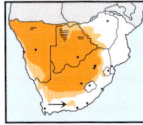

A: Swartbandlangstertjie
Z: Ujengosifubesimnyama
Ss: Seqeshe-Thwalakgauntsho
G: Brustbandprinie

br.

DRAKENSBERG PRINIA

Forest fringes and marshy scrub. Brown upperparts, yellowish eyebrows and lightly streaked underparts, and long tail. **14 cm**

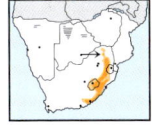

A: Drakensberglangstertjie **Z:** Ujenga Wokhahlamba
X: Injwiza **G:** Gelbbauchprinie

STIERLING'S WREN-WARBLER

Woodland thickets.
Dark brown upperparts,
and white underparts with
blackish barring.
11.5–13 cm

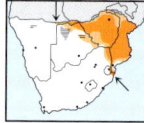

A: Stierlingsanger
Z: Isadube
G: Stierling-Bindensänger

CINNAMON-BREASTED WARBLER

Dry, rocky bushveld.
Dark brown upperparts,
cinnamon forehead,
lower breast and
vent, and pale
throat with
dark barring.
13–14 cm

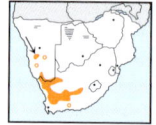

A: Kaneelborssanger
Z: Ujamelidwalobomvu
G: Zimtbrustsänger

BARRED WREN-WARBLER

Woodland thickets.
Dark brown upperparts,
and buffy underparts with
brown barring; breast is
dark in summer.
13–15 cm

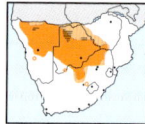

A: Gebande Sanger
Z: Isanyendle
G: Bindensänger

br.

non-br.

NAMAQUA WARBLER

Karoo thorn scrub. Dark
brown upperparts, white
underparts, lightly spotted
breast, and buffy flanks
and vent. 14 cm

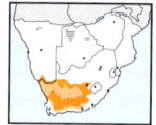

A: Namakwalangstertjie
Z: Ujenga Womfula
Ss: Seqeshe-Sa-Bophirima
G: Namasänger

GARDEN WARBLER

Thickets, parks and gardens. Plain dark brown upperparts and paler underparts; no prominent features.
15 cm

A: Tuinsanger **Z:** Umnqumo
Ss: Swamahlaka-Sa-Jarete
G: Gartengrasmücke

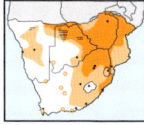

SAND MARTIN

Inland waters and estuaries. Dark brown upperparts, white underparts, narrow breast band, and shallowly forked tail. 12 cm

A: Europese Oewerswael
Z: Inhlolamfula
Ss: Lekabelane-La-Mangope
G: Europäische Uferschwalbe

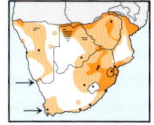

LITTLE RUSH WARBLER

Dense vegetation over water. Dark brown upperparts, pale eye-stripe and underparts, and faintly marked upper breast. 17 cm

A: Kaapse Vleisanger
Z: Umavelashona
G: Sumpfbuschsänger

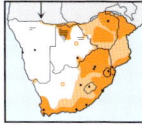

BROWN-THROATED MARTIN

Inland rivers, estuaries and sandbanks. Dark brown upperparts, white belly, and shallowly forked tail; some birds are all brown.
13 cm

A: Afrikaanse Oewerswael
Z: Inhlolamazi
Ss: Lekabelane-Kodusootho
G: Braunkehl-Uferschwalbe

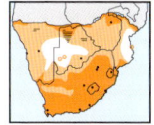

ROCK MARTIN

Cliffs, bridges and buildings. Dark brown upperparts, buffy underparts, and square tail with white 'windows'. **15 cm**

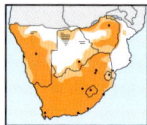

A: Kransswael
Z: Inhlolamvula Yamadwala
X: Unongubende
Ss: Lekabelane-La-Mawa
G: Steinschwalbe

AFRICAN PALM SWIFT

Vicinity of palm trees. Brown, with slender wings and deeply forked tail. **17 cm**

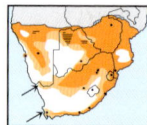

A: Palmwindswael
Z: Ijiyankomelimlotha
Tw: Phetla Ya Mokolwane
N: !unihai sōsowob
Ss: Lehaqasi La Palema
G: Palmensegler

BANDED MARTIN

Inland waters and moist grassland. Dark brown upperparts, white underparts, wide brown breast band, white eyebrows, and square tail. **17 cm**

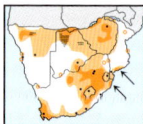

A: Gebande Oewerswael
Z: Inhlolamvulebhandensundu
Ss: Lekabelane-Kodutshweu
G: Weißbrauenschwalbe

NEDDICKY (S & SE race)

Woodland and thickets. Rufous cap, brown upperparts, and blue-grey underparts. **10–11 cm**

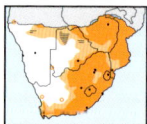

A: Neddikkie
Z: Incede
X: Incede
Ss: Motintinyane-O-Moputswa
Sp: Setwaneng
G: Brauner Zistensänger

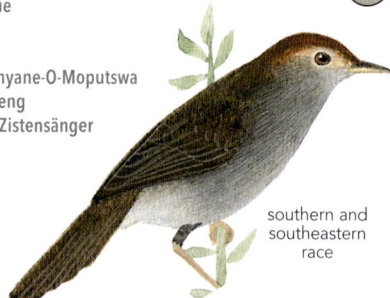

southern and southeastern race

LEVAILLANT'S CISTICOLA

Reed beds and rank grass. Dark brown upperparts with streaked back, pale underparts, and rufous-washed face, breast and flanks. 12–13 cm

A: Vleitinktinkie
Z: Umdokwe
X: Umvila
G: Uferzistensänger

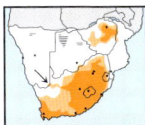

CAPE SISKIN

Mountain slopes. Dark brown upperparts, streaky crown, and yellow underparts; female has streaking on breast. 13 cm

A: Kaapse Pietjiekanarie
Z: Umbhalane WaseKapa
G: Hottentottengirlitz

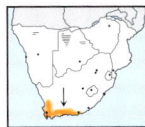

RATTLING CISTICOLA

Grassy bushveld scrub. Buff and dark brown upperparts and pale underparts; distinctive rattle at end of song. 14–16 cm

A: Bosveldtinktinkie
Z: Iqodo
G: Rotscheitel-Zistensänger

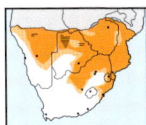

DRAKENSBERG SISKIN

Mountain slopes. Dark brown upperparts and streaky head; male has greenish-yellow underparts; female is buffy below with streaky breast. 13 cm

A: Bergpietjiekanarie
Z: Umbhalane Wokhahlamba
Ss: Swaswi
G: Drakensberggirlitz

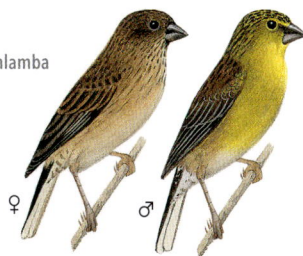

BROWN-BACKED HONEYBIRD

Woodland. Dark brown upperparts, white outer-tail feathers, pale underparts with dusky breast, and black bill. 13 cm

A: Skerpbekheuningvoël
Z: Unomtsheketche
Sp: Kgogo Ya Mokolosotho
Tw: Tshetlho Ya Mokotlarokwa
N: ≠gama-‖ã dani!khõdanab
Ss: Modisadinotshi Wa Mokokotlosootho
G: Schmalschnabel-Honiganzeiger

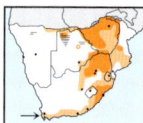

GREATER HONEYGUIDE

Mixed woodland. Adult has dark brown upperparts and whitish underparts; male has pink bill and dark throat patch; female has black bill; imm. is yellowish below. 19-20 cm

imm.

A: Grootheuningwyser
Z: Ingede
Nd: Ingede
Sh: Tsoro
N: kai dani!khõdanab
Ss: Tsetlo E Kgolo
G: Schwarzkehl-Honiganzeiger

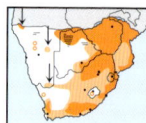

♀
♂

LESSER HONEYGUIDE

Woodland. Dark greenish-brown upperparts, grey head, white outer-tail feathers, pale underparts with dusky breast, and black bill with white patch. 15 cm

A: Kleinheuningwyser
Z: Ingedana
Tw: Tshetlho E Nnyenyane
N: ≠khari dani!khõdanab
Ss: Tsetlo E Nnyenyane
G: Kleiner Honiganzeiger

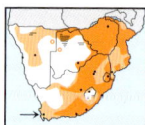

AFRICAN DUSKY FLYCATCHER

Forest fringes. Dark grey-brown upperparts and breast, whitish throat and underbelly, and indistinct smudges on breast. 12-13 cm

A: Donkervlieëvanger
Z: Usikhothambuzane
X: Unomaphelaphelane
Ss: Kapantsi-Thokwana
G: Dunkelschnäpper

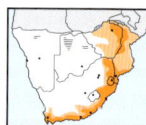

SPOTTED FLYCATCHER

Mixed woodland. Dark grey-brown upperparts, dark-streaked crown, and distinct streaking on breast and flanks.
14–15 cm

A: Europese Vlieëvanger
Z: Usonambuzane
Ss: Kapantsi-Tubatubi
G: Grauschnäpper

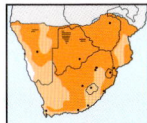

PALE FLYCATCHER

Broad-leaved woodland. Dull grey-brown, with paler throat, and pale eye-rings.
18 cm

A: Muiskleurvlieëvanger **Z:** Isangundwane
G: Fahlschnäpper

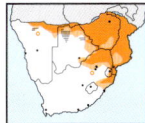

MARICO FLYCATCHER

Acacia thornveld.
Dark brown upperparts and crisp white underparts.
18 cm

A: Maricovlieëvanger **Z:** Isagundwane SaseNtshonalanga
G: Maricoschnäpper

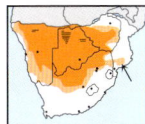

BLUE-MANTLED CRESTED FLYCATCHER

Forest canopy and fringes. Crested head, dark upper-parts, white wingbar and underparts; male has black throat and breast; female has finely spotted breast.
17–18 cm

A: Bloukuifvlieëvanger
Z: Uqholwane **X:** Igotyi
G: Blaumantel-Schopfschnäpper

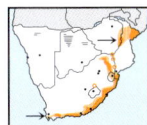

♂

CHAT FLYCATCHER

Arid scrubland. Grey-brown upperparts, pale-edged wing feathers, and whitish underparts with brown-washed breast and belly. 20 cm

A: Grootvlieëvanger **Z:** Isagundwanesikhulu **G:** Drosselschnäpper

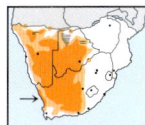

FAMILIAR CHAT

Rocky ground and farmlands.
Dark brown upperparts,
paler underparts, chestnut-
brown rump and tail,
and black central
tail feathers.
15 cm

A: Gewone Spekvreter
Z: UmBexe
X: Isikretyane
Sp: Letlerenyane
Tw: Kgatatswe
Ss: Letleretsane-La-Masaka
G: Rostschwanzschmätzer

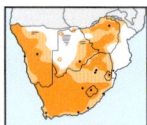

BUSH BLACKCAP

Montane forest fringes
and scrub. Black cap, brown
wings and tail, grey breast,
and red bill and legs.
17 cm

A: Rooibektiptol
Z: Unosigqokomnyama
Ss: Mmameru-Hlohontsho
G: Buschschwarzkäppchen

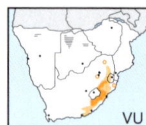

SICKLE-WINGED CHAT

Open grassland scrub.
Dark brown upperparts,
rufous-edged wing feathers,
pale chestnut rump, white
underparts, and dusky
breast. 15 cm

A: Vlaktespekvreter
Z: Umbexe Wezintaba
Ss: Letleretsane-La-Maloti
G: Oranjeschmätzer

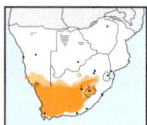

ANT-EATING CHAT

Short grasslands. Dark
brown or blackish-brown;
male darker with white
shoulder patch; in flight,
shows pale wing
feathers. 18 cm

A: Swartpiek
Z: Indlantuthwane
Ss: Thoromedi-Thokwa
G: Termitenschmätzer

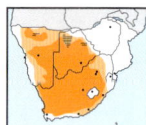

KAROO SCRUB ROBIN

Karoo veld. Dark brown upperparts, paler underparts, white eyebrows and throat, and black spots on vent.
17 cm

A: Slangverklikker
Z: Ugaganompunga
G: Karruheckensänger

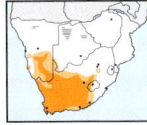

DARK-BACKED WEAVER

Dense riverine and valley forests. Dark brown upperparts, yellow underparts, and pale bill and legs.
16 cm

A: Bosmusikant
Z: Idonsi
G: Waldweber

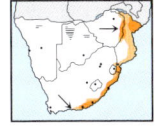

MOUNTAIN WHEATEAR ♀

Boulder-strewn slopes. Dark brown, with white rump and outer-tail feathers. 17–20 cm

A: Bergwagter
Z: Ikhwelentabeni
Ss: Kgalodi
G: Bergschmätzer

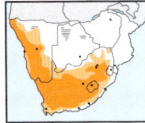

WHITE-BROWED SPARROW-WEAVER

Thornveld. Dark brown upperparts with white-edged feathers, white eyebrows, wingbars, and underparts, black bill and pink legs.
18 cm

A: Koringvoël
Z: Usoqhawe
Ss: Mohale
G: Mahaliweber

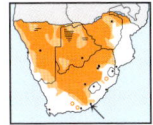

THICK-BILLED WEAVER

Reed beds and adjacent bush. Male dark brown, with white spot on wing and forehead when breeding; female has whitish underparts with heavy dark streaking.
18 cm

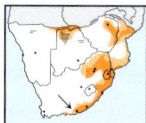

A: Dikbekwewer
Z: Usiqhophokezi
G: Weißstirnweber

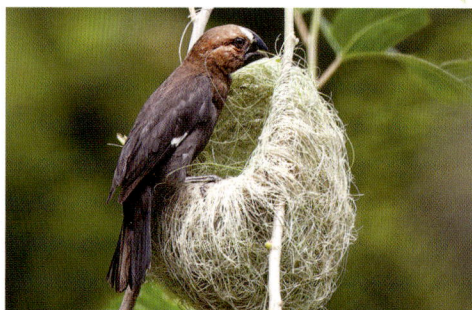

WHITE-EARED BARBET

Coastal forest fringes. Dark brown, with white ear stripe and belly.
18 cm

A: Witoorhoutkapper
Z: Intunjana
Ss: Mankotlo Wa Tsebesweu
G: Weißohr-Bartvogel

RED-BILLED BUFFALO WEAVER

Mixed woodland. Dark brown with red bill; female is paler with streaky underparts.
24 cm

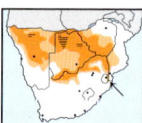

A: Buffelwewer
Z: Usoqhawomnyama
G: Büffelweber

THREE-BANDED PLOVER

Freshwater shores. Brown upperparts, white underparts, and two black breast bands.
18 cm

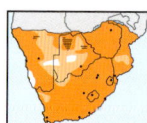

A: Driebandstrandkiewiet
Z: Igwigwi
X: Inqatha
Ts: N'watshekulana
N: daoxa xoexoes
Ss: Mororwane Wa Metjhatoraro
Tw: Thatswane Ya Meelediraro
G: Dreiband-Regenpfeifer

PEARL-SPOTTED OWLET

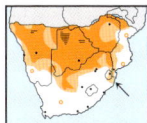

Woodland. Dark brown-grey upperparts with white spots, black ' false eyes' on the back of the head, and brown-and-white streaked underparts.
15–18 cm

A: Witkoluil
Z: Inkovana
Tw: Pelekekae
N: !uri-!khai !hûros
Ss: Morubisi Ya Sefubametjhato
G: Perlkauz

AFRICAN BARRED OWLET

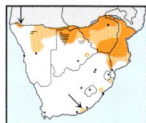

Woodland. Dark brown-grey upperparts with white barring and wing spots, and white underparts with grey-brown bars and spots.
20 cm

A: Gebande Uil
Z: Inkovanemidwa
Tw: Morubisana
Ts: Xikhodlane
N: !khai-|gā !hûros
Ss: Morubsi Ya Sefubadirothi
G: Kapkauz

AFRICAN SCOPS OWL

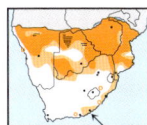

Mixed bushveld. Black-streaked grey-brown plumage, resembling tree bark, yellow eyes, and prominent ear tufts.
15–18 cm

A: Skopsuil **Z:** Umadletshana
Ss: Makgohlwana
Sp: Leribišane
Tw: Sekopamarumo
Ts: Xikotlwa
Sh: Chimbori
N: ≠gae |honnes
H: Okasivi Kautui Outiți
G: Afrikanische Zwergohreule

grey morph   brown morph

DUSKY LARK

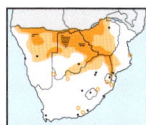

Broad-leaved woodland. Dark brown scalloped upperparts, heavily streaked underparts and bold facial markings. 19 cm

A: Donkerlewerik
Z: Ungqwashomnyama
G: Drossellerche

WOOD SANDPIPER

Freshwater shores.
Dark brown upperparts
with white speckling, white
eyebrows and belly,
buffy breast, and
yellow-green legs.
20 cm

A: Bosruiter
Z: Umakhwifikwifi
Ss: Mosalakatane Wa Moru
N: hai!khuwi!gûb
G: Bruchwasserläufer

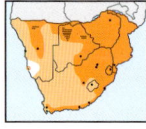

AFRICAN CRAKE

Reed beds. Dark brown
scalloped upperparts, grey
head and chest, and black-
and-white barred belly
and flanks. 20-23 cm

A: Afrikaanse Riethaan
Z: UmJekejeke WaseAfrika
Ss: Kgoholelhaka Ya Afrika
Tw: Kgogoletlhaka Ya Aforika
N: Afrika ≠ā-anib
G: Steppenralle

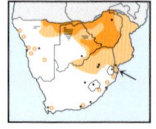

COMMON SANDPIPER

Freshwater shores.
Dark brown upperparts
and breast band, white
shoulder and underparts;
in flight shows white wingbar.
20 cm

A: Gewone Ruiter
Z: Ucijomhlope
Ss: Mosalakatane Wa Lebopo
Tw: Mosalakatane Wa Letshitshi
N: !ā !khuwi!gûb
G: Flußuferläufer

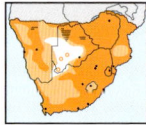

LITTLE GREBE

Inland waters. Dark brown
upperparts, pale underparts,
distinctive creamy patch
at base of bill; br. ad. has
chestnut face and neck.
20 cm

A: Kleindobbertjie
Z: Imvukwane
X: Unolwilwilwi
Sp: Kudupana Ye Nnyane
Tw: Senwedi Se Sennye
N: ≠khari dûb
Ss: Thoboloko E Nnyenyane
G: Zwergtaucher

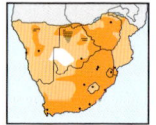

BLACK-NECKED GREBE

Pans and saline waters. Blackish-brown upperparts, and red eyes; br. ad. has golden ear coverts and flanks; non-br. has whitish underparts. 28 cm

A: Swartnekdobbertjie
Z: Ivukelintamemnyama
Ss: Thoboloko E Molalantsho
Tw: Sen wedi Sa Molalantsho
N: ≠nū-!ao dûb
G: Schwarzhalstaucher

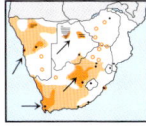

non-br.

br.

DARK-CAPPED BULBUL

Woodland and gardens. Dark brown, with tufted head, dusky white underparts and yellow vent. 20–22 cm

A: Swartoogtiptol
Z: Iphothwe
X: Ikhwebula
Sp: Rankgwetšhe
Ts: Mabyitana
Sh: Gwenhure
Ss: Hlakahlothwana-Ihlotsho
G: Graubülbül

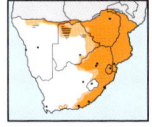

TERRESTRIAL BROWNBUL

Forests and thickets. Dark brown upperparts, dusky underparts, and white throat. 21–22 cm

A: Boskrapper
Z: Igedezi
X: Ikhalakandla
Sp: Seruane
G: Laubbülbül

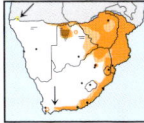

AFRICAN RED-EYED BULBUL

Woodland and gardens. Dark brown upperparts, dusky white underparts, yellow vent, tufted black head and red eye-ring. 21 cm

A: Rooioogtiptol
Z: Iphothwelimehlabomvu
Ss: Hlakahlothwana-Ihlofubedu
G: Maskenbülbül

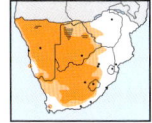

CAPE BULBUL

Coastal scrub and gardens. Dark brown, with tufted head, white eye-ring and yellow vent. 21 cm

A: Kaapse Tiptol
Z: Iphothwelimehlamhlophe
Sp: Lekolo
G: Kapbülbül

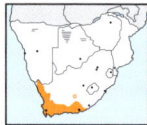

YELLOW-BILLED OXPECKER

Woodland and areas with game or cattle. Brown head and body, yellow-buff rump and underparts, yellow bill with red tip, and yellow eyes. 22 cm

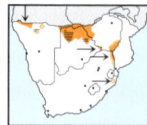

A: Geelbekrenostervoël
Z: Ihlalanyathi
Ss: Tsomi
Sp: Legame
Sh: Shakahuni
G: Gelbschnabel-Madenhacker

RED-BILLED OXPECKER

Woodland and areas with game or cattle. Brown head and body, yellow-buff rump and underparts, red bill and eyes, and yellow eye-ring. 20–22 cm

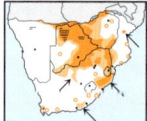

A: Rooibekrenostervoël
Z: Ihlalanyathi **Ss:** Kalla-Tjepa
Sp: Tšhomi **Ts:** Ndzandza
G: Rotschnabel-Madenhacker

KURRICHANE THRUSH

Broad-leaved woodland. Greyish-brown upperparts, orange bill, eye-ring, flanks and legs, white belly, and black moustachial streaks. 22 cm

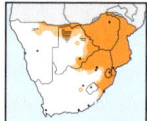

A: Rooibeklyster
Z: Insansane
Ss: Setsipitsipi-Koduphatshwa
G: Rotschnabeldrossel

GROUNDSCRAPER THRUSH

Open woodland. Dark grey-brown upperparts, white face and underparts with bold black markings, black-and-orange bill, and orange legs.
22 cm

A: Gevlekte Lyster
Z: Insansa
G: Akaziendrossel

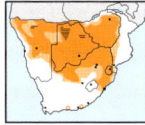

KAROO THRUSH

Woodland, scrubland and gardens. Dark grey-brown with orange belly, and orange-yellow bill and legs.
24 cm

A: Geelbeklyster
Z: Umunswomduba
Ss: Setsipitsipi-Sa-Moru Bokone
G: Karoodrossel

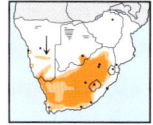

SPOTTED GROUND THRUSH

Coastal forests. Dark brown upperparts with white wingbars, white face and underparts with bold black markings, black bill and pink legs.
23 cm

A: Natallyster
Z: UmuNswi Wehlathi
G: Fleckengrunddrossel

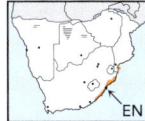

OLIVE THRUSH

Montane forests and gardens. Dark olive-brown upperparts, speckled throat, orange belly, pale vent, and orange-yellow bill and legs; highveld race has brown breast.
24 cm

A: Olyflyster
Z: UmuNswili
Ss: Setsipitsipi-Sa-Bokone
X: Umswi
G: Kapdrossel

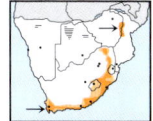

TAMBOURINE DOVE

Forest fringes. Dark brown upperparts, and white eyebrows, forehead and underparts. **23 cm**

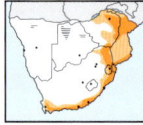

A: Witborsduifie
Z: Isikhombazane-sehlathi
Ss: Mokodunyane Wa Sefubasweu
Sp: Sekgwaranyane Sa Sehubašweu
G: Tamburintaube

RÜPPELL'S PARROT ♀

Arid woodland. Dark brown, with yellow shoulders, and blue rump, underbelly and vent. **23 cm**

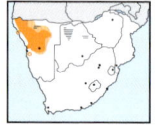

A: Bloupenspapegaai
Ss: Heka Ya Mpatalalehodimo
Sh: Hwenga
N: ≠hoa-!nã ‖giririb
G: Rüppellpapagei

MEYER'S PARROT

Woodland. Brown upper-parts, pale blue back, green belly and rump, and yellow forehead and shoulders. **23 cm**

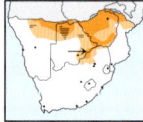

A: Bosveldpapegaai
Z: Isikhwenenesimahlombaphuzi
Tw: Heka Ya Phatlasehla
N: !huni-!ũ ‖giririb
G: Goldbugpapagei

ARROW-MARKED BABBLER

Mixed bushveld and thicket. Dark brown upperparts, grey-brown to tawny under-parts with white arrow marks, and orange eyes with red eye-ring. **23–25 cm**

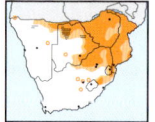

A: Pylvlekkatlagter
Z: Ihelkehle
Ss: Sekganoha
G: Braundroßling

HARTLAUB'S BABBLER

Riverine woodland.
Dark brown upperparts
and breast, white-fringed
feathers, white rump, belly
and vent, and yellow eyes
with red eye-ring.
26 cm

A: Witkruiskatlagter
G: Weißbürzeldroßling

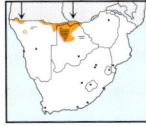

BLACK-WINGED LAPWING

Grasslands and open
woodland. Dark olive-brown
back and wings, grey head
and upper breast,
white forehead,
and white under–
parts; in flight, shows
black and white
underwings. 29 cm

A: Grootswartvlerkkiewiet
Z: Ititihoye
Ss: Lekekeruane La Motjhatontsho
G: Schwarzflügelkiebitz

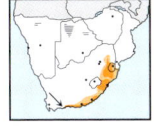

SENEGAL LAPWING

Moist grasslands. Brown
upperparts, grey head, neck
and upper breast, and white
forehead and underparts;
in flight, shows black and
white underwings.
23 cm

A: Kleinswartvlerkkiewiet
Z: Umahambehlala
G: Trauerkiebitz

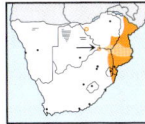

COLLARED PRATINCOLE (br.)

Estuaries, waterside banks
and farmlands. Dark brown
upperparts, buff throat and
breast, black collar, and white
belly and rump. 25 cm

A: Rooivlerksprinkaanvoël **Z:** Iwamba
Ss: Lehlakangwato La Lepheofubedu **G:** Brachschwalbe

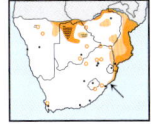

br.

BLACK-WINGED PRATINCOLE (non-br.)

Edges of wetlands and farmlands. Dark brown upperparts, buff throat and breast, and white belly and rump, and black underwings; br. ad. has thin black collar.
25 cm

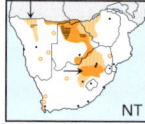

A: Swartvlerksprinkaanvoël
Z: Iwambelimaphikamnyama
N: ≠nü-‖gawo !khuwiswaweli
Ss: Lehlakangwato La Lepheontsho
G: Schwarzflügel-Brachschwalbe

non-br.

PIED STARLING

Open habitats and roadsides. Very dark brown with white underbelly and vent, whitish eyes and orange gape.
25–27 cm

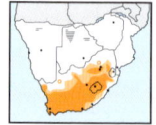

A: Witgatspreeu
Z: Ingwangwa
X: Iqiyogiyo
Ss: Lehodi-Phatshwa
G: Zweifarbenstar

COMMON MYNA

Towns. Brown, with black head, mantle and breast, white belly, and yellow bill, facial skin and legs.
25 cm

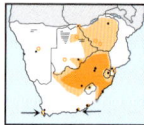

A: Indiese Spreeu
Z: Usothathizwe
Ss: Lehodi-Tlabotjha
G: Hirtenmaina

NATAL SPURFOWL

Riverine bush. Dark brown streaked upperparts, black and white speckled underparts, yellow-and-red bill, and red legs.
30–38 cm

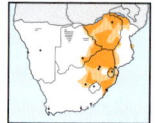

A: Natalse Fisant
Z: Unomemeza
X: Isakhwehle
Ss: Kgwale Ya Molomolamunu
Tw: Segweba
Ts: Nghwari Ma Ntshengwhayi
G: Natalfrankolin

RED-BILLED SPURFOWL

Dry scrub and thickets. Dark brown finely barred upperparts, black-and-white barred underparts, red bill and legs, and yellow eye-ring. 30–38 cm

A: Rooibekfisant
Z: Isikhwehlesimlomobomvu
Ss: Kgwale Ya Molomofubedu
Nd: Letšankgarane
N: ǀawa-am ≠nanas
H: Ongwari
G: Rotschnabelfrankolin

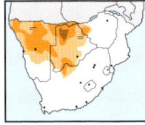

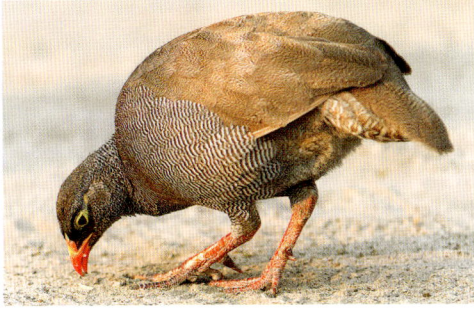

SWAINSON'S SPURFOWL

Open grass woodlands. Dark brown body, red facial and throat skin, black-tipped red bill, and dark grey legs. 34–39 cm

A: Bosveldfisant
Z: Inkwali
Ss: Kgwale Ya Leotontsho
Sp: Lehoho La Leotoso
Nd: Rakodukhubidu
Ts: Nghwari Ya Xidhaka
N: ≠nū|nū ≠nanas
H: Ongwari Yovihua Vyo Mokuti
G: Swainsonfrankolin

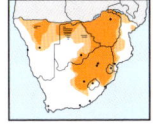

RED-NECKED SPURFOWL
(eastern races)

Dense bush. Dark brown streaked upperparts, black underparts with white streaks, and red facial and throat skin, bill and legs. 32–44 cm

eastern morph

A: Rooikeelfisant
Z: Isikhwehlesimqalabomvu
Ss: Kgwale Ya Mmetsofubedu
X: Inkwali
Sh: Nhindiro
G: Rotkehlfrankolin

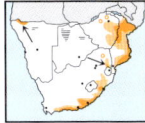

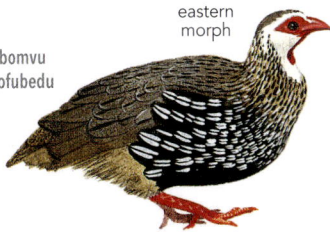

CAPE SPURFOWL

Wooded kloofs, fynbos and gardens. Dark brown upperparts with pale-edged feathers, black underparts with white streaks, and red bill and legs. 40–45 cm

A: Kaapse Fisant
Z: Isikhwehle SaseKapa
Ss: Kgwale Ya Kapa
Tw: Lesogo La Kapa
N: !khawaga ≠nanas
G: Kapsperling

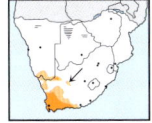

AFRICAN RAIL

Reed beds. Dark brown upperparts, grey head and underparts, black-and-white barred belly and flanks, and red bill and legs. 36 cm

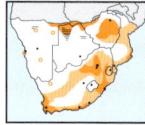

A: Grootriethaan
Z: Isizinzi
Ss: Mopakapaka
Ts: Nwatsekutseku
N: kai ≠ā-anib
G: Kapralle

BROWN-HEADED PARROT

Broad-leaved woodland. Brown head and neck, and green body and wings. 40 cm

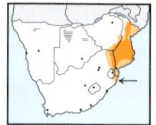

A: Bruinkoppapegaai
Z: Isikhwenenesikhandansundu
Tw: Heka Ya Tlhogorokwa
Ts: Yhokwe
G: Braunkopfpapagei

AFRICAN OLIVE PIGEON

Forests and plantations. Dark purple-brown with grey head, purple-grey neck, white spots on wings and belly, and bright yellow eye-rings, bill and legs. 36–40 cm

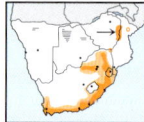

A: Geelbekbosduif
Z: Ivukuthu-lehlathi
X: Izuba
Ss: Leebamphapane
Tw: Leebaphepane
Ts: Ngalakana
G: Oliventaube

SOUTHERN WHITE-FACED OWL

Woodland. Grey with dark streaks, black-bordered white facial disc, and orange eyes. 25–28 cm

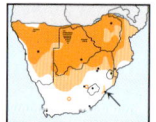

A: Witwanguil
Z: Umandubulu
Tw: Kukuruma
Nd: Umandubulo
N: !uri-ai |honnes
G: Weißgesicht-Ohreule

WESTERN BARN OWL

Open savanna and farmland. Grey-and-tawny spotted upperparts, pale spotted underparts, and whitish heart-shaped facial disc. 30–33 cm

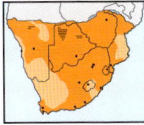

A: Nonnetjie-uil **Z:** UmZwelele
Ss: Sephooko Sa Hae
Tw: Sekea **Ts:** Madzukuya
Ve: Tshikwitha-mpembe
Sw: Umsomi
Nd: Umzwelele
N: |hû≠guib / sereb
H: Onjimbi
G: Schleiereule

AFRICAN GRASS OWL

Moist grasslands. Dark brown upperparts with small white spots, and creamy underparts with small brown spots; lacks 'ear' tufts. 34–37 cm

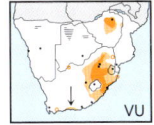

A: Grasuil
Z: Isikhova sotshani
Ss: Sephooko Sa Naga
Tw: Lekutikurru
Ts: Musoho
G: Graseule

AFRICAN WOOD OWL

Dense forests and woodlands. Dark brown upperparts and whitish underparts with fine brown barring; lacks 'ear' tufts. 30–36 cm

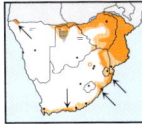

A: Bosuil
Z: Umabhengwane
X: Ibengwana
N: !huni-am |honnes
Ss: Morubisi Wa Molomosehla
G: Woodfordkauz

MARSH OWL

Vleis and marshes. Dark brown upperparts, pale buff underparts, and small 'ear' tufts; in flight, shows chestnut in primaries. 36 cm

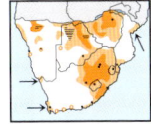

A: Vlei-uil
Z: Isikhova Sexhaphozi
Ss: Morubisi Ya Mohlaka
Sh: Zizi Bani
G: Kapohreule

SPOTTED EAGLE-OWL

Lightly wooded areas. Dark brown upperparts, finely barred and blotched underparts, prominent 'ear' tufts, dark-bordered facial disc, and yellow eyes.
43–50 cm

A: Gevlekte Ooruil
Z: Isikhovamponjwama
Ss: Sehihi **Tw:** Leghonda
Ts: Xiyinha
Sh: Jichidza
N: !khai ≠uwib
G: Fleckenuhu

AFRICAN GREY HORNBILL

Mixed bushveld. Dark brown upperparts with mottled wings, grey head, and white eyebrows and belly; male has black bill with casque; female has smaller casque. 43–48 cm

A: Grysneushoringvoël
Z: UmKholwanomlotha
Ss: Korwe Ye Putswa
Tw: Korwemodimo
Ts: Manteveni
N: |hai kököseb
H: Etoko Evahe
G: Grautoko

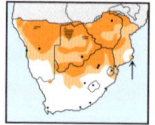

CAPE EAGLE-OWL

Rocky valleys. Dark brown upperparts, buffy blotched underparts, prominent 'ear' tufts, dark-bordered facial disc, and orange eyes.
48–55 cm

A: Kaapse Ooruil
Z: Isikhovampondo
Ss: Mohwe
Tw: Morubise
N: !khawaga ≠uwib
G: Kapuhu

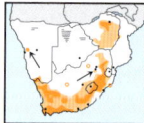

CROWNED HORNBILL

Riverine and valley forest. Dark brown upperparts, white underparts, and large red bill with yellow base.
50–57 cm

A: Gekroonde Neushoringvoël
Z: UmKhololwane
X: Umkholwane
Ss: Korwe Ya Moqhaka
Tw: Kgoropo Kg Serokwa
Ts: Nkorhonyarhi
Sh: Woto
H: Etoko Rotjinkorone
G: Kronentoko

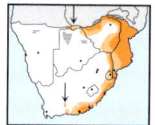

MONTEIRO'S HORNBILL

Broad-leaved woodland and rocky areas. Dark brown upperparts, head and breast, white underparts, and red bill with white base.
54–58 cm

A: Monteironeushoringvoël
Tw: Korwe Ya Lefukasweu
N: !uri-||gawo kōkōseb
G: Monteirotoko

AFRICAN BLACK DUCK

Rivers. Dark brown with white-spotted upperparts, grey bill and orange legs.
51–54 cm

A: Swarteend
Z: Idadelimnyama
Ss: Letata La Noka
Tw: Sehudi Se Sentsho
N: ≠nū ≠naras
H: Ombaka Ondurozu
G: Schwarzente

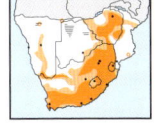

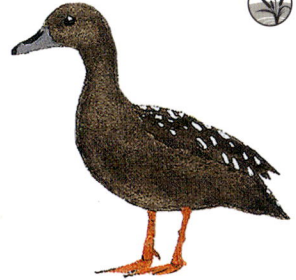

MACCOA DUCK ♀

Inland waters. Dark brown body and cheek stripe, white neck and grey bill.
46 cm

A: Bloubekeend **Z:** Idadelikhandamnyama
Ss: Letata La Molomo-Talalehodimo
Tw: Pidipidi Ya Molomo-talalegodimo
H: Ombaka Yoviva Ovisupi Novizorondu **G:** Maccoa-Ente

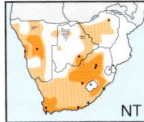

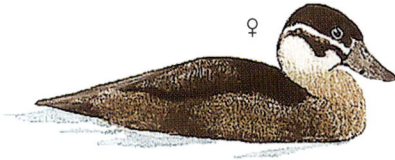

YELLOW-BILLED DUCK

Dams and rivers. Dark brown upperparts with white-edged feathers, paler underparts, and yellow bill with black saddle. 53–58 cm

A: Geelbekeend
Z: Idadelimlomophuzi
Ss: Letata La Molomosehla
Tw: Sehudi Sa Molomosetlha
N: !huni-am ≠naras
H: Ombaka Yotjinyatjingara
G: Gelbschnabelente

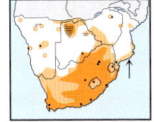

GREAT CRESTED GREBE

Pans and open waters. Dark brown upperparts and white underparts; br. ad. has 'horned' crest and golden flanks; non-br. ad. has white head and neck. 50 cm

A: Kuifkopdobbertjie
Z: Ivukelikhulu
Ss: Thoboloko E Kgolo
Tw: Senwedi E Segolo
Ts: Ripetani
G: Haubentaucher

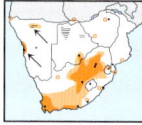

REED CORMORANT (imm.)

Inland waters, estuaries and coastal lagoons. Dark brown upperparts, pale brown underparts and dull yellow bill. 60 cm

A: Rietduiker
Z: Iphishamanzi
Ss: Ntodi Ya Lehlaka
N: ≠ā ≠nũ-anis
G: Riedscharbe

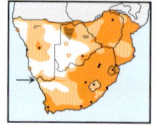

imm.

SOUTHERN POCHARD

Deep dams and pans. Male is dark brown with bronzy flanks; female has paler underparts and white facial markings. 51 cm

A: Bruineend **Z:** Isankawu
Ss: Letata La Leihlofubedu
Tw: Pidipidi Ya Leitlhohubidu
Ts: Xinyankakeni
G: Rotaugenente

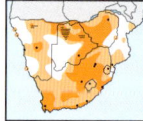

AFRICAN FINFOOT

Quiet rivers. Brown-and-white barred plumage, and red bill and legs; male has grey back and neck; female has white throat. 63 cm

A: Watertrapper
Z: Igwedlamanzi
Ss: Sehatametsi
Tw: Segatametsi
N: ||gamdāb
G: Afrikanische Binsenralle

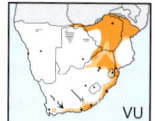

VU

HAMERKOP

Estuaries, dams and freshwater edges. Dark brown, with hammer-shaped head, and black bill and legs. 56 cm

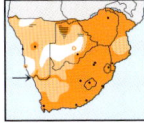

A: Hamerkop
Z: Uthekwane
X: Uthekwane
Ss: Mmamasianoke
Tw: Mmamasiloanoka
Ts: Nghondzwe
Nd: Uthekwane **Sh:** Vakondo
N: hamerdanas **H:** Otjiuru Mbike
G: Hammerkopf

AFRICAN GOSHAWK

Mixed woodlands and forested valleys. Dark brown upperparts, rufous-banded underparts, and yellow eyes and legs; male greyer above; immature browner. 40 cm

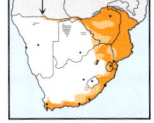

A: Afrikaanse Sperwer
Z: Ushomheshe, Imvumvuyane
X: Ukholo
Ss: Fiolo Y Afrika
Tw: Segodi Sa Aforika
N: Afrika ani!khāb
G: Afrikahabicht

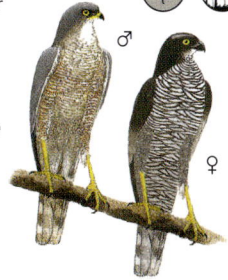

AFRICAN CUCKOO-HAWK

Mixed woodland. Dark upperparts, grey head and barred tail, and rufous barring on breast, belly and underwing coverts. 40 cm

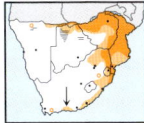

A: Koekoekvalk
Z: Usomthende
Ss: Fiolo-lehopoho
Tw: Segodi-Tlhotlhamedupe
N: hō-hōse hīsabes
G: Kuckucksweih

BAT HAWK

Riverine forests and veld. Dark brown, with pale eyes and white legs. 45 cm

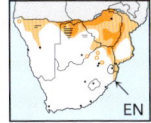

A: Vlermuisvalk
Z: Umahlwithilulwane
Ss: Fiolo Ya Mmankgane
G: Halsband-Feinsänger

AFRICAN MARSH HARRIER

Marshlands. Dark brown with paler underparts, and well-barred underwings. 44–49 cm

A: Afrikaanse Vleivalk
Z: Umamhlangenonsundu
Ss: Mmankgodimohlaka Wa Afrika
Tw: Mmankgodimolapo Wa Aforika
H: Orukoze Romarindi WaAfrika
G: Afrikanische Rohrweihe

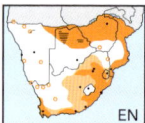

AUGUR BUZZARD ♂

Wooded rocky hills. Dark brown upperparts, white underparts, rufous tail, and dark-edged white underwings. 44–53 cm

A: Witborsjakkalsvoël
Sp: Segodi
Tw: Ntswana Ya Sehubasweu
Sh: Nyamudzura
N: !uri-ǀgā anitsēbeb
G: Augurbussard

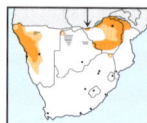

JACKAL BUZZARD

Hilly regions. Dark greyish-brown, with rufous breast and tail, and distinctive black-and-white underwings. 44–53 cm

A: Rooiborsjakkalsvoël
Z: Inhlandlokazi
Ss: Kgajwane Ya Sefubafubedu
Tw: Ntswana Ya Sehubahubidu
G: Felsenbussard

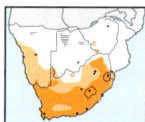

COMMON BUZZARD

Open country. Plumage variable; dark brown to red-brown, with darker upperparts, and streaked and banded underparts. 45 cm

A: Bruinjakkalsvoël
Z: Isanxa **X:** Isigoloda
Ss: Kgajwane E Tshootho
Tw: Ntswana E Rokwa
N: ≠gama anitsēbeb
G: Mäusebussard

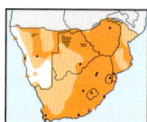

dark morph

red-brown morph

FOREST BUZZARD

Alien plantations. Dark brown upperparts, and white underparts with brown blotches, with breast usually white. 45 cm

A: Bosjakkalsvoël
Z: Uklebe Lwehlathi
Ss: Kgajwane Ya Moru
Tw: Ntswana Ya Sekgwa
G: Bergbussard

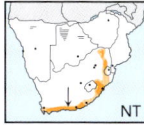

YELLOW-BILLED KITE

Open bushveld and mixed woodlands. Dark brown, with yellow bill and and legs, and deeply forked tail.
55 cm

A: Geelbekwou **Z:** Unhloyile
X: Untloyiya
Ss: Mmankgodi Wa Molomosehla
Ts: Mangatlwana
N: !huni-am hīsabes
H: Ombirinyama
G: Schmarotzermilan

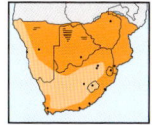

EUROPEAN HONEY BUZZARD

Mixed woodland and suburbia. Dark brown upperparts, variable underparts, from white with brown spots to dark brown, and well-barred underwings.
54–60 cm

A: Wespedief
Z: Umanyovini
Ss: Lejanotshi
Tw: Lejanotshe
N: !hawu-≠ūxa hīsabes
G: Wespenbussard

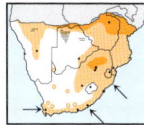

OSPREY

Lakes and lagoons. Dark brown upperparts and face mask, white underparts and pale grey legs.
55–63 cm

A: Visvalk
Z: Inkwazana
Sp: Sepekwahlapi
Tw: Phakwetlhapi
N: ||auhīsabes
G: Fischadler

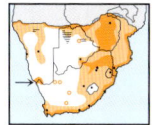

BOOTED EAGLE

Open wooland and semi-arid bush. Dark brown upperparts, dark brown, buff or white underparts, and pale yellow cere and feet. 48–52 cm

A: Dwergarend
Z: Ukhozolumadladla
Ss: Ntsu E Nnyenyane
Tw: Ntsu E Nnye
N: ≠khari !khās
G: Zwergadler

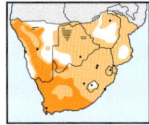

BATELEUR (juv.)

Game reserves and open woodlands. Dull brown, with slate-grey facial skin and legs, and a short tail. 55–70 cm

A: Berghaan
Z: Ingqungqulu
X: Ingqanga
Ss: Petleke
Sp: Kgwadira
Nd: Ingqungqulu
Sh: Chapungu
N: !nuwu-≠are !khās
G: Gaukler

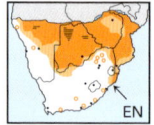

juv.

WAHLBERG'S EAGLE

Woodland and areas with game or cattle. Dark brown, with yellow cere and feet, narrow parallel wings and square tail.
55–60 cm

A: Bruinarend
Z: Ukhozolusisila
Ss: Ntsu Ya Motlwenyakgutshwane
Tw: Ntsu Ya Setlopokhutshwane
Sh: Chingaira
N: !nuwu-!amxadana !khās
G: Wahlbergs Adler

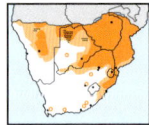

AFRICAN HAWK-EAGLE

Open and riverine woodland. Dark brown upperparts, white underparts, dark-streaked breast, white windows in under-wings, and black terminal tail band. 60–65 cm

A: Grootjagarend
Z: Ukhozolumidwayidwa
Ss: Ntsutjheke E Kgolo
Sp: Ntšhumebalabala Ye Kgolo
Tw: Ntsukgweba E Kgolo
N: kai-anxa !khās
G: Habichtsadler

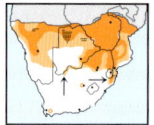

BLACK-CHESTED SNAKE EAGLE

Mixed wooded and grass bushveld. Dark brown upperparts, pale underparts and yellow eyes; pale underwings visible in flight. 63–68 cm

A: Swartborsslangarend
Z: Indlanyokemnyama
Ss: Lejanoha La Sefubantsho
Ts: Xithaklongwa
N: ≠nū-ǀgā ǀao!khas
G: Schwarzbrust-Schlangenadler

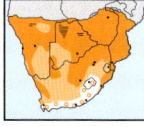

TAWNY EAGLE (dark morph)

Woodland. Various colour forms: light brown, tawny and ginger-brown; tawny has black dappling on upperwing covert only; all have black flight feathers and tail, and yellow cere and legs. 65–72 cm

A: Roofarend
Z: Ukhozolunsundu
Sp: Ntšhukobokobo
Tw: Ntsu E Tshetlha
N: ≠gama !khās
H: Orukoze Ohonimdumbu
G: Raubadler

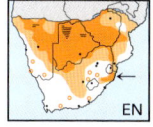

LESSER SPOTTED EAGLE

Woodland and areas with game or cattle. Dark brown, with yellow cere and feet; immature has white spots on wings. 65 cm

A: Gevlekte Arend
Z: Ukhozolumabala
Ss: Ntsudirothi E Nnyenyane
Tw: Ntsudimarabana E Nnye
N: !khai-ǁgawo !khās
G: Schreiadler

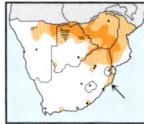

AFRICAN FISH EAGLE

Dams, lagoons and rivers. White head, mantle and breast, rufous body, dark brown wings, and yellow cere and legs. 63–73 cm

A: Visarend
Z: Inkwazi
X: Inkwaza
Ss: Ntsuhlapi
Tw: Audi
Ts: Nghunghwa
Nd: Iwunkwe
N: huri-am!ari!khās
H: Orukoze Yomahundju
G: Schreiseeadler

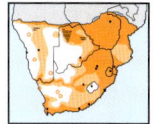

BROWN SNAKE EAGLE

Woodland. Dark brown, with yellow eyes and whitish legs; distinctive upright stance.
71-76 cm

A: Bruinslangarend
Z: Indlanyokensundu
Ss: Lejanoha Le Lesootho
N: ≠gama ǀao!khās
H: Orukoze Yonoka
G: Brauner Schlangenadler

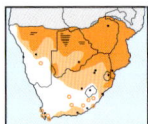

MARTIAL EAGLE

Woodland. Dark brown upperparts and breast, white belly and legs with brown spots, grey cere and yellow feet. 78-83 cm

A: Breëkoparend
Z: Isihuhwa
Ss: Ntsu E Kgolo
Sp: Mmakgwana
Tw: Ntsu E Thamaga
Ts: Manole
H: Orukoze Havita
G: Kampfadler

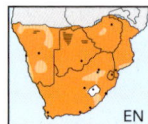

STEPPE EAGLE

Woodland. Dark brown, with orange yellow gape and feet. 75 cm

A: Steppe-arend
Z: Ukhozimuhlwa
Ss: Ntsu Ya Naga
Tw: Ntsu Ya Naga
H: Orukoze Omaheke
G: Steppenadler

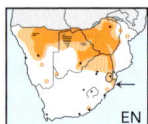

CROWNED EAGLE

Well-wooded areas. Dark upperparts, heavily mottled underparts, with barred tail and rufous underwings visible in flight.
80-90 cm

A: Kroonarend
Z: Isihuhwa
Ss: Makgwana
N: gao-aoǀgapa !khās
G: Kronenadler

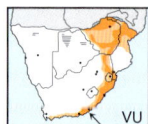

HOODED VULTURE

Game reserves and open woodlands. Dark, with pink face and neck, and white downy hood, pectoral feathers and thighs.
70 cm

A: Monnikaasvoël
Z: Inqelincane
Ss: Kgonyaito
Tw: Lenong Le Lerokwa
N: ≠gama kai-anis
G: Kappengeier

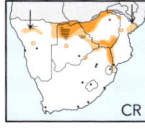

WHITE-BACKED VULTURE (imm.)

Game reserves and open woodlands. Dark brown, with white-streaked underparts, blackish head and neck with white downy covering.
90–98 cm

A: Witrugaasvoël
Z: Inqe Lehlanze
Ss: Leaka
Sp: Lenong La Mokološweu
Tw: Lenong Le Letuba
N: !uri-ǁã kai-anis
G: Weißrückengeier

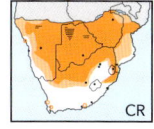

imm.

ad.

WHITE-HEADED VULTURE

Game reserves and open woodlands. Dark brown upperparts and upper breast, white crown, nape and belly, pink face and feet; female has white inner secondaries.
85 cm

A: Witkopaasvoël
Z: Ukhandelimhlope
Ss: Lenong La Hlohosweu
Sp: Lenong La Sehubašweu
Tw: Lenong La Tlhogosweu
Ts: Khoti Mpenyani
H: Onguviyetjiuru Otjivapa
G: Wollkopfgeier

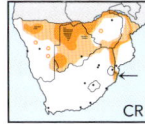

♀

CAPE VULTURE (imm.)

Arid open bushveld and cliffs. Brown, with pale-streaked underparts, reddish head, neck and breast patches, with white downy covering.
105–115 cm

A: Kransaasvoël
Z: Idlanga Lentaba
X: Ihlanga **Ss:** Lening La Selomo
Sp: Rrantšwe **Tw:** Diswaane
Ts: Khoti Mavalanga
N: ǁhoa kai-anis
H: Onguvi YaKapa
G: Kapgeier

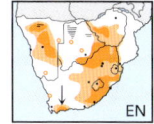

imm.

ad.

LAPPET-FACED VULTURE

Game reserves and open woodlands. Dark brown upperparts, white underparts, dark brown breast streaks, and red head and neck.
115 cm

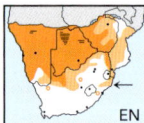

A: Swartaasvoël **Z:** Indlangamandla
Ss: Letlakapipi
Sp: Lenong Er Leso
Tw: Bibing
Ts: Khoti Mfumo
Sh: Gohora **N:** ≠nũ kai-anis
H: Onguvi Ondorozu
G: Ohrengeier

HADADA IBIS

Open moist grass, farmlands and gardens. Dull grey-brown with iridescent greenish-black wings.
76 cm

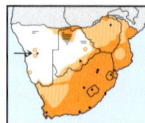

A: Hadeda
Z: Inkankane
X: Ing'ang'ane
Ss: Lengaangane
Sp: Lehaahaa
Tw: Tshababarwa
Ts: Man'An'Ani
N: |hai ≠khani||khâbams
G: Hagedasch-Ibis

GLOSSY IBIS

Pans and moist grassland. Bronze brown with iridescent green on wings, and long, curved bill. 71 cm

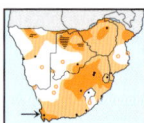

A: Glansibis
Z: Umacibudaka
Ss: Mokgotlwana
N: ≠khaira ≠khani||khâbams
G: Brauner Sichler

br.

non-br.

ABDIM'S STORK

Grassveld and bushveld. Dark brown upperparts and breast, white belly and rump, and whitish legs; bill horn-coloured in summer.
76 cm

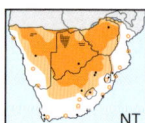

A: Kleinswartooievaar
Z: Umahlombamhlophe
Ss: Lekololwane
Sh: Ngauzani
N: ≠hoa-ai oefari
G: Abdimsstorch

AFRICAN WOOLLY-NECKED STORK

Wooded wetlands. Dark brown with white head and neck, and dark red bill and legs. 86 cm

A: Wolnekooievaar
Z: Isithandamanzi
Ss: Mokotatsie Wa Molomosweu
Sp: Leakabosane
N: !uri-!ao oefari
G: Wollhalsstorch

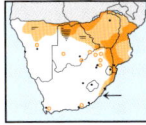

SPUR-WINGED GOOSE (imm.)

Large inland waters and croplands. Dark brown, with red bill. 102 cm

A: Wildemakou **Z:** Ihhoye **X:** Ihoye **Ss:** Letshikgwi
Tw: Letsukwe **N:** ||khü||gawo !kharas
G: Sporngans

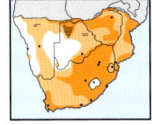

imm.

WHITE-BREASTED CORMORANT

Inland and coastal waters. Dark brown, with white face and breast, and black-edged wing feathers. 90 cm

A: Witborsduiker
Z: Iwondelimhlope
X: Umxwiqa
Ss: Ntodi Ya Sefubasweu
Tw: Ntodi Ya Sehubasweu
Ts: Ngulukwani
N: !uri||khaib
G: Weißbrustkormoran

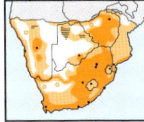

COMMON OSTRICH ♀

Grasslands and woodland. Brown-grey plumage with whitish head, neck, legs and some wing feathers. 2 m

A: Volstruis
Z: Intshe
X: Inciniba
Ss: Mpshe
Tw: Ntshe
Ts: Yinca
Nd: Intshe
Sh: Mhou
N: |amib
H: Ombo
G: Strauß

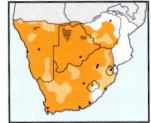

First impression
LIGHT BROWN PLUMAGE

Many birds with this coloration are waders, such as Kittlitz's Plover, or those that frequent dry regions, such as Yellow-throated Sandgrouse. For many species, light brown is also the colour of the drab plumage of females or non-breeding males.

How does light brown plumage serve a bird?

Light brown plumage usually occurs on a bird's upperparts, allowing the bird to appear less conspicuous on sandy terrain or mudflats when viewed from above.

NESTING HABITS

Birds' nests primarily serve as a place in which to lay eggs and raise young. Nests are fairly varied in terms of shape, materials used and location.

Weaver nests: Weaver nests are as variable as the materials used to build them. The Spectacled Weaver constructs a long tunnel entrance to its nest, which may serve to deter predators; the Thick-billed Weaver's nest is made of the finest materials; and the Red-headed Weaver builds a nest of pliable, hairy twigs. The hairy covering of the twigs causes them to lock firmly together, but, since the twigs are brown, the nest appears to be old from the outset, deterring predators. Sociable Weavers take nest building to the extreme. Their massive nest structures, with 50 or more separate chambers, are added to constantly, and may eventually break under their own weight.

Cup-shaped nests: Perhaps the most widely used nest type is the conventional cup-shaped nest of thrushes, robins, wagtails, flycatchers, shrikes, and even of larger birds like storks and eagles. For some birds, such as plovers and thick-knees, the nest is just a shallow scrape on open ground.

Strange nests: Many swallows build nests of mud, while bee-eaters burrow into the side of river banks or road cuttings. Hornbill males use mud to lock the female into a nest hole, in order to protect the eggs and chicks from predators. Falcons and kestrels, on the other hand, make no nest at all, and lay their eggs straight onto a rock ledge.

RED-BILLED FIREFINCH

Riverine bush. Male has grey-brown wings and reddish head and underparts; female is brown with paler underparts, and red lores and rump. 10 cm

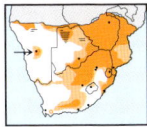

A: Rooibekvuurvinkie **Z:** Inkashana
Ss: Mphubetswana-Lomofubedu **G:** Senegal-Amarant

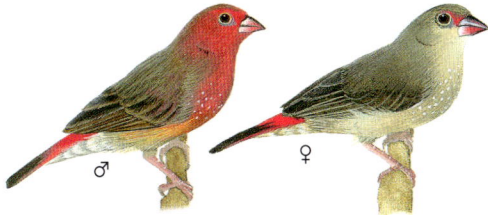

RED-HEADED FINCH

Thornveld. Grey-brown upperparts, speckled underparts, and heavy bill; male has red head; female's plain brown. 13 cm

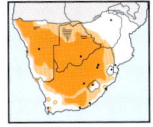

A: Rooikopvink **Z:** Ugazini **G:** Rotkopfamadine

COMMON WAXBILL

Reed beds and moist grasslands. Red mask, bill and central belly, and brown-barred underparts. 13 cm

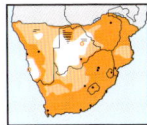

A: Rooibeksysie
Z: Intiyanelijwayelekile
X: Intshiyane
Ss: Borane-Mpatsoku
G: Wellenastrild

CUT-THROAT FINCH

Dry woodland. Speckled brown with white bill; male has broad red throat band. 12 cm

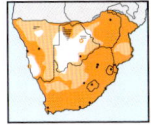

A: Bandkeelvink
Z: Unongilonegazi
G: Bandfink

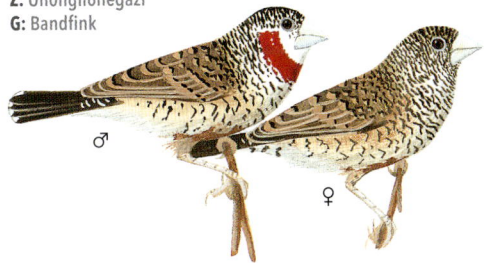

RED-BILLED QUELEA

Croplands. Streaky brown back; male has red or pinkish bill; br. male has blackish face. 13 cm

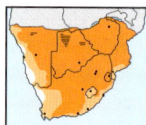

A: Rooibekkwelea
Z: Isicibilili
G: Blutschnabelweber

non-br. ♀

br. ♂

br. ♂

SOCIABLE WEAVER

Dry acacia woodland. Scaled pale grey-brown above with light brown cap, black lores and chin, and white underparts. 14 cm

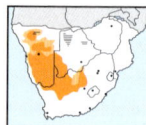

A: Versamelvoël
Z: Unosidlekekazi
G: Siedelweber

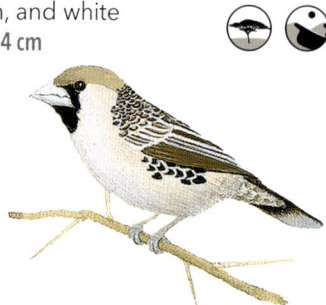

SCALY-FEATHERED WEAVER

Thornveld. Light brown with black-and-white scaling on wing feathers. 11 cm

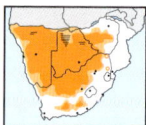

A: Baardmannetjie **Z:** Usontshetshana
G: Schnurrbärtchen

LARK-LIKE BUNTING

Arid regions. Light brown upperparts, buffy feather edges, pale cinnamon underparts, and pale eyebrows. 14 cm

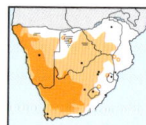

A: Vaalstreepkoppie
Z: Usokhandamidwa Wasehlane
Ss: Mmaborokwanyana
G: Lerchenammer

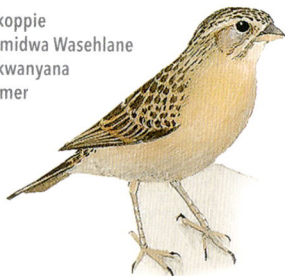

CAPE BUNTING

Various arid habitats. Black-and-white streaked head, rufous upperparts and grey-brown-washed underparts.
16 cm

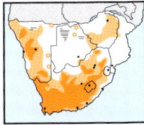

A: Rooivlerkstreepkoppie
Z: Usokhandamidwonsundu
Ss: Mmaborokwane-Nyaopedi
G: Kapammer

STREAKY-HEADED SEEDEATER

Woodland. Grey-brown upperparts, streaky crown, white eyebrows, pale underparts, and stout, blackish bill. 16 cm

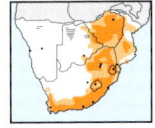

A: Streepkopkanarie
Z: UmBhalanonsundu
Ss: Tswere-Hlohokgwaba
G: Brauengirlitz

BLACK-EARED SEEDEATER

Woodland. Black mask, grey-brown upperparts, with streaking on head, and paler streaking on breast.
13–14 cm

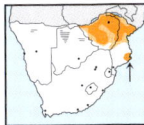

A: Swartoorkanarie
G: Schwarzwangengirlitz

WHITE-THROATED CANARY

Thicket and scrub. Greyish-brown, with yellow rump, and heavy bill. 14–15 cm

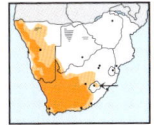

A: Witkeelkanarie
Z: Umbhalanongilemhlophe
Ss: Tswere-Kodutshwana
G: Weißkehlgirlitz

PROTEA CANARY

Protea woodland. Mainly drab grey-brown with pale wingbars and heavy, grey bill. 16 cm

A: Witvlerkkanarie
Z: Umbhalane Wesiqalaba
G: Proteagirlitz

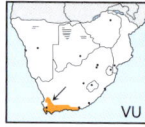

CAPE SPARROW

Farmlands and suburbia. Chestnut mantle, black-and-white wings; male has black-and-white head and breast; female has grey-and-white head. 15 cm

A: Gewone Mossie **Z:** Undlunkulu **X:** Unondlwane
Ss: Serobele-Hlohophatshwa **Sp:** Lemphorokgohlo La Kapa
H: Oyatuhere RwaKapa **G:** Kapsperling

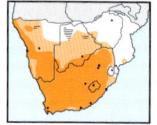

BLACK-THROATED CANARY

Grassy woodland. Greyish upperparts, pale underparts, yellow rump, and black throat. 11–12 cm

A: Bergkanarie
Z: Unogilomnyama
Ss: Tswere-Koduntsho
G: Angolagirlitz

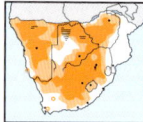

HOUSE SPARROW ♀

Farmlands and suburbia. Pale brown with mottled upperparts, and buffish eyebrows. 14 cm

A: Huismossie
Z: Ujolwane Wekhaya
G: Haussperling

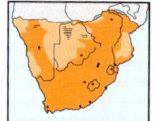

SOUTHERN GREY-HEADED SPARROW

Woodland and gardens. Plain grey head, chestnut upperparts, whitish underparts and stout black or horn-coloured bill. 15–16 cm

A: Gryskopmossie
Z: Ujolwanokhandaphunga
G: Graukopfsperling

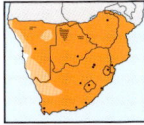

MARICO SUNBIRD ♀

Thornveld. Light brown upperparts, pale orange-yellow underparts, dusky throat; bill longer than head. 13–14 cm

A: Maricosuikerbekkie
Z: Insonsi
G: Bindennektarvogel

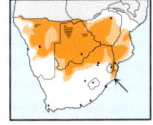

GREAT SPARROW

Dry thornveld. Grey crown, chestnut nape, back and wings, small white wingbar; male has conspicuous black bib. 15–16 cm

A: Grootmossie
Z: Ujolwanomkhulu
Ss: Serobele-Se-Seholo
G: Rotbrauner Sperling

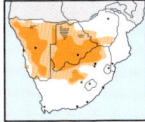

GREATER DOUBLE-COLLARED SUNBIRD ♀

Moist forest edges, kloofs and gardens with nectar-bearing flowers. Dull grey-brown, with paler underparts; bill longer than head. 14 cm

A: Groot-rooibandsuikerbekkie
Z: Incuncu
Ss: Pinyane-Petakgubedu
G: Großer Halsband-Nektarvogel

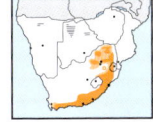

SOUTHERN DOUBLE-COLLARED SUNBIRD ♀

Woodlands, fynbos and gardens. Dull grey-brown, with paler underparts; bill is same length as head. 12 cm

A: Klein-rooibandsuikerbekkie
Z: Incuncwana
Ss: Pinyane-Petakgubetswana
G: Halsband-Nektarvogel

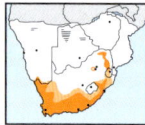

AMETHYST SUNBIRD ♀

Woodland and gardens. Light brown upperparts, cream-white underparts, creamish moustachial streak, and dark, mottled throat. 15 cm

A: Swartsuikerbekkie
Z: Insusha
G: Amethyst-Glanzköpfchen

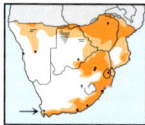

WHITE-BROWED SCRUB ROBIN

Bushveld thickets. Light brown upperparts, rufous rump and uppertail, white eyebrows, well-streaked breast, and white wing-markings. 15 cm

A: Gestreepte Wipstert **Z:** Ugaganomidwa
G: Weißbrauen-Heckensänger

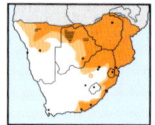

KALAHARI SCRUB ROBIN

Kalahari thornveld. Light brown upperparts, greyish cap and white eyebrows, rufous rump and uppertail, and pale underparts. 16–17 cm

A: Kalahariwipstert **Z:** Ugagana LwaseNtshonalanga
G: Kalahariheckensänger

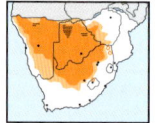

BEARDED SCRUB ROBIN

Broad-leaved and riverine woodland thickets. Light brown upperparts, black-and-white facial markings, and orange breast. 16–18 cm

A: Baardwipstert **Z:** Ugaganontshebe
G: Brauner Bartheckensänger

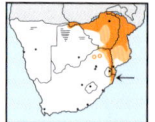

COLLARED PALM THRUSH

Palm savanna. Rufous upperparts and vent, grey neck, cream throat patch and black collar.
19 cm

A: Palmmôrelyster
Z: Umunswi Wasemalaleni
G: Morgenrötel

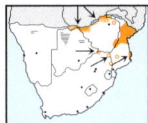

TRACTRAC CHAT

Arid plains and scrub. Southern race pale grey-brown above; Namibian race very pale brown above; both white below. 14–15 cm

A: Woestynspekvreter
Z: Umbexomhlophe
G: Namibschmätzer

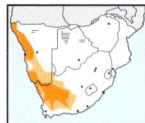

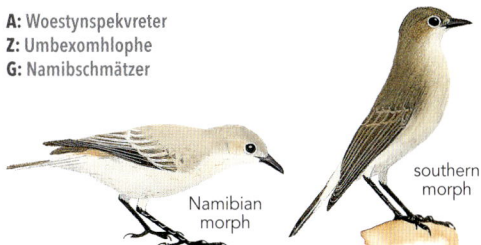

Namibian morph

southern morph

BUFF-STREAKED CHAT ♀

Rocky grassland. Buffy underparts; male has black throat, face and wings; female has warm brown upperparts; lively, demonstrative behaviour.
15–17 cm

A: Bergklipwagter
Z: Inkolotsheni
Ss: Sethwena-Majweng
Sp: Tantabe
G: Fahlschulterschmätzer

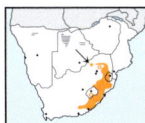

♀

♂

KAROO CHAT

Karoo scrub. Namibian race has light brown upperparts, breast and rump, white belly, vent and outer-tail feathers; southern race grey.
15–18 cm

A: Karoospekvreter
Z: Umbexe Wasehlane
G: Bleichschmätzer

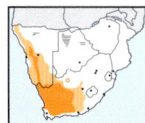

Namibian race

HERERO CHAT

Arid, rocky ground. Light brown upperparts, rufous rump and outer-tail feathers; white underparts with faint brown streaks, black facial mask and white eyebrows. 17 cm

A: Hererospekvreter
G: Namibschnäpper

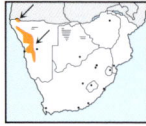

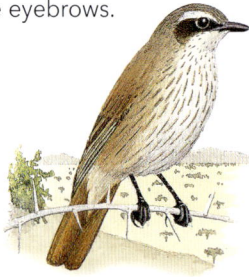

RED-CAPPED LARK

Dry pans and short grass. Light brown upperparts, rufous cap and pectoral tufts, and whitish underparts. 15 cm

A: Rooikoplewerik **Z:** UmNtoli **X:** Intibane
Ss: Tsirwane-E-Tlopo **G:** Rotscheitellerche

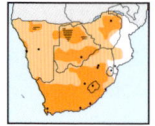

FLAPPET LARK

Stony grassland. Brown, streaked upperparts, and rufous head and wing edges, and streaked back. Distinctive spurts of territorial wing-clapping in flight when breeding. 16 cm

A: Laeveldklappertjie **Z:** Ungqangendlela **G:** Baumklapperlerche

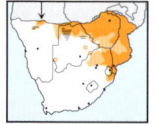

SABOTA LARK

Woodland. Well-streaked, dark grey and buff upperparts, distinctive white eyebrows, and pale outer-tail feathers. 15 cm

A: Sabotalewerik
Z: Unqothi
Ss: Nketsisane-Otonala
G: Sabotalerche

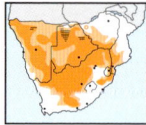

RUFOUS-NAPED LARK

Grassland with bush. Rufous wash on body; eastern race has rufous crest and wings; western race is paler and greyer. 18–19 cm

A: Rooineklewerik **Z:** Untilontilo **X:** Iqabathule
Ss: Tsirwane-Pheotsoku **Sp:** Pulaekhudile **Sh:** Tsotso
G: Rotnackenlerche

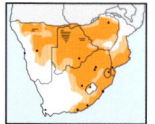

eastern race

western race

KAROO LONG-BILLED LARK

Scrubland. Brownish upperparts, whitish underparts, rufous wash on spotted breast, and conspicuous long bill. 20-22 cm

A: Karoolangbeklewerik
G: Karru-Langschnabellerche

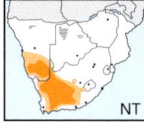

NT

LITTLE STINT (non-br.)

Shorelines and shallow water. Sandy brown with white-edged feathers, white underparts, and black bill and legs. 14 cm

A: Kleinstrandloper **Z:** Unothwayizana
Ss: Tsititsiti **N:** ≠khari huri-am!gûb
G: Zwergstrandläufer

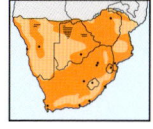

non-br.

SHAFT-TAILED WHYDAH

Thornveld. Red bill and legs, and buffy underparts; br. male has black upperparts and very long tail shafts. 12 cm (br. male 34 cm)

A: Pylstertrooibekkie
Z: Ibhakelimsilosihlaku
G: Königswitwe

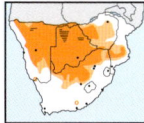

br. ♂

♀

AFRICAN PIPIT

Open grassland. Light brown body, bold facial features and boldly marked breast. 16 cm

A: Gewone Koester
Z: Ingcelekeshe
Ss: Tshase-Ya-Dithota
Sp: Serala
Ts: Mjonjo
G: Zimtspornpieper

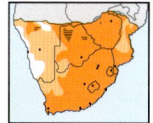

CHESTNUT-BANDED PLOVER ♂

River and dam sandflats. Light brown upperparts, white forehead, face and underparts, and narrow chestnut or buffy throat band. 15 cm

A: Rooibandstrandkiewiet **Z:** Unosongo Wechweba
G: Fahlregenpfeifer

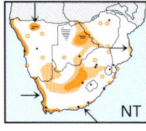

KITTLITZ'S PLOVER

Edges of estuaries, rivers and inland waters. Light brown upperparts, black-and-white bands on head and neck, buff breast and white belly. 16 cm

A: Geelborsstrandkiewiet **Z:** Umatatazela
Ss: Mororwane Wa Sehubasehla **N:** !huni-|ga xoexoes
G: Hirtenregenpfeifer

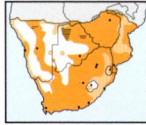

THREE-BANDED PLOVER

Freshwater shores. Brown upperparts, white underparts, and two black breast bands. 18 cm

A: Driebandstrandkiewiet **Z:** Igwigwi **X:** Inqatha
Ss: Mororwane Wa Metjhatoraro **Tw:** Thatswane Ya Meelediraro
N: daoxa xoexoes **G:** Dreiband-Regenpfeifer

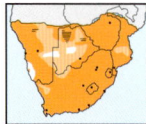

COMMON RINGED PLOVER

Shorelines of estuaries and inland waters. Brown upperparts, white underparts; br. ad. has black mask and bold black neckband. 18 cm

A: Ringnekstrandkiewiet
Z: Unosongo
Tw: Thatswane Ya Sehubantsho
N: râi-|haro xoexoes
G: Sandregenpfeifer

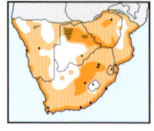

br.

WHITE-FRONTED PLOVER

Coastal and river shores and pans. Sandy brown upperparts, and white forehead and underparts; male has darker forecrown. 18 cm

A: Vaalstrandkiewiet
Z: Umathantatha
X: Unotelela
Ss: Mororwane Wo Mosehla
N: !huni xoexoes
G: Weißstirn-Regenpfeifer

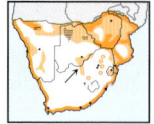

COMMON QUAIL

Grasslands and cultivated fields. Rufous upperparts with black-and-white streaks and pale eyebrows, buffy underparts and white-streaked flanks; male has dark throat. **18 cm**

A: Afrikaanse Kwartel
Z: Isagwacesjiwayelekile
Ss: Sekweqe
Tw: Sekhwiri se Serokwa
Ts: Mavolwane
N: ≠gama !nabaris
G: Wachtel

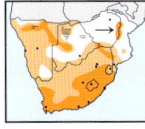

YELLOW-BILLED OXPECKER

Woodland and areas with game or cattle. Brown head and body, yellow-buff rump and underparts, yellow bill with red tip, and yellow eyes. **22 cm**

A: Geelbekrenostervoël
Z: Ihlalanyathi
Ss: Tsomi
Sp: Legame
Sh: Shakahuni
G: Gelbschnabel-Madenhacker

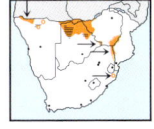

RED-BILLED OXPECKER

Woodland and areas with game or cattle. Brown head and body, dark rump, buff underparts, red bill and eyes, and yellow eye-ring. **20–22 cm**

A: Rooibekrenostervoël
Z: Ihlalanyathi **Ss:** Kalla-Tjepa
Sp: Tšhomi **Ts:** Ndzandza
G: Rotschnabel-Madenhacker

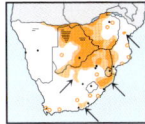

SOUTHERN WHITE-CROWNED SHRIKE

Woodland. Light brown mantle, belly and vent, dark wings, lores and ear coverts, and white crown and breast. **23–25 cm**

A: Kremetartlaksman
Z: Unomqhelomhlophe
Sp: Leagakametlwa
Ts: Ghengele
G: Weißscheitelwürger

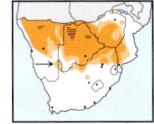

EMERALD-SPOTTED WOOD DOVE

Woodland. Fawn upperparts, rufous flight feathers, glossy green wing spots, and black bars on the back. 20 cm

A: Groenvlekduifie **Z:** Isikhombazane-sehlanze
X: Ivukazana **Ss:** Mokodunyane Wa Dirothitala
Tw: Mokodunyane Wa Marabanatalatlhaga
Ts: Wariba **Sh:** Mutondo
N: ǁhopob
H: Onguti Yotjivavize
G: Bronzeflecktaube

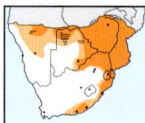

WHITE-BACKED MOUSEBIRD

Dry bush and suburbia. Grey upperparts and upstanding crest, white back, buff underparts, black-tipped white bill, and red legs. 30–34 cm

A: Witkruismuisvoël
Z: Indlazemhlanomhlophe
Ss: Mmasehlothwana Wa Nkotosweu
Sp: Letšhee
Tw: Marungwane
N: ǃuri-ǀnana ǀkhenni
G: Weißrücken-Mausvogel

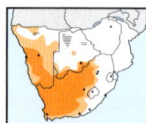

NAMAQUA DOVE

Farmlands and thornveld. Light brown upperparts, purple wing spots, and paler underparts; male has black mask. 27 cm

A: Namakwaduifie **Z:** Unkombose **X:** Isavukazana
Ss: Mokgorwane **Tw:** Mokgwarinyane **Ts:** Xivhambalana Xa Ncila **Sh:** Dzembe **N:** flôb **G:** Kaptäubchen

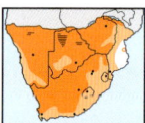

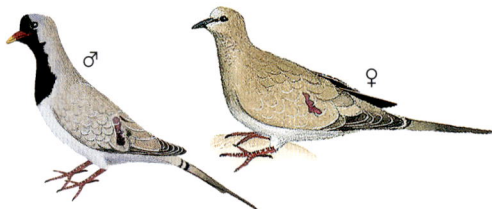

RED-FACED MOUSEBIRD

Thornveld and suburbia. Light brown upperparts, grey-white rump and underparts, blue eyes, black bill, and red mask and legs. 32–34 cm

A: Rooiwangmuisvoël **Z:** UmTshivovo **X:** Intshili **Ss:** Letsiababa
Ts: Ncivovo **Sh:** Swenya **N:** ǀawa-ai ǀkhenni
G: Rotzügel-Mausvogel

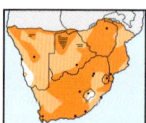

SPECKLED MOUSEBIRD

Bush and suburbia. Brown upperparts, light brown crest and underparts, black mask and upper mandible, white lower mandible, and black legs. 30–35 cm

A: Gevlekte Muisvoël
Z: Indlazi
X: Indlazi
Sp: Letswiokoko
Tw: Moririmothlofe
Ts: Nhlazi
G: Braunflügel-Mausvogel

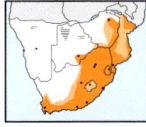

GURNEY'S SUGARBIRD

Mountain slopes with proteas and aloes. Brown upperparts, rufous cap and breast, and long tail. 25–29 cm

A: Rooiborssuikervoël
Z: Unosiqalaba
Ss: Mmanotswane
G: Gurneys Honigfresser

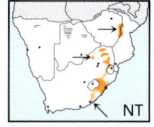

CAPE SUGARBIRD

Coastal fynbos scrub and mountains with flowering proteas. Brown upperparts, light brown breast, dark malar streak, and long tail. 24 cm female, 44 cm male

A: Kaapse Suikervoël **Z:** Unosiqalaba WaseKapa
G: Kap-Honigfresser

DOUBLE-BANDED SANDGROUSE

Broad-leaved woodland. Female speckled; male has brown back with white spots, plain fawn head and breast, and black-and-white breast band. 25 cm

A: Dubbelbandsandpatrys **Z:** Unogwadule Wehlanze
Sp: Sebopa Sa Melabedi **Ts:** Xighwaraghwara
N: !nuwu≠are !nabaris **G:** Nachtflughuhn

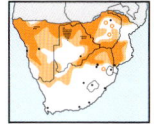

BURCHELL'S SANDGROUSE

Sandveld. Cinnamon with heavy white speckling; male has grey face; female has yellowish face.
25 cm

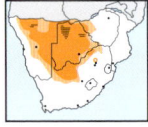

A: Gevlekte Sandpatrys Z: Unogwadulogqabhagqabha
Ss: Kokwi Ya Leramatalalehodimo Tw: Legorwagorwana
N: ≠hoa-ai !nabaris G: Fleckenflughuhn

NAMAQUA SANDGROUSE

Desert. Ochre head and long, pointed tail; male has plain head and breast, and black-and-white breast band; female is mottled. 28 cm

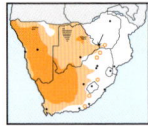

A: Kelkiewyn Z: Unogwadule Ss: Lekgwakgwa Tw: Lekotokobii
N: gāxū≠are !nabaris G: Namaflughuhn

YELLOW-THROATED SANDGROUSE

Thornveld. Cream-yellow face and throat; male has black collar; female is mottled. 30 cm

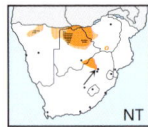

A: Geelkeelsandpatrys Z: Unogwadulontamephuzi
Ss: Kokwi Ya Mmetsosehla Tw: Photi-mpha-bogogo
N: !hunidom !nabaris G: Gelbkehl-Flughuhn

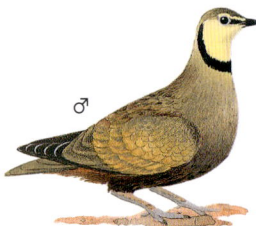

RED-WINGED FRANCOLIN

Grassy hills. Dark brown, blotched upperparts, rufous ear coverts and neck stripe, black-and-white mottled breast, and streaked, pale rufous underparts. 38–40 cm

A: Rooivlerkpatrys Z: Ithendelelibomvu
Ss: Kgwale Ya Lepheofubedu G: Rotflügelfrankolin

ORANGE RIVER FRANCOLIN

Dry grasslands. Dark grey-brown, mottled upperparts, rufous, black-and-white head, white throat, and dappled, rufous underparts. 33–35 cm

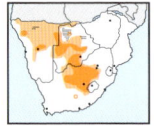

A: Kalaharipatrys
Z: Isikhwehle Sehlane
Ss: Kgwale Ya Kgalagadi
N: !aub !nowoṣ
G: Rebhuhnfrankolin

COQUI FRANCOLIN ♂

Bushveld and woodland. Tawny head, light brown body, and fine black barring on chest. 28 cm

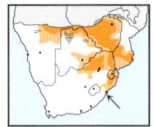

A: Swempie Z: Inswempe Ss: Lebudiane
Tw: Letsiekwane Sh: Horgwe N: !huni|awa-dana !nowos
G: Coquifrankolin

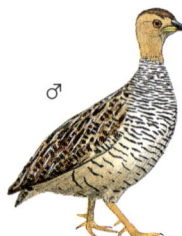

CRESTED FRANCOLIN

Mixed bushveld and forest fringes. Rufous-brown upperparts, black-and-white facial marks, well-spotted breast, and red legs. 32 cm

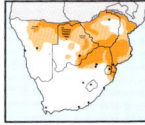

A: Bospatrys Z: Isikhwehlesiqhova Ss: Lesogo
Tw: Lekweekwane N: !amxadana !nowos
H: Ongwari Ozondomba G: Schopffrankolin

GREY-WINGED FRANCOLIN

Grassy hills. Tawny, mottled upperparts, rufous head markings, white throat with black spots, and grey underparts. 31–33 cm

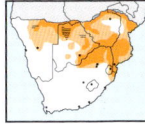

A: Bergpatrys Z: Ithendelelimlotha
Ss: Kgwale Ya Thaba G: Grauflügelfrankolin

SHELLEY'S FRANCOLIN

Grassy woodland. Mottled, dark grey-brown upperparts, white underparts, blotched red-brown breast, and black-barred belly. 33 cm

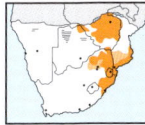

A: Laeveldpatrys Z: Isikhwehlesimqhalomhlophe Ss: Kgwale Ya Botjhabela Ts: Njenjele Sh: Marenge G: Shelleyfrankolin

TEMMINCK'S COURSER

Short grassland. Light brown upperparts and breast, rufous cap and lower breast, black eye-stripe, and white eyebrows, belly and legs. 20 cm

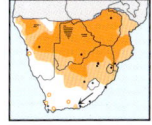

A: Trekdrawwertjie Z: Unobulongwana
Ss: Mokopjwane Wa Leboya N: |awa-gao-ao|gapa !naeb
G: Temminckrennvogel

DOUBLE-BANDED COURSER

Arid grasslands. Mottled light brown upperparts, white underparts and two narrow black breast bands. 22 cm

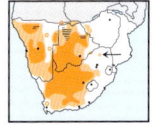

A: Dubbelbanddrawwertjie
Z: Unobulongwonesifociya
Ss: Mokopjwane Wa Metjhatobedi
N: |awa-||gawo !naeb
G: Doppelband-Rennvogel

BURCHELL'S COURSER

Short grassland. Chestnut, with grey nape, and white belly and legs. 23 cm

A: Bloukopdrawwertjie
Z: Unobulongwe
X: Ingegane
Ss: Mokopjwane Wa Bophirima
N: ≠hoa-gao-ao|gapa !naeb
G: Rostrennvogel

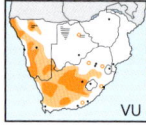

VU

THREE-BANDED COURSER

Dry woodland. Mottled light brown upperparts, white throat, chestnut V-shaped collar and lower breast band, and dark brown breast band. 28 cm

A: Driebanddrawwertjie
Z: Unobulongwonomgexe
Ss: Mokopjwane Wa Metjhatoraro
Tw: Segolagola
N: !uri-dom !naeb
G: Bindenrennvogel

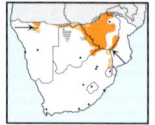

BRONZE-WINGED COURSER

Woodland. Light brown upperparts and breast, dark mask, white eyebrows, throat and underparts, and red eye-rings and legs. 25 cm

A: Bronsvlerkdrawwertjie
Z: Unobulongwonsundu
Ss: Mokopjwane Wa Lepheoporonse
Tw: Mmadithsipi
Ts: Tshembyana
N: ≠ai|uri-||gawo !naeb
G: Amethystrennvogel

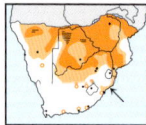

CASPIAN PLOVER ♂

Dry plains and pans. Light brown upperparts, white face and belly, and dusky (non-br.) or broad chestnut (br.) breast band. 21–23 cm

A: Asiatiese Strandkiewiet
Z: Unomvula
Ss: Mororwane Wa Sefubafubedu
N: |awa-|gã xoexoes
G: Wermutregenpfeifer

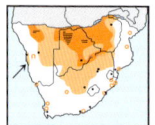

br.

non-br. ♂

MARSH SANDPIPER

Coastal and inland waters. Sandy brown upperparts with white-edged feathers, white underparts, slender black bill, and long yellow-green legs. 23 cm

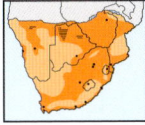

A: Moerasruiter **Z:** Unothwayiza
Ss: Mosalakatane Wa Molhaka
N: gãxū-|nū !khuwi!gûb
G: Teichwasserläufer

STRIPED CRAKE ♂

Flooded grasslands. Dark brown upperparts with white-edged feathers, and buffy-brown underparts. 24 cm

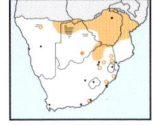

A: Gestreepte Riethaan **Tw:** Kgogoletlhaka Ya Meeledi
G: Graukehl-Sumpfhuhn

RUFF

Shallow inland and coastal waters. Light brown head and neck, dark brown back and wings with pale-edged feathers, and white underparts; adult has orange legs; immature has dark legs. 24–30 cm

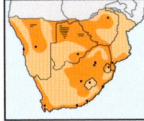

A: Kemphaan
Z: Unogqabakazi
Ss: Seyalelebopo Sa Motlwenya
Tw: Seyalelebopo Sa Setlopo
N: |gare|û huri-am!gûb
G: Kampfläufer

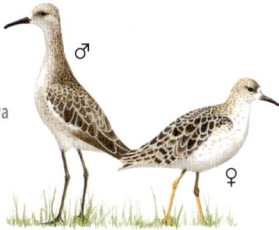

LITTLE BITTERN

Reed beds. Buffy brown; male has black crown, back and flight feathers and pale streaks on neck; female has dark brown upperparts and dark streaks on neck. 26 cm

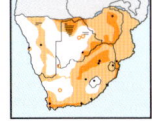

A: Kleinrietreier **Z:** Umacuthomncane **X:** Ihashe
Ss: Kgwitwana Ya Mokokotlontsho **N:** ≠khari ||nowab
G: Zwergrohrdommel

juv.

CROWNED LAPWING

Dry open veld. Light brown upperparts, neck and breast, black crown with white band, white belly, yellow eyes, and red bill and legs.
30 cm

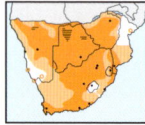

A: Kroonkiewiet
Z: Ititihoyelimqhele
Ss: Lekekeruane La Moqhaka
Tw: Lerweerwee
N: ǁgāxaris
H: Ongurukungwini
G: Kronenkiebitz

WHITE-CROWNED LAPWING

Sandbanks of major rivers. Brown back, grey head and neck, white crown and underparts, black and white wings, and yellow bill, wattles and legs.
30 cm

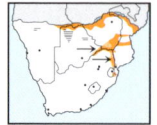

A: Witkopkiewiet
Z: Ititihoyelimqhelomhlophe
Ss: Lekekeruane La Hlahellalelele
Tw: Lerrane La Lebodulelele
N: !uri-gao-aoǀgapa xaixais
G: Langspornkiebitz

LONG-TOED LAPWING

Floodplains. Light brown upperparts, black-and-white head and breast, white wings in flight, and red bill and legs. 30 cm

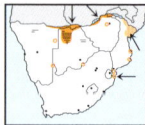

A: Witvlerkkiewiet
Z: Ititihoye Lamazibu
Tw: Lerrane La Dikubu
G: Langzehenkiebitz

AFRICAN WATTLED LAPWING

Moist grassland. Light grey-brown, with white forecrown, black-streaked neck, and yellow wattles, bill and legs. 35 cm

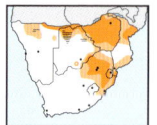

A: Lelkiewiet
Z: Umadevaphuzi
Ss: Lekekeruane La Hlahellakgutshwane
Tw: Lerrane La Lebodukhutshwane
N: ǀawa-!ū xaixais
G: Senegalkiebitz

COMMON GREENSHANK

Coastal and inland waters. Brown upperparts with white-edged feathers, white underparts, slightly upturned black bill, and long greenish legs. 32 cm

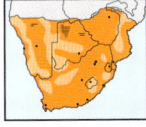

A: Groenpootruiter
Z: Unompempe
X: Uphendu
Ss: Mosalakatane Wa Leototala
N: !am-|nŭ !khuwi!gûb
G: Grünschenkel

BLUE-BILLED TEAL

Shallow pans and dams. Dark brown hood and wing feathers, creamy brown underparts with black spotting, and blue-grey bill. 35 cm

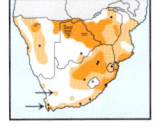

A: Gevlekte Eend **Z:** Idadelincane
Ss: Sefudi Sa Molomo-Talalehodimo
Tw: Sehudi Sa Molomo-Talalegodimo
H: Ombaka Yehi Rowakwena
G: Pünktchenente

AFRICAN SNIPE

Marshes. Buff upperparts and breast, white breast with dark brown streaks, and very long, straight black bill. 32 cm

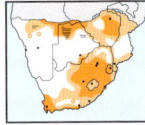

A: Afrikaanse Snip **Z:** Unununde **Ss:** Motjodi-Matsana **Sp:** Kwekwe Ya Afrika **Tw:** Maphari
N: Afrika ||hâigôa-ams
G: Afrikanische Bekassine

CAPE TEAL

Brackish pans. Dark brown upperparts with cream-edged feathers, pale head and underparts with brown spots, and pink bill. 46 cm

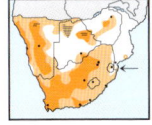

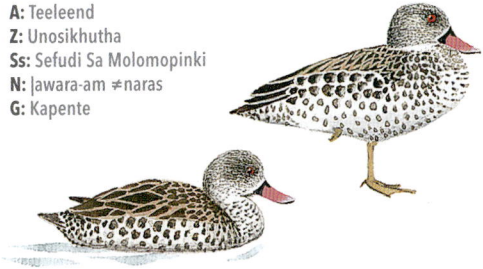

A: Teeleend
Z: Unosikhutha
Ss: Sefudi Sa Molomopinki
N: |awara-am ≠naras
G: Kapente

RED-BILLED TEAL

Dams, pans and floodplains. Dark brown hood and upperparts with cream-edged feathers, buffy neck, mottled underparts, and red bill. 48 cm

A: Rooibekeend **Z:** Idadelimlomobomvu
Ss: Sefudi Sa Molomofubedu
N: ǀawa-am ≠naras
H: Ombaka Yoheya
G: Rotschnabelente

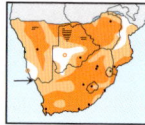

WHITE-BACKED DUCK

Secluded pans and dams. Brown-barred upperparts, buff neck, and black bill with white spot at the base. 43 cm

A: Witrugeend
Z: Inszwinzwi
Ss: Letata La Mokokotlosweu
Tw: Pidipidi Ya Mokotlasweu
G: Weißrückenente

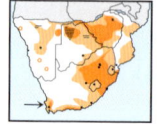

SQUACCO HERON

Lakes, lagoons and streams. Buffy, with white wings and belly (visible in flight); non-br. is more tawny with brown streaks. 43 cm

A: Ralreier **Z:** Umacuthomhlophe
Ss: Kokolofitwe Ya Molomotalalehodimo
N: ≠hoa-am ǀgurikhoeseb
G: Rallenreiher

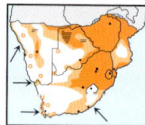

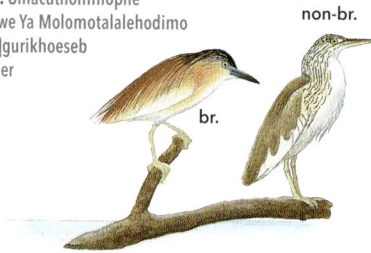

non-br.

br.

FULVOUS WHISTLING DUCK

Inland freshwater pans and dams. Rufous head and body, dark brown back and wings, and white flank feathers. 46 cm

A: Fluiteend
Z: Inzwinzwinzebomvu
Ss: Lewewe La Melodi
N: ≠namxa ≠naras
G: Gelbe Baumente

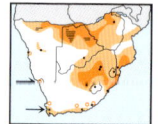

WATER THICK-KNEE

Near water edge. Buffy with dark streaks, dark moustachial stripe, distinctive black-edged grey wingbar, large yellow eyes and long yellow legs. **40 cm**

A: Waterdikkop
Z: Isiwelewele
Ss: Tapiane
Tw: Mongwangwa
Ts: Xigidavusiku
H: Okakungutuwa
G: Wassertriel

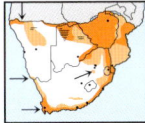

RUFOUS-BREASTED SPARROWHAWK

Wooded patches in hills. Dark grey upperparts, rufous underparts, barred underwings and tail, and yellow eyes and legs. 33–40 cm

A: Rooiborssperwer **Z:** Uheshanobomvu
X: Ukhetshe Womlambo **Ss:** Fiolo Ya Sefubafubedu
G: Rotbauchsperber

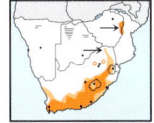

SPOTTED THICK-KNEE

Stony grassland. Dark-streaked buffy upperparts and white underparts, dark moustachial stripe, large yellow eyes and long yellow legs. **44 cm**

A: Gewone Dikkop
Z: UmBangaqhwa
Ss: Kgwadira
Tw: Tswangtswang
Ts: Mpyempye
H: Ipingizupauda
G: Kaptriel

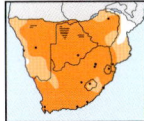

AFRICAN CUCKOO-HAWK

Riverine woodland. Grey head and barred tail, brown upperparts, and whitish underparts with light brown barring. **40 cm**

A: Koekoekvalk
Z: Usomthende
Ss: Fiolo-lehopoho
Tw: Segodi-Tlhotlhamedupe
N: hō-hōse hīsabes
G: Kuckucksweih

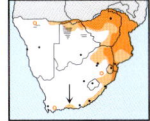

BLACK-BELLIED BUSTARD

Moist grasslands and fields. Tawny above, black markings on neck; pale yellow legs; male has black-and-white head marking and black belly; female is white below. 58–65 cm

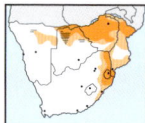

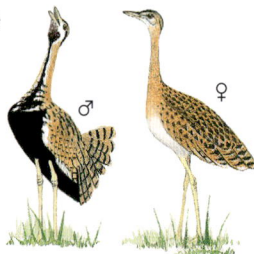

A: Langbeenkorhaan
Z: Ufumba
Ss: Lekakarane La Mpantsho
Tw: Mokgweba
Sh: Gunja
G: Schwarzbauchtrappe

SOUTHERN BLACK KORHAAN

Karoo renosterveld. Buffy barred upperparts and bright yellow legs; male has black head, neck and underparts; female has black belly. 53 cm

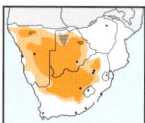

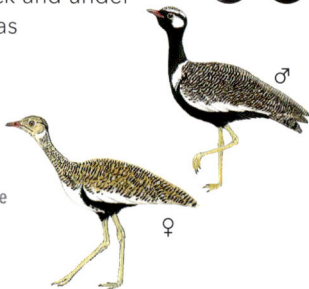

A: Swartvlerkkorhaan
Z: Iseme LaseKapa
X: Ikhalukhalu
Ss: Tlatlawe Ya Borwa
G: Gackeltrappe

NORTHERN BLACK KORHAAN

Karoo and savanna scrub. Buffy barred upperparts and bright yellow legs; male has black head, neck and under-parts; female has black belly. 53 cm

A: Witvlerkkorhaan
Z: Iseme Lethafa
Ss: Tlatlawe Ya Leboya
Tw: Tlatlawe ya Bokone
N: ‖haragas
G: Monteirotoko

RED-CRESTED KORHAAN

Mixed woodland. Brown upperparts with cream chevrons; male has greyish neck; rufous crest visible only during courtship. 53 cm

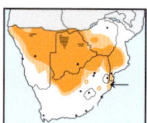

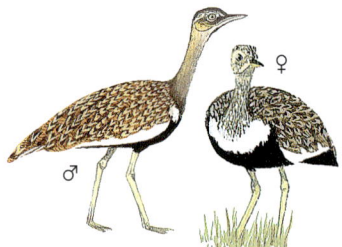

A: Boskorhaan
Z: Umngqithi
Sp: Kgwarakgwara
Tw: Khoba
Ts: Ntsukwani
H: Etuva
G: Rotschopftrappe

KAROO KORHAAN

Arid areas. Light cinnamon-brown, with plain head, greyish neck and black throat patch.
56–60 cm

A: Vaalkorhaan
Z: Umbexe Wasehlane
Ss: Lekakarane La Karu
N: ≠naubas
G: Namatrappe

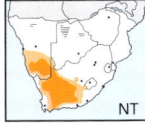

AFRICAN HAWK-EAGLE (juv.)

Woodland and riverine valleys. Dark brown upperparts, and buffy head and underparts.
60–65 cm

A: Grootjagarend
Z: Ukhozolumidwayidwa
Ss: Ntsutjheke E Kgolo
N: kai-anxa !khãs
G: Habichtsadler

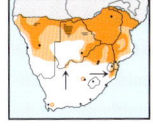

juv.

RÜPPELL'S KORHAAN

Arid plains. Light brown upperparts, white underparts; male has pale grey head and neck with black-and-white markings.
56–60 cm

A: Woestynkorhaan
Ss: Lekakarane La Lefeella
N: !noars!oars
G: Rüppelltrappe

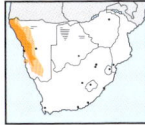

♂

AFRICAN HARRIER-HAWK (GYMNOGENE) (juv.)

Mixed woodland and suburbia. Birds in first plumage are light brown, with darker flight feathers and tail. 60–66 cm

A: Kaalwangvalk
Z: Ijikanyawo
Ss: Seitlhwaeledi
Ts: N'watimhakweni
N: !huni-ai hĩsabes
G: Höhlenweihe

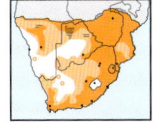

juv.

juv.

TAWNY EAGLE

Woodland. Various colour forms: light brown, tawny and gingery-brown; tawny form has black dappling on upperwing covert only; all have black flight feathers and tail; cere and legs yellow.
65–72 cm

A: Roofarend **Z:** Ukhozolunsundu
Sp: Ntšhukobokobo
Tw: Ntsu E Tshetlha
N: ≠gama !khās
H: Orukoze Ohonimdumbu
G: Raubadler

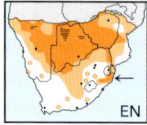

MARTIAL EAGLE (imm.)

Woodland. Light brown upperparts, speckled neck, and white underparts.
78–83 cm

A: Breëkoparend
Z: Isihuhwa
Ss: Ntsu E Kgolo
Sp: Mmakgwana
Tw: Ntsu E Thamaga
Ts: Manole
N: !ari!khās
H: Orukoze Havita
G: Kampfadler

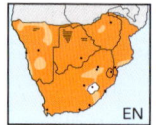

imm.

STEPPE EAGLE (imm.)

Woodland. Light brown, with darker flight feathers with a white trailing edge.
75 cm

A: Steppe-arend
Z: Ukhozimuhlwa
Tw: Ntsu Ya Naga
H: Orukoze Omaheke
G: Steppenadler

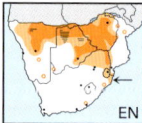

imm.

WHITE-BACKED VULTURE

Woodland and areas with game or cattle. Grey-brown, with white back, and black flight feathers, neck and bare parts.
90–98 cm

A: Witrugaasvoël
Z: Inqe lehlanze
Ss: Leaka
Sp: Lenong La Mokološweu
Tw: Lenong Le Letuba
N: !uri-||â kai-anis
G: Weißrückengeier

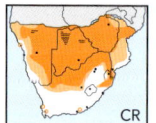

BEARDED VULTURE

High-altitude montane cliffs. Rufous body, dark brown wings and tail, black mask and beard, and white face. 110 cm

A: Baardaasvoël
Z: Ugaganontshebe
Ss: Seodi
G: Bartgeier

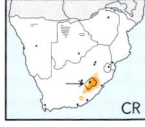

CAPE VULTURE

Arid open bushveld and cliffs. Light brown body and wings, blue-grey neck, black flight feathers and tail, and honey-coloured eyes. 105–115 cm

A: Kransaasvoël
Z: Idlanga lentaba
X: Ihlanga
Ss: Lenong La Selomo
Sp: Rrantšwe
Tw: Diswaane
Ts: Khoti Mavalanga
H: Onguvi YaKapa
G: Kapgeier

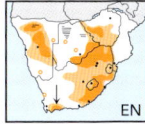

LUDWIG'S BUSTARD

Karoo and Namib plains. Brown back, dark foreneck and upperwings, and white belly. 75–90 cm

A: Ludwigpou **Z:** Iseme
Ss: Kgupa Ya Mmetsosootho
N: ≠gamadom !huib **G:** Ludwigstrappe

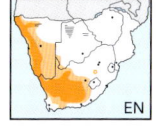

DENHAM'S BUSTARD

Hilly grasslands. Brown back, ash-grey foreneck, black cap, and black-and-white upperwings. 86–110 cm

A: Veldpou **Z:** iSeme **Ss:** Kgupa Ya Mmetsoputswa
N: |haidom !huib **G:** Stanleytrappe

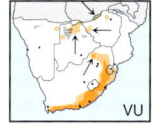

KORI BUSTARD

Woods and grasslands. Light brown upperparts, grey neck, black-and-white upperwings, white underparts. 134 cm

A: Gompou **Z:** Isemelikhulu **Ss:** Kgori **Ts:** Mithisi
Nd: Itjeme **Sh:** Ngomanyuni **N:** kai !huib
H: Etwangema **G:** Riesentrappe

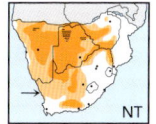

First impression
SPECKLED PLUMAGE
(including freckled, dappled, brindled and mottled)

Many birds appear speckled or dappled, which is a result of feathers having pale margins, giving a scalloped effect, or having dark centres, stripes or spots. These feathers may also be overlaid with stripes or bars of black or white, creating a spotty pattern as seen, for example, in the African Snipe or the Spotted Eagle-Owl. In several cases, these birds are best told by bill shape, length or colour, or leg length or colour. These features, coupled with their spotted plumage, are the surest clue to their identity.

How does speckled plumage serve a bird?

Camouflage: Speckled plumage provides excellent camouflage, which is particularly useful for species that nest on the ground, such as the cryptically patterned nightjars. In the Crowned Lapwing, both eggs and hatchlings are remarkably well camouflaged resulting in a lower risk of detection by predators.

CANNIBALISM

Owls are carnivores, and the prey they take is determined by the bird's size. Small owls prey on insects, other birds and small rodents, while large owls feed on larger prey. What is surprising, though, is that many owls prey on other owls. **Verreaux's Eagle-Owl**, for example, will prey on other owls, even those as large as the **Spotted Eagle-Owl** or a **Pel's Fishing Owl**, a bird equal to it in size.

CUT-THROAT FINCH

Dry woodland. Dark grey, flecked upperparts, barred head, finely barred under-parts, black primaries and tail; male has a red throat band. **12 cm**

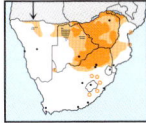

A: Bandkeelvink
Z: Unongilonegazi
G: Bandfink

AFRICAN SPOTTED CREEPER

Broad-leaved woodland. Dark brown upperparts with heavy white spotting, barred white underparts, and slender, decurved bill. **15 cm**

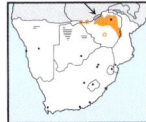

A: Boomkruiper
Z: Inkwelamthini

CHESTNUT-BACKED SPARROW-LARK ♀

Bare areas in grassland. Mottled chestnut upperparts, white-edged wing feathers, white hindcollar, streaked white underparts, black belly, and white bill and legs. **12 cm**

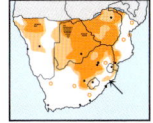

A: Rooiruglewerik **Z:** Intakajolwane
Ss: Mmadiberwane-Nkatakgunong **G:** Weißwangenlerche

BLACK-EARED SPARROW-LARK ♀

Karoo scrublands. Dappled rufous upperparts, streaked white underparts, and white bill and legs. **12–13 cm**

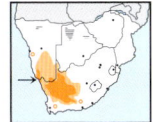

A: Swartoorlewerik **Z:** Intakajolwanemnyama
G: Schwarzwangenlerche

GREY-BACKED SPARROW-LARK ♀

Semi-arid grasslands. Mottled greyish upperparts, white-edged wing feathers, streaked breast, black belly, and white bill and legs. **12–13 cm**

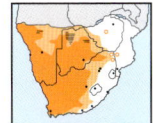

A: Grysruglewerik **Z:** Intakajolwane Yasehlane
Ss: Mmadiberwane-Nkataputswa **G:** Nonnenlerche

COMMON QUAIL

Bushveld and grasslands. Rufous upperparts with black and white streaks and pale eyebrows, buffy underparts and white-streaked flanks; male has dark throat.
18 cm

A: Afrikaanse Kwartel
Z: Isagwacesjiwayelekile
Ss: Sekweqe
Tw: Sekhwiri Se Serokwa
Ts: Mavolwane
N: ≠gama !nabaris
G: Wachtel

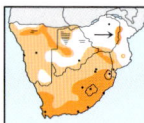

AFRICAN SCOPS OWL

Mixed bushveld. Black-streaked grey-brown plumage, resembling tree bark, yellow eyes, and prominent ear tufts.
15–18 cm

A: Skopsuil **Z:** UmaDletshana
Sp: Leribišane
Tw: Sekopamarumo
Ts: Xikotlwa
Sh: Chimbori
N: ≠gae |honnes
H: Okasivi Kautui Outiṭi
G: Afrikanische Zwergohreule

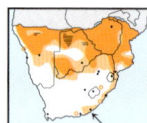

grey morph   brown morph

PEARL-SPOTTED OWLET

Woodland. Dark brown-grey upperparts with white spots, black ' false eyes' on the back of the head, and brown-and-white streaked underparts.
15–18 cm

A: Witkoluil **Z:** Inkovana
Ss: Morubisi Ya Sefubametjhato
Tw: Pelekekae
N: !uri-!khai !hûros
G: Perlkauz

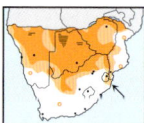

AFRICAN BARRED OWLET

Woodland. Dark brown-grey upperparts with white barring and wing spots, and white underparts with grey-brown bars and spots.
20 cm

A: Gebande Uil
Z: Inkovanemidwa
Ss: Morubsi Ya Sefubadirothi
Tw: Morubisana
Ts: Xikhodlane
N: !khai-|gā !hûros
G: Kapkauz

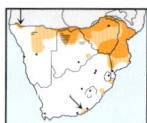

COMMON STARLING (non-br.)

Suburbia. Dark upperparts with tawny spots, tawny-edged wing feathers, and greenish-black underparts with white spots. 20-22 cm

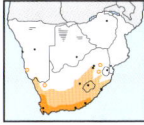

A: Europese Spreeu **Z:** Ikhwinsi LaseYurobhu
Ss: Lehodi-Papapa **G:** Star

non-br.

VIOLET-BACKED STARLING ♀

Broad-leaved woodland. Brown upperparts, and white belly with brown speckles. 18-19 cm

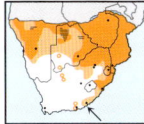

A: Witborsspreeu **Z:** Ikhwezelimacwebi
Ss: Lehodi-Kokotlopherese **G:** Amethystglanzstar

♀

NIGHTJARS

Mixed woodland. Heavily mottled, barred and spotted rufous, dark brown, black and white; species can only be told apart by call or wing and tail patterns. 23-28 cm

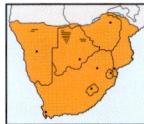

A: Naguile **G:** Nachtschwalben

Fiery-necked

DOUBLE-BANDED SANDGROUSE

Broad-leaved woodland. Female speckled; male has brown back with white spots, plain fawn head and breast, and black-and-white breast band. 25 cm

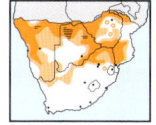

A: Dubbelbandsandpatrys **Z:** Unogwadule Wehlanze
Sp: Sebopa Sa Melabedi **Ts:** Xighwaraghwara
N: !nuwu≠are !nabaris **G:** Nachtflughuhn

♀   ♂

BURCHELL'S SANDGROUSE

Sandveld. Usually in pairs or flocks at waterholes. White-spotted rufous underparts; male has grey face; female has yellowish face. 25 cm

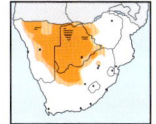

A: Gevlekte Sandpatrys **Z:** Unogwadulogqabhagqabha
Tw: Legorwagorwana **N:** ≠hoa-ai !nabaris
G: Fleckenflughuhn

♂   ♀

NAMAQUA SANDGROUSE

Arid grass- and scrublands. Ochre head and long, pointed tail; female densely mottled except on throat and underbelly; male has plain head and breast, and black-and-white breast band. 28 cm

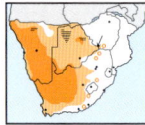

A: Kelkiewyn **Z:** Unogwadule **Ss:** Lekgwakgwa
Tw: Lekotokobii **N:** gãxü≠are !nabaris **G:** Namaflughuhn

YELLOW-THROATED SANDGROUSE ♀

Short grass and cultivated lands. Heavily mottled cream and blackish-brown, with yellow face and throat, dusky belly and rufous vent.
30 cm

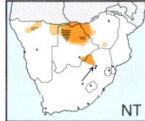

A: Geelkeelsandpatrys
Z: Unogwadulontamephuzi
Ss: Kokwi Ya Mmetsosehla
Tw: Photi-mpha-bogogo
N: !hunidom !nabaris
G: Gelbkehl-Flughuhn

GREY-WINGED FRANCOLIN

Grassy hills. Tawny, mottled upperparts, rufous head markings, white throat with black spots, and grey underparts. 31–33 cm

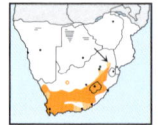

A: Bergpatrys **Z:** Ithendelelimlotha **Ss:** Kgwale Ya Thaba
G: Grauflügelfrankolin

ORANGE RIVER FRANCOLIN

Dry grasslands. Dark grey-brown, mottled upperparts, rufous, black and white head, white throat, and dappled, rufous underparts. 33–35 cm

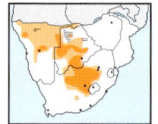

A: Kalaharipatrys
Z: Isikhwehle Sehlane
Ss: Kgwale Ya Kgalagadi
N: !aub !nowos
G: Rebhuhnfrankolin

SHELLEY'S FRANCOLIN

Grassy woodland. Mottled, dark grey-brown upperparts, white underparts, blotched red-brown breast, and black-barred belly. 33 cm

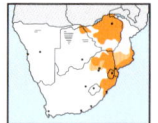

A: Laeveldpatrys **Z:** Isikhwehlesimqhalomhlophe
Ss: Kgwale Ya Botjhabela **Ts:** Njenjele **Sh:** Marenge
G: Shelleyfrankolin

RED-WINGED FRANCOLIN

Grassy hills. Dark brown, blotched upperparts , rufous ear coverts and neck stripe, black-and-white mottled breast, and streaked, pale rufous underparts. 38–40 cm

A: Rooivlerkpatrys
Z: Ithendelelibomvu
Ss: Kgwale Ya Lepheofubedu
G: Rotflügelfrankolin

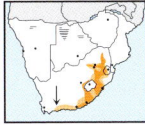

NATAL SPURFOWL

Granite koppies. Dark brown-streaked upperparts, black-and-white speckled underparts, yellow and red bill, and red legs. 30–38 cm

A: Natalse Fisant
Z: Unomemeza
X: Isakhwehle
Ss: Kgwale Ya Molomolamunu
Tw: Segweba
Ts: Nghwari Ma Ntshengwhayi
G: Natalfrankolin

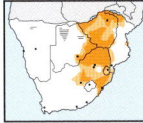

AFRICAN OLIVE PIGEON

Forests and wooded areas. Dark purple-brown with grey head, purple-grey neck, white spots on wings and belly, and bright yellow eye-rings, bill and legs. 36–40 cm

A: Geelbekbosduif **Z:** Ivukuthu-lehlathi **X:** Izuba
Ss: Leebamphapane **Tw:** Leebaphepane **Ts:** Ngalakana
G: Oliventaube

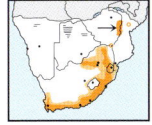

WOOD SANDPIPER

Freshwater shores. Dark brown upperparts with white speckling, white eyebrows and belly, buffy breast, and yellow-green legs. 20 cm

A: Bosruiter **Z:** UmaKhwifikwifi **Ss:** Mosalakatane Wa Moru
N: hai!khuwi!gûb **G:** Bruchwasserläufer

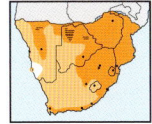

MARSH SANDPIPER

Freshwater and river shores. Sandy brown upperparts with white-edged feathers, white underparts, slender black bill, and long yellow-green legs. 23 cm

A: Moerasruiter **Z:** Unothwayiza **Ss:** Mosalakatane Wa Molhaka
N: gāxū-|nū !khuwi!gûb **G:** Teichwasserläufer

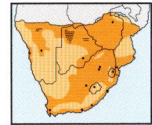

RUDDY TURNSTONE (non-br.)

Shorelines. Speckled chestnut upperparts, black-and-white head, neck and breast, and white underparts. 22 cm

A: Steenloper Z: UmaPhendulamatshe
Ss: Lekitinyane N: |ui!gûb G: Steinwälzer

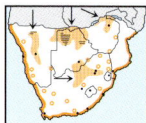

non-br.

GREY PLOVER (non-br.)

Tidal flats. Mottled upper-parts, white forehead and eyebrow, black 'armpits' in flight. 30 cm

A: Grysstrandkiewiet
Z: UmaKhwaphamnyama
N: |hai xoexoes
G: Kiebitzregenpfeifer

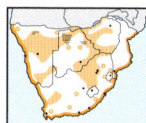

non-br.

RUFF (non-br.)

Shallow coast and inland waters. Light brown head and neck, dark brown back and wings with pale-edged feathers, and white underparts; adult has orange legs; immature has dark legs.
24–30 cm

A: Kemphaan
Z: Unogqabakazi
Ss: Seyalelebopo Sa Motlwenya
Tw: Seyalelebopo Sa Setlopo
N: |gare|û huri-am!gûb
G: Kampfläufer

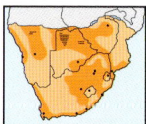

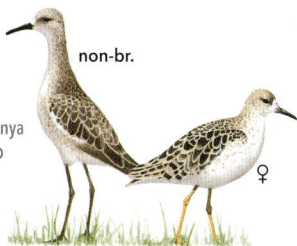

non-br.

♀

AFRICAN SNIPE

Marshes. Buff upperparts and breast, white belly with dark brown streaks, and very long, straight black bill.
32 cm

A: Afrikaanse Snip
Z: Unununde
Ss: Motjodi-Matsana
Sp: Kwekwe Ya Afrika
Tw: Maphari
N: Afrika ||hâigôa-ams
G: Afrikanische Bekassine

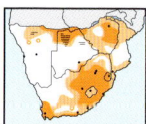

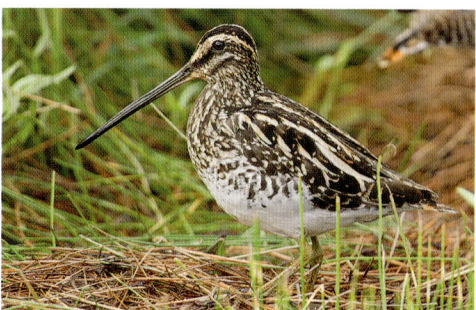

AMUR FALCON ♀

Open grasslands. Grey upperparts, white under-parts with dark chevrons, and red or orange eye-ring, cere and legs. 28–30 cm

A: Oostelike Rooipootvalk **Z:** Oklebeklebe
Ss: Phakwe Ya Leotolamunu
N: ai≠oa |awa-≠ai |aub **G:** Amur-Rotfußfalke

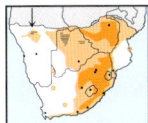

BLUE-BILLED TEAL

Shallow pans and dams. Dark brown hood and wing feathers, creamy brown underparts with black spotting, and blue-grey bill. 35 cm

A: Gevlekte Eend **Z:** Idadelincane
Ss: Sefudi Sa Molomo-Talalehodimo
H: Ombaka Yehi Rowakwena **G:** Pünktchenente

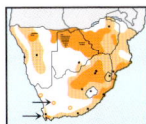

CAPE TEAL

Brackish pans. Dark brown upperparts with cream-edged feathers, pale head and underparts with brown spots, and pink bill. 46 cm

A: Teeleend **Z:** Unosikhutha **Ss:** Sefudi Sa Molomopinki
N: |awara-am ≠naras **G:** Kapente

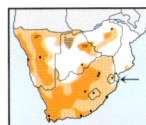

RED-BILLED TEAL

Dams, pans and floodplains. Dark brown hood and upperparts with cream-edged feathers, buffy neck, mottled underparts, and red bill. 48 cm

A: Rooibekeend **Z:** Idadelimlomobomvu
Ss: Sefudi Sa Molomofubedu
N: |awa-am ≠naras
H: Ombaka Yoheya
G: Rotschnabelente

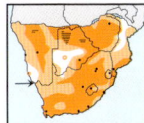

SPOTTED THICK-KNEE

Stony grassland. Dark-streaked buffy upperparts and white underparts, dark moustachial stripe, large yellow eyes and long yellow legs.
44 cm

A: Gewone Dikkop
Z: UmBangaqhwa
Ss: Kgwadira
Tw: Tswangtswang
Ts: Mpyempye
H: Ipingizupauda
G: Kaptriel

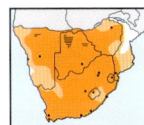

WHITE-BACKED DUCK

Secluded pans and dams. Brown-barred upperparts, buff neck, and black bill with white spot at the base. 43 cm

A: Witrugeend **Z:** Inszwinzwi **Ss:** Letata La Mokokotlosweu
Tw: Pidipidi Ya Mokotlasweu **G:** Weißrückenente

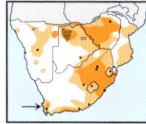

AFRICAN BLACK DUCK

Rivers. Dark brown with white-spotted upperparts, grey bill and orange legs. 51–54 cm

A: Swarteend **Z:** Idadelimnyama **Ss:** Letata La Noka
Sp: Letata **Tw:** Sehudi Se Sentsho **N:** ≠nū ≠naras
H: Ombaka Ondurozu **G:** Schwarzente

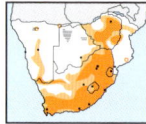

YELLOW-BILLED DUCK

Dams and rivers. Dark brown upperparts with white-edged feathers, paler underparts, and yellow bill with black saddle. 53–58 cm

A: Geelbekeend **Z:** Idadelimlomophuzi
Ss: Letata La Molomosehla **Tw:** Sehudi Sa Molomosetlha
N: !huni-am ≠naras **H:** Ombaka Yotjinyatjingara
G: Gelbschnabelente

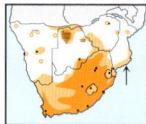

CAPE SHOVELER

Shallow inland and tidal waters and lagoons. Dark brown-speckled grey body, broad-tipped black bill, and orange-yellow legs; male has paler head; in flight, shows pale blue-green on upperwings. 53 cm

A: Kaapse Slopeend
Z: Unofosholo
Ss: Letatakgaba La Borwa
N: ||goa-am ≠naras
G: Kaplöffelente

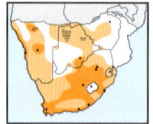

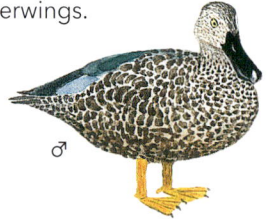

♂

EURASIAN WHIMBREL

Lagoons and tidal flats. Dark brown upperparts mottled white, white underparts with brown streaking on breast and flanks, striped crown, and long, decurved bill. 43 cm

A: Kleinwulp
Z: Unokhifi
Ss: Keowe E Nnyenyane
N: ≠khari !hoa-ams
G: Regenbrachvogel

EURASIAN CURLEW

Estuaries and lagoons. Buffy upperparts and breast with dark brown streaks, white-edged wing feathers, white underbelly and long, decurved bill. **59 cm**

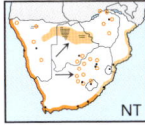

A: Grootwulp
Z: Unokhifomkhulu
Ss: Seyalelebopo Sa Molomokgopo
N: !hoa-am huri-am!gûb
G: Großer Brachvogel

CAPE EAGLE-OWL

Rocky valleys. Dark brown upperparts, buffy blotched underparts, prominent 'ear' tufts, dark-bordered facial disc, and orange eyes. **48–55 cm**

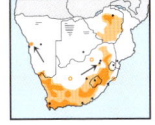

A: Kaapse Ooruil
Z: Isikhovampondo
Ss: Mohwe
Tw: Morubise
N: !khawaga ≠uwib
G: Kapuhu

SPOTTED EAGLE-OWL

Lightly wooded areas. Dark brown upperparts, finely barred and blotched underparts, prominent 'ear' tufts, dark-bordered facial disc, and yellow eyes. **43–50 cm**

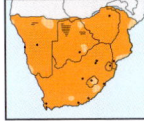

A: Gevlekte Ooruil
Z: Isikhovamponjwama
Ss: Sehihi
Sp: Leribiši La Leihlosehla
Tw: Leghonda
Ts: Xiyinha
Sh: Jichidza
N: !khai ≠uwib **G:** Fleckenuhu

CROWNED EAGLE (imm.)

Well-wooded river and hillside forests. Dark brown upperparts with white-edged feathers, pale head and underparts with brown and orange speckling. **80–90 cm**

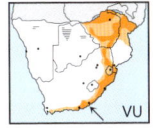

imm.

A: Kroonarend
Z: Isihuhwa
Ss: Makgwana
Sp: Makgwana
Tw: Makgwana
G: Kronenadler

COLLARS AND BREAST BANDS

Collars or bands are found in many bird species and are excellent recognition features.

Collars are bands of colour on a bird's neck or throat. They are usually at the front of the neck, but may be on the hindneck only, as in Kittlitz's Plover, or may completely encircle the lower neck, as in the Common Ringed Plover.

Breast bands are bands of colour, often black, that span the bird's breast or chest. Breast bands may number as many as three, as in the Three-banded Plover, although a single band is most common. Some birds have a wide breast band, for example, the Bokmakierie, and this is usually called a gorget. In some species, such as the Black-chested Prinia, the breast band is found only during the breeding season, and it will fade or disappear completely during the non-breeding season.

BROOD PARASITES

Brood parasites are birds that lay their eggs in the nest of an unrelated species and take no part in raising their own young. While cuckoos are well known for this behaviour, within southern Africa brood parasitism is also practised by other species, such as the **Cuckoo Finch**, **honeyguides**, **whydahs** and related **widow-finches**. Most cuckoos in the region are summer visitors that parasitise a range of other species. The **Red-chested Cuckoo** favours the robin group, while the **Diederik Cuckoo** prefers weavers and bishops. The eggs of these two cuckoos normally hatch before those of the host, and the chick ejects the eggs of its foster siblings. Young **honeyguides** also hatch early and are initially equipped with a sharp bill-hook, which is used to break the eggs of its host or to kill the chicks. In contrast, **whydahs** and **indigobirds** parasitise **waxbills** and other small **finches** in a much gentler manner. The whydah and indigobird chicks resemble those of the host in several ways, and grow up in harmony with them. The **Cuckoo Finch**, a parasitic weaver, usually parasitises **cisticolas** and **prinias** and, as far as is known, the chick does not deliberately dispose of its foster siblings.

SAND MARTIN

Inland waters and river estuaries. Dark brown upperparts, white under-parts, narrow breast band, and shallowly forked tail. **12 cm**

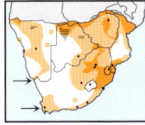

A: Europese Oewerswael
Z: Inhlolamfula
Ss: Lekabelane-La-Mangope
G: Europäische Uferschwalbe

WHITE-THROATED SWALLOW

Near open water and moist grasslands. Metallic blue upperparts, orange forehead, white underparts, black breast band, and forked tail. **17 cm**

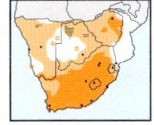

A: Witkeelswael
Z: Inkonjanemqalomhlophe
X: Unocel' Izapholo
G: Weißkehlschwalbe

BANDED MARTIN

Marsh- and grasslands. Dark brown upperparts, white underparts, wide brown breast band, white eyebrows, and square tail. **17 cm**

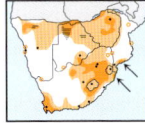

A: Gebande Oewerswael
Z: Inhlolamvulebhandensundu
Ss: Lekabelane-Kodutshweu
G: Weißbrauenschwalbe

BARN SWALLOW

Moist bushveld. Metallic blue upperparts, orange forehead and chin, black throat, white underparts, and forked tail. **18 cm**

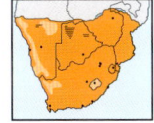

A: Europese Swael
Z: Inkonjane YaseYutobhu
Ss: Lepeolane
G: Rauchschwalbe

juv.

ALPINE SWIFT

Mountains. Dark brown breast band, and white chin and belly. 22 cm

A: Witpenswindswael **Z:** Inhlolazulu
X: Irulumente **Ss:** Lehaqasi La Mpasweu
Tw: Phetla Ya Mpasweu
N: !ur-!nã sõsowob **G:** Alpensegler

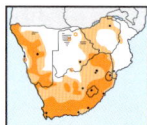

YELLOW-BREASTED APALIS

Bushveld and mixed forest fringes. Olive upperparts, white throat and belly, and yellow breast; some males have a small black bar below breast. 10–12 cm

A: Geelborskleinjantjie
Z: UmanKolophuzi
X: Umhlantonono
G: Gelbbrust-Feinsänger

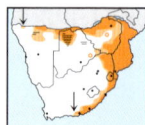

♂

RUDD'S APALIS

Coastal bush. Olive upperparts, grey cap, white underparts and black breast band. 10.5–12 cm

A: Ruddkleinjantjie **Z:** UmaNkole
G: Rudds Feinsänger

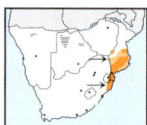

♂

♀

BAR-THROATED APALIS

Forests and woodland. Olive-grey upperparts and white or yellow underparts; all races have a black collar. 12–13 cm

A: Bandkeelkleinjantjie **Z:** UmaBilwane
X: Ugxakhweni **Ss:** Pilipili-Mpasehla
G: Halsband-Feinsänger

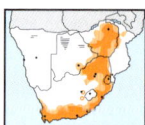

yellowest morph

CUT-THROAT FINCH ♂

Dry broad-leaved woodland. Speckled brown, with broad red collar. **12 cm**

A: Bandkeelvink **Z:** Unongilonegazi
G: Bandfink

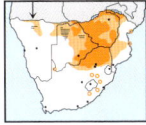

CAPE BATIS

Forest fringes. Black and white with grey cap; male has broad black breast band; female has rufous throat and breast band.
12-13 cm

A: Kaapse Bosbontrokkie
Z: Udokotela
Ss: Swamahlaku-Sa-Kapa
G: Kapschnäpper

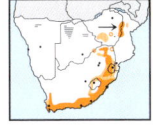

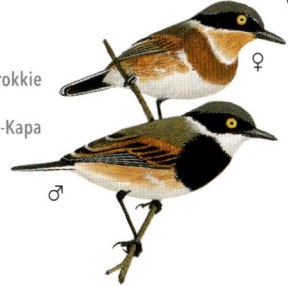

PRIRIT BATIS ♂

Dry thornveld. Dark grey upperparts, white underparts and broad black breast band.
12 cm

A: Priritbosbontrokkie **Z:** Incwaba YaseNtshonalanga
Ss: Swamahlaku-Sa-Bophirima **G:** Priritschnäpper

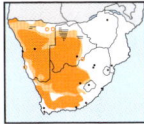

CHINSPOT BATIS

Mixed woodland. Black and white with grey cap and yellow eyes; male has broad black breast band; female has rufous breast and chin spot. **12-13 cm**

A: Witliesbosbontrokkie
Z: Incwaba
X: Unondyola
Ss: Swamahlaku-Sa-Bokone
G: Weißflankenschnäpper

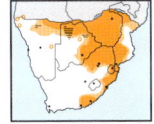

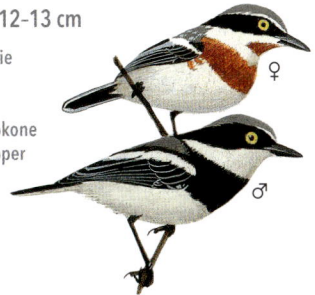

BLACK-CHESTED PRINIA
(br. ad)

Dry thornveld. Dark brown upperparts, white underparts and black breast band.
13–15 cm

A: Swartbandlangstertjie
Z: Ujengosifubesimnyama
Ss: Seqeshe-Thwalakgauntsho
G: Brustbandprinie

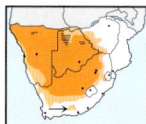

br.

SOUTHERN DOUBLE-COLLARED SUNBIRD ♂

Woodlands, fynbos and gardens. Glossy green head and mantle, narrow blue and red breast bands, and greyish belly. 12.5 cm

A: Klein-rooibandsuikerbekkie
Z: Incuncwana
Ss: Pinyane-Petakgubetswana
G: Halsband-Nektarvogel

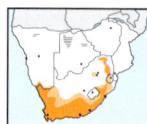

♂

RUFOUS-EARED WARBLER

Semi-arid scrub. Rufous mask and ear coverts, white underparts, and black breast band. 14 cm

A: Rooioorlangstertjie
Z: Ujenga Wehlane
G: Rotbackensänger

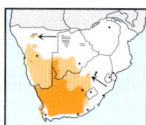

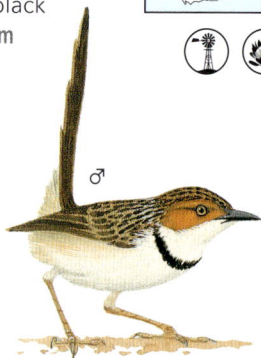

♂

MARICO SUNBIRD ♂

Thornveld. Glossy green upperparts, head and upper breast, purple and red breast bands, and black belly.
13–14 cm

A: Maricosuikerbekkie
Z: Insonsi
G: Bindennektarvogel

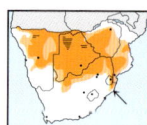

♂

GREATER DOUBLE-COLLARED SUNBIRD ♂

Moist forest edges, kloofs and gardens. Glossy green head and mantle, narrow blue and wide red breast bands, and greyish belly. 14 cm

A: Groot-rooibandsuikerbekkie
Z: Incuncu
Ss: Pinyane-Petakgubedu
G: Großer Halsband-Nektarvogel

LITTLE BEE-EATER

Riverine bush. Green upperparts, rufous underparts, yellow throat and black throat patch. 17 cm

A: Kleinbyvreter
Z: Inkothana
Ss: Thlapolome E Nnyenyane
Tw: Seselamarumo Se Sennye
N: ≠khari nīb
G: Zwergspint

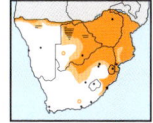

ORANGE-BREASTED SUNBIRD ♂

Protea slopes. Glossy green head and throat, purple breast band, and orange underparts. 15 cm

A: Oranjeborssuikerbekkie **Z:** Incwincwi YaseKapa
G: Goldbrust-Nektarvogel

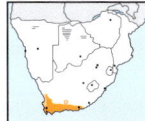

BLACK-THROATED WATTLE-EYE

Riverine and coastal thickets. Black upperparts, red eye wattle, and white underparts; female has all-black breast; male has narrow black breast band. 18 cm

A: Beloogbosbontrokkie
Z: UmaShiyabomvu
G: Schwarzkehl-Lappenschnäpper

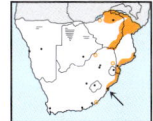

COLLARED PALM THRUSH

Palm savanna. Rufous upperparts and vent, black collar, cream throat, and grey flanks. 19 cm

A: Palmmôrelyster
Z: UmuNswi Wasemalaleni
G: Morgenrötel

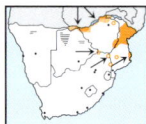

CAPPED WHEATEAR

Cultivated fields and open short grass. Brown upperparts, white throat and breast, and broad black gorget. 18 cm

A: Hoëveldskaapwagter
Z: Uqolomhlophe
G: Erdschmätzer

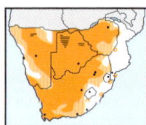

AFRICAN PIED WAGTAIL

Lowland rivers. Black and white, with a broad black breast band. 20 cm

A: Bontkwikkie
Z: UmVemvolunga
Ss: Motjodi-Phatshwa
Sp: Moselakatane
Sh: Kamujana
G: Witwenstelze

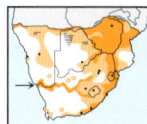

MOUNTAIN WAGTAIL

Mountain streams. Grey, black and white, with black breast band. 19–20 cm

A: Bergkwikkie
Z: UmVemventabe
G: Langschwanzstelze

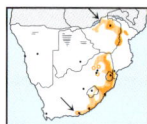

CAPE WAGTAIL

Wetlands and gardens. Greyish-brown, with white throat and black breast band. 18 cm

A: Gewone Kwikkie **Z:** UmNcishu
Ss: Motjodi-Thokwana **G:** Kapstelze

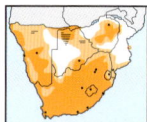

RED-COLLARED WIDOWBIRD (br. ♂)

Bushveld vleis. Black, with red collar and long tail; collar often difficult to see unless bird is perched.
15 cm (br. male 40 cm)

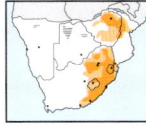

A: Rooikeelflap **Z:** Ujojo **X:** Ujojo **Ss:** Molepe-Lalafubedu
G: Schildwida

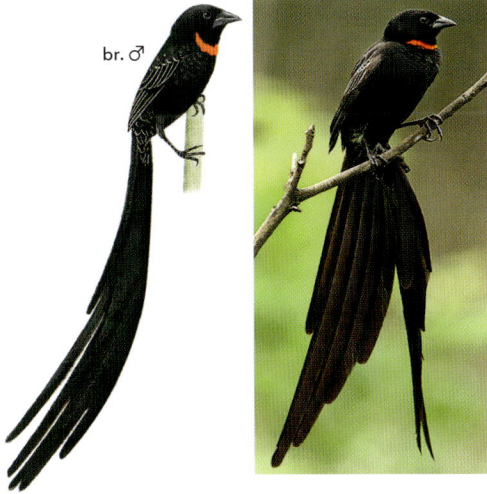

br. ♂

CHESTNUT-BANDED PLOVER ♂

Pans and gravel pits. Light brown upperparts, white forehead, face and underparts, and narrow chestnut or buffy throat band. 15 cm

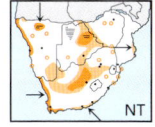

A: Rooibandstrandkiewiet
Z: Unosongo Wechweba
G: Fahlregenpfeifer

♂

THREE-BANDED PLOVER

Freshwater shores. Brown upperparts, white underparts, and two black breast bands. 18 cm

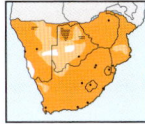

A: Driebandstrandkiewiet **Z:** Igwigwi **X:** Inqatha
Ss: Mororwane Wa Metjhatoraro **Tw:** Thatswane Ya Meelediraro
N: daoxa xoexoes **G:** Dreiband-Regenpfeifer

KITTLITZ'S PLOVER

Edges of estuaries, rivers, pans and inland waters. Light brown upperparts, black and white bands on head and neck, buff breast and white belly.
16 cm

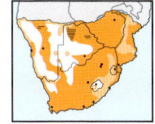

A: Geelborsstrandkiewiet
Z: UmaTatazela
Ss: Mororwane Wa Sehubasehla
Tw: Thatswane Ya Sefubasetlha
N: !huni-ǀgã xoexoes
G: Hirtenregenpfeifer

COMMON RINGED PLOVER

Shorelines of estuaries and inland waters. Brown upperparts, white underparts; male has black mask and bold black neckband. 18 cm

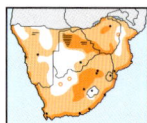

A: Ringnekstrandkiewiet
Z: Unosongo
Tw: Thatswane Ya Sehubantsho
N: râi-|haro xoexoes
G: Sandregenpfeifer

YELLOW-THROATED LONGCLAW

Open woodland. Grey-brown upperparts, yellow eyebrows, throat and underparts, and black gorget. 20 cm

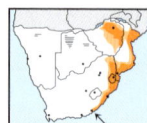

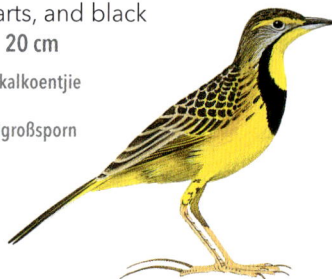

A: Geelkeelkalkoentjie
Z: Itoyiya
G: Gelbkehlgroßsporn

CAPE LONGCLAW

Short moist grassland. Grey-brown upperparts, yellow eyebrows and underparts, and orange throat with black gorget. 20 cm

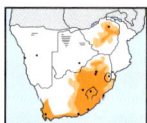

A: Oranjekeelkalkoentjie
Z: Inqomfi
X: Inqilo
Ss: Lethwele
G: Kapgroßsporn

GORGEOUS BUSHSHRIKE ♂

Dense bush thickets. Olive upperparts, red chin and throat, black gorget, and yellow eyebrows and belly. 20 cm

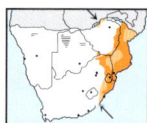

A: Konkoit **Z:** Ingongoni
G: Vierfarbenwürger

BOKMAKIERIE

Bush and urban areas. Grey crown and mantle, olive upperparts, yellow underparts and black gorget. 23 cm

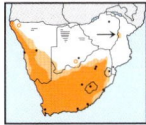

A: Bokmakierie
Z: Inkovu
X: Ingqwangi
Ss: Ptjemptjete
Sp: Mpherwane
G: Bokmakiri

DOUBLE-BANDED COURSER

Arid grasslands. Mottled light brown upperparts, white underparts and two narrow black breast bands. 22 cm

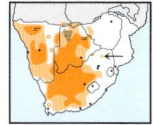

A: Dubbelbanddrawwertjie
Z: Unobulongwonesifociya
Ss: Mokopjwane Wa Metjhatobedi **N:** |awa-||gawo !naeb **G:** Doppelband-Rennvogel

BRONZE-WINGED COURSER

Woodland. Light brown upperparts and breast, dark mask, white eyebrows, throat and underparts, and red eye-rings and legs. 25 cm

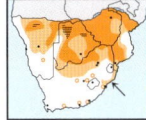

A: Bronsvlerkdrawwertjie **Z:** Unobulongwonsundu
Ss: Mokopjwane Wa Lepheoporonse **Tw:** Mmadithsipi
Ts: Tshembyana **G:** Amethystrennvogel

THREE-BANDED COURSER

Dry woodland. Mottled light brown upperparts, white throat, chestnut V-shaped collar and lower breast band, and dark brown breast band. 28 cm

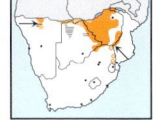

A: Driebanddrawwertjie
Z: Unobulongwonomgexe
Ss: Mokopjwane Wa Metjhatoraro
Tw: Segolagola
N: !uri-dom !naeb
G: Bindenrennvogel

CASPIAN PLOVER

Dry plains and pans. Light brown upperparts, white face and belly, and dusky (non-br.) or broad chestnut (br.) breast band.
21–23 cm

A: Asiatiese Strandkiewiet
Z: Unomvula
Tw: Thatswane Ya Sehubahubidu
N: ǀawa-ǀgā xoexoes
G: Wermutregenpfeifer

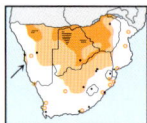

br.

non-br.

GREATER PAINTED-SNIPE

Pond fringes. Rufous face, nape and breast, olive back, white band over shoulders and belly, and yellow legs.
28–32 cm

A: Goudsnip
Z: UmaKhwaneni
Ss: Kwekwe Ya Kgauta
G: Goldschnepfe

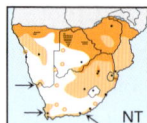

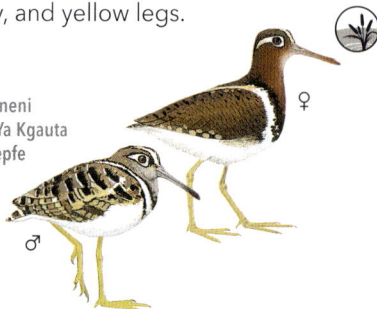

♀

♂

NT

COLLARED PRATINCOLE (br.)

Floodplains and estuaries. Dark brown upperparts, buff throat and breast, black collar, and white belly and rump. 25 cm

A: Rooivlerksprinkaanvoël **Z:** Iwamba
Ss: Lehlakangwato La Lepheofubedu **G:** Brachschwalbe

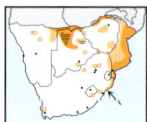

br.

SWALLOW-TAILED BEE-EATER

Dry woodland. Green upperparts and upper breast, yellow throat with blue band, and blue belly and forked tail. 20–22 cm

A: Swaelstertbyvreter
Z: Inkothesankonjane
Ss: Thlapolome Ya Setonolekabelane
Tw: Sabotlhoko
N: swawel-≠are nīb
H: Ondera Yotjiongo
G: Schwalbenschwanzspint

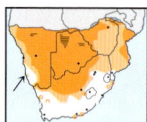

EUROPEAN BEE-EATER

Mixed woodland. Chestnut, yellow and green upperparts, yellow throat, black collar, and blue forehead and underparts. 25–29 cm

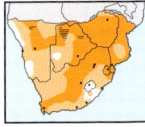

A: Europese Byvreter **Z:** Inkothanyosi
Ss: Thlapolome Ya Leboya
Tw: Seselamarumo Ya Bokone
Sh: Gamanyuchi
H: Ondera Yazonjutji
G: Europäischer Bienenfresser

MOURNING COLLARED DOVE

Riverine woodland. Grey head, black hindcollar, pinkish breast, and yellow eyes. 30 cm

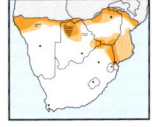

A: Rooioogtortelduif **Z:** Ihobhelililayo
Ss: Mokuru Wa Leihlosehla
N: !huni-mû ≠nais
G: Angolaturteltaube

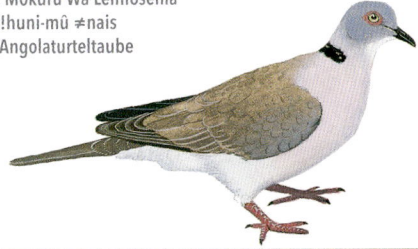

PIED KINGFISHER

Waterbodies. Pied, with stout black bill; male has double breast band; female has single band with gap in centre. Hovers over water before plunging. 28–29 cm

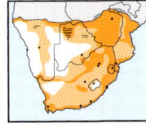

A: Bontvisvanger
Z: Ihlabahlabane
Ss: Seinodi Se Setjhekeho
Tw: Mmatlhapi Yo Monala
H: Ongambura Mahundju Ombonde
G: Graufischer

RED-EYED DOVE

Woodland and suburbia. Pinkish head and breast, broad black hindcollar, and red eyes. 33–36 cm

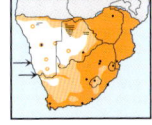

A: Grootringduif
Z: Ihobhelimehlabombu
X: Indlasidudu
Ss: Leebamosu
Tw: Letseba
Ts: Khopola
Sh: Bvukutirwo
N: ǀawa-mû ≠nais
G: Halbmondtaube

RED-CHESTED CUCKOO

Woodland and suburbia.
Grey upperparts, rufous
breast band, barred
underparts, and yellow
eye-ring, lower mandible
and legs. 28 cm

A: Piet-my-vrou
Z: Uphezukomkhono
X: Uphezukomkhono
Ss: Tlo-Nke-Tsoho
Sp: Bjalapeu
Tw: Tlhotlhamedupe Ya Sehubahubidu
Ts: Tsheketani
N: ǀawaǀgã hõhõseb
G: Einsiedlerkuckuck

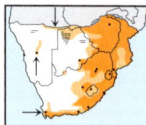

YELLOW-THROATED SANDGROUSE ♂

Short grass and cultivated
lands. Greyish-brown
upperparts, cream-yellow
face and throat, and black
collar. 30 cm

A: Geelkeelsandpatrys
Z: Unogwadulontamephuzi
Ss: Kokwi Ya Mmetsosehla
Tw: Photi-mpha-bogogo
N: !hunidom !nabaris
G: Gelbkehl-Flughuhn

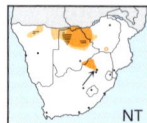

DOUBLE-BANDED SANDGROUSE ♂

Broad-leaved woodland
Brown back with white spots,
plain fawn head and breast,
and black and white breast
band. 25 cm

A: Dubbelbandsandpatrys
Z: Unogwadule Wehlanze
Sp: Sebopa Sa Melabedi
G: Nachtflughuhn

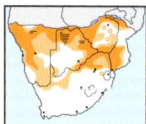

NAMAQUA SANDGROUSE ♂

Arid grass- and scrublands.
Ochre head and long,
pointed tail, buffy underparts,
and black-and-white breast
band. 28 cm

A: Kelkiewyn **Z:** Unogwadule
Ss: Lekgwakgwa **Tw:** Lekotokobii
N: gäxü≠are !nabaris
G: Namaflughuhn

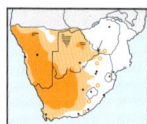

CROWNED LAPWING

Dry open veld. Light brown upperparts, neck and breast, black breast band, black crown with white band, white belly, yellow eyes, and red bill and legs. 30 cm

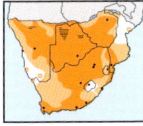

A: Kroonkiewiet
Z: Ititihoyelimqhele
Ss: Lekekeruane La Moqhaka
Tw: Lerweerwee
Sw: Gwegwezi
N: ǁgãxaris
H: Ongurukungwini
G: Kronenkiebitz

LONG-TOED LAPWING

Wetland marshes and flooded areas. Light brown upperparts, black-and-white head, black breast band, and red bill and legs; in flight, shows white wings. 30 cm

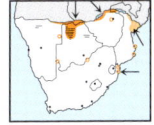

A: Witvlerkkiewiet
Z: Ititihoye Lamazibu
Sp: Thapšane Ya Lephegošweu
Tw: Lerrane La Dikubu
G: Langzehenkiebitz

BLACK-WINGED LAPWING

Hilly grassland. Brown back, grey head, neck and upper breast, black breast band, and white forehead and underparts. 29 cm

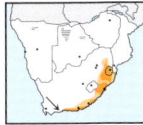

A: Grootswartvlerkkiewiet
Ss: Lekekeruane La Motjhatontsho
Z: Ititihoye
G: Schwarzflügelkiebitz

AFRICAN MARSH HARRIER (juv.)

Marshlands. Dark brown with broad white breast band. 44–49 cm

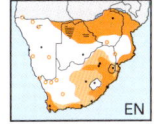

A: Afrikaanse Vleivalk
Z: UmaMhlangenonsundu
Ss: Mmankgodimohlaka Wa Afrika
H: Orukoze Romarindi WaAfrika
G: Froschweihe

juv.

THE IMPACT OF CLIMATE CHANGE ON BIRDS

Shannon Conradie

UNIVERSITY OF CAPE TOWN

Climate change has become one of the hottest topics of the 21st century, with weather records over recent decades revealing unquestionable patterns of rising temperatures and a trend for more frequent and intense heatwaves. However, climate change is not restricted to rising temperatures, but rather overall changes in weather patterns including unpredictable rainfall, droughts, floods and wildfires. These changes are occurring at an unprecedented rate and together with human activities are altering habitats and landscapes affecting virtually all aspects of biodiversity.

Birds are particularly sensitive to the effects of climate change due to them being predominantly small, mostly diurnal and highly active. In order to survive and reproduce successfully, birds need to maintain a constant body temperature, within a narrow range. When environmental temperatures become too hot for them to do so, it leads to behavioural or physical responses.

Range shifts

When temperatures become inhospitable for birds, they may move or shift their ranges to cooler areas, which generally means higher latitudes and/or elevations. For example, in the 1970s the Common Swift extended its range by approximately 1,000 km, from central Namibia to the Cape Peninsula, where it is commonly found today.

Seasonal (phenological) changes

Rising temperatures may result in birds shifting the timing of their migration and breeding to coincide with more favourable conditions. For example, atlas data show that the Red-backed Shrike departs from southern Africa earlier than it did 30 years ago.

Body size changes

In some instances, higher temperatures can lead to decreased body mass. In southern Africa, birds such as the Common Fiscal and Southern Yellow-billed Hornbill have been found to reduce feeding rates of nestlings during hot weather, resulting in slower growth rates and overall smaller nestlings. Appendage size may also change in response to rising temperatures. For instance, a study in Australia revealed that cockatoos and parrots have increased their beak size by 4–10% since the late 1800s, correlated with increases in average temperatures. This adaptation is believed to aid in thermoregulation, as increased beak size can contribute to enhanced heat dissipation, helping these birds cool down more effectively in warmer climates.

In already hot environments, rising temperatures are threatening the ability of birds to survive in these extreme environments or to maintain body temperatures at sublethal levels. Birds exposed to air temperatures above 45 °C over short periods (hours to days) are at risk of perishing due to dehydration as a result of panting, or hyperthermia. Recently a heat-related mortality event was reported in Pongola Nature Reserve in KwaZulu-Natal, when air temperatures exceeded 45 °C, claiming a number of passerines (approximately 47 species), including Blue Waxbills, Fork-tailed Drongos and Green-winged Pytilias, as well as approximately 60 Wahlberg's Epauletted Fruit Bats. While climate change has the potential to increase the risk of such mortalities, the consequences of rising temperatures are generally manifested through more subtle processes and over longer time periods.

Over longer periods (weeks to months) of sustained hot weather these subtle risks arise due to trade-offs between thermoregulation (for example, panting) and activities such as foraging, meaning that it is physically challenging to feed while panting. Under these conditions, birds' foraging efficiency may be compromised to the point where they are unable to maintain body mass at healthy levels, resulting in a number of consequences, including reduced breeding success. Species such as the Southern Yellow-billed Hornbill have been shown to be particularly vulnerable to these subtle risks. A recent study in the Kalahari Desert suggests that if current warming trends persist over the next few years, hornbills in this region are likely to stop breeding entirely by 2027. While most species seem to be negatively affected by climate change, some will thrive. For instance, Pied Crow numbers have dramatically increased in arid parts of southern Africa, which appears to be linked to temperature increases in the region.

There are luckily a few mitigation strategies we can still implement to prevent extinctions across southern Africa. Essential conservation tools include measures such as identifying and maintaining critical sources of water and shade, and providing insulated nest boxes for cavity-breeding birds. In the long-term, conservation efforts need to focus on preserving and maintaining areas that are warming less rapidly, to buffer the effects of climate change on biodiversity.

CITIZEN SCIENCE AND CONSERVATION DATA
Ernst Retief

BIRDLIFE SOUTH AFRICA

Citizen science

Citizen science is a collaborative approach to scientific research that involves members of the public. Volunteers contribute their time and efforts to collect data or participate in other scientific activities. This approach enhances the scale of scientific research, while simultaneously promoting public engagement and awareness.

South Africa has a rich history of citizen science projects, most notably those collecting data on birds. Through projects such as the South African Bird Ringing Unit (SAFRING), Co-ordinated Waterbird Counts (CWAC) and the Southern African Bird Atlas Projects 1 and 2 (SABAP1 and 2), birders have contributed a wealth of knowledge on birds in southern Africa, and even the rest of Africa. These projects have collected a variety of data, such as the distribution of bird species (SABAP2), biometric data such as weight and moult (SAFRING), as well as population data for waterbirds (CWAC). Data collection follows specific scientific-based protocols, meaning that the data can be used for academic and conservation purposes.

The accessibility of digital applications such as **BirdLasser** have enabled the public to seamlessly contribute to the collection of bird data in the areas they visit. Institutions such as **BirdLife South Africa** play a crucial role in bird conservation and environmental advocacy in the region. Consider becoming a member of this group to help support the important work they do in conservation.

Southern African Bird Atlas Project and how the data are used

SABAP2 started in 2007 and is ongoing. Since then, more than 2,000 birders have submitted more than 17 million records to the project. All records are automatically vetted, ensuring that the data in the database are accurate. SABAP2 follows on SABAP1, which ran from 1986 to 1993. Although there are differences in the protocols between the two projects, distribution data can be compared, allowing for analyses over more than three decades, for example, to detect changes in the distribution from 1990 to now.

The data are extremely valuable, and are used to inform bird guides and apps, and for academic and conservation purposes. Most bird field guides and apps now use SABAP2 maps to develop their bird distribution maps. Recently, **BirdLife South Africa's** *GoBirding* website (**https://gobirding.birdlife.org.za/**) added a checklist function, using SABAP2 data. More than 150 scientific papers and 700 articles have used data from SABAP1 and 2.

The red listing of birds is the process of assigning conservation categories, such as Endangered or Vulnerable. Red listing is an important project, as it guides conservation efforts. When **BirdLife South Africa** published a red list in 2015, it made extensive use of data from SABAP1 and 2.

Recently, the data have been used to inform conservation planning in South Africa. The Department of Forestry, Fisheries and the Environment has used SABAP2 data in conjunction with habitat suitability models to inform environmental impact assessments.

The value of these datasets cannot be overstated. Through the efforts of citizens who diligently collect data, at their own time and cost, our knowledge of birds and their distribution has grown significantly. Without their contribution, this would not have been possible.

To join the community of citizen scientists and to participate in this important initiative, visit **https://sabap2.birdmap.africa/howto**.

BIRD NAMES IN THE AFRICAN LANGUAGES OF SOUTHERN AFRICA

Johan Meyer
CHAIR, SOUTH AFRICAN NAMES FOR SOUTH AFRICAN BIRDS (SANSAB)

Birds have historically been known by common names in different languages around the world, predating the scientific binomial naming system introduced by Carolus Linnaeus. Over time, these common names became more species-specific, particularly for birds of cultural or economic significance. However, regional variations in bird names persisted within languages.

With increased global communication and globalisation, there was a growing need to standardise bird names, which has been recently accomplished at an international level for languages such as English, French and Spanish. Locally, the Afrikaans Bird Name Group standardised regional Afrikaans bird names.

Most bird guides in southern Africa now include scientific names and either English or Afrikaans names for each bird species.

However, many speakers of African languages use generic names for various bird species. Efforts to create species-specific bird names in African languages began with Hermann Kolberg's list for Herero in 1986 and continued with Charles Mlingwa's list for Swahili in 1997, among others.

To address this gap, the South African Names for South African Birds (SANSAB) working group was established to develop species-specific common names for birds in all official traditional languages, reflecting cultural and linguistic diversity. To achieve this, SANSAB aims to involve researchers, ornithologists, linguists and mother-tongue speakers of these languages. Initially, SANSAB focused on isiZulu and Sepedi (Northern Sotho). In other African languages, general names for bird groups exist, but species-specific names are rare. Translating names from English to other languages is not a simple task, as new names must capture the essence of birds in the relevant culture.

The naming of birds in African languages encompasses a variety of complex issues, including one name for many species, multiple names for a single species, spelling variations, and different noun classes. Some bird species or groups may lack known names, particularly those not found in specific regions. In African languages, larger and culturally significant birds tend to have species-specific names, while smaller, similar-looking species such as larks may have fewer specific names. Overall, research on bird names in African languages, including KhoeSan languages, is ongoing, aiming to appreciate and conserve the rich birdlife of southern Africa.

USEFUL INFORMATION

Birding information
GoBirding - BirdLife South Africa (birding sites, local guides and accommodation): www.gobirding.birdlife.org.za

Conservation organisations
BirdLife International: www.birdlife.org
BirdLife South Africa: www.birdlife.org.za
BirdLife Botswana: www.birdlifebotswana.org.bw
BirdLife Zimbabwe: www.birdlifezimbabwe.org
World Wildlife Fund for Nature: wwf.org.za
SANCCOB: www.sanccob.co.za
WESSA: www.wessa.org.za

Citizen science
Birdlasser: www.birdlasser.com
Biodiversity & Development Institute: www.thebdi.org

Academic bodies
South African National Biodiversity Institute (SANBI): www.sanbi.org
Southern African Bird Atlas Project: www.sabap2.birdmap.africa
Animal Demography Unit: www.adu.org.za

FitzPatrick Institute of African Ornithology: www.science.uct.ac.za/fitzpatrick

Bird rescue organisations
South African Wildlife Rehabilitation Centre: www.sawrc.org.za/
Vulpro: www.vulpro.com
African Raptor Centre: www.africanraptor.co.za
Mabula Ground Hornbill Project: www.ground-hornbill.org.za
Endangered Wildlife Trust: www.ewt.org.za
Nature's Valley Trust: www.naturesvalleytrust.co.za
Bird of Prey & Rehabilitation Centre: www.birdsofprey.co.za

Social media
Newman's Birds: @newmansbirds (Instagram/Facebook/Telegram)
BirdLife South Africa: @birdlife_sa (Instagram/Facebook)
SA Rare Bird News: sa-rarebirdnews@googlegroups.com
The Birding Life (digital birding magazine and podcasts): www.thebirdinglife.com

Visit **www.newmansbirds.com** or scan the QR code for more information.

REFERENCES

Barnes, K.N. (ed.) 1998. *The Important Bird Areas of Southern Africa*. BirdLife South Africa, Johannesburg. Reference framework presenting estimated numbers of threatened species in the region's most important bird conservation localities.

Barnes, K.N. (ed.) 2000. *The Eskom Red Data Book of Birds of South Africa, Lesotho and Swaziland*. BirdLife South Africa, Johannesburg. Focuses on the conservation of and threats facing the region's endangered species.

BirdLife International. 2022. Mapping of global threats using the IUCN Red List reveals hunting and trapping is the most prevalent threat to birds. http://datazone. birdlife.org/2022-annual-update.

Blondel, J. 2022. How do birds adapt to a changing climate? *Encyclopedia of the Environment*. https://www.encyclopedie-environnement.org/en/life/how-birds-adapt-changing-climate.

Chittenden, H., Davies, G. & Weiersbye, I. 2016. *Roberts Bird Guide*. Jacana, Johannesburg. Condensed version of the voluminous *Roberts Birds of Southern Africa*, focusing on field identification.

Harfoot, M.B.J., Johnston, A., Balmford, A., Burgess, N.D., Butchart, S.H.M., Dias, M.P., Hazin, C., Hilton-Taylor, C., Hoffman, M., Isaac, N.J.B., Iversen, L.L., Outhwaite, C.L., Visconti, P. & Geldmann, J. 2021. Using the IUCN Red List to map threats to terrestrial vertebrates at global scale. *Nat. Ecol. Evol.*, 5:1510–1519.

Maia, R., D'Alba, L. & Shawkey, M.D. What makes a feather shine? A nanostructural basis for glossy black colours in feathers. *Proc. Biol. Sci.* 2011 Jul 7;278(1714):1973–80. Cornell Lab of Ornithology, Ithaca, NY, USA. https://doi.org/10.1098/rspb.2010.1637. Epub 2010 Dec 1. PMID: 21123257; PMCID: PMC3107640.

Newman, K. 2003. *What's that Bird? A starter's guide to birds of southern Africa*. Struik Nature, Cape Town. Introduces the reader to the region's rich bird diversity by highlighting the main bird groups.

Newman, V. & Newman, K. 2010. *Newman's Birds of Southern Africa*. Struik Nature, Cape Town. Comprehensive field guide to birds of the southern African region.

RSPB.org.uk. https://www.rspb.org.uk/birds-and-wildlife/wildlife-guides/birdwatching/how-to-identify-birds/abnormal-colouration-of-birds/.

Van Grouw, H. The dark side of birds: melanism – facts and fiction. *Bulletin of the British Ornithologists' Club*, 137(1), 12–36, (13 March 2017). https://bioone.org/journals/bulletin-of-the-british-ornithologists-club/volume-137/issue-1/bboc.v137i1.2017.a9/The-dark-side-of-birds-melanismfacts-and-fiction/10.25226/bboc.v137i1.2017.a9.full.

Winkler, D.W., Billerman, S.M., & Lovette, I.J. 2020. Family Procellariidae: shearwaters and petrels (Procellariidae), version 1.0. In Billerman, S.M., Keeney, B.K., Rodewald, P.G. & Schulenberg, T.S. (eds), *Birds of the World*. Cornell Lab of Ornithology, Ithaca, NY, USA. https://doi.org/10.2173/bow.procel3.01.

Yin, H., Shi, L., Sha, J., Li, Y., Qin, Y., Dong, B., Meyer, S., Liu, X., Zhao, L. & Zi, J. Iridescence in the neck feathers of domestic pigeons. *Phys. Rev. E*. Stat Nonlin Soft Matter Phys. 2006 Nov; 74(5 Pt 1):051916. Cornell Lab of Ornithology, Ithaca, NY, USA. https://doi.org/10.1103/PhysRevE.74.051916. Epub 2006 Nov 22. PMID: 17279948.

GLOSSARY

Band
A horizontal stripe of colour, as in tail band.

Cap
Top of the head above the eyes.

Casque
Horny cap or protuberance on the bill or head.

Cere
Soft base of the beak in parrots, pigeons and birds of prey.

Coverts
Feathers that cover the ears, wings, etc.

Crest
Plume or tuft of feathers on a bird's head.

Crown
Topmost part of the head.

Culmen
Top ridge of the bird's upper mandible.

Eye-stripe
A band of colour, often black, in front of and behind the eye.

Gape
Corner of the mouth where the mandibles are hinged.

Gular region
Sides of the throat.

Hood
Colouring of the top of the head when it extends to below the eyes.

Lore
Area between the eye and the beak on either side of a bird's head.

Mandibles
Upper and lower jaws of a bird.

Mantle
The upper back adjacent to the lower back.

Mask
A wide area of colour (wider than an eye-stripe) surrounding the eyes.

Moustachial streak
A line of colour extending from the bird's gape.

Nape
Back of the head.

Pectoral region
Sides of the upper breast.

Primaries
Major flight feathers on the outer part of the wing.

Rectrices
Tail feathers; rectrix in the singular.

Secondaries
Second most important flight feathers lying between the primary feathers and the body.

Speculum
Patch of iridescent colour on secondary upperwing feathers of some ducks.

Streak
A vertical mark, longer than a spot.

Underwing coverts
Contour feathers covering the forward part of a bird's wing.

Vent
Feathered region covering the bird's anus.

Wattles
Fleshy appendages, usually highly coloured, that hang from the gape or the lores.

ACKNOWLEDGEMENTS

I want to take a moment to express my deepest gratitude and heartfelt appreciation to all those who have supported me in completing this book. I am incredibly grateful to my family and friends, who have provided me with unwavering encouragement, support and understanding throughout this journey. To my late father and mother, Ken and Ursula, for countless trips into the bush and for quiet, percolated knowledge. To Elmarie, who has been my constant source of support, even checking if I'm still in touch with reality when I've spent too long staring at a screen. Your calmness, ability to break down problems into manageable solutions, and unwavering belief in me has been invaluable and I thank you more than words can express.

I would also like to thank my sisters for their support and encouragement, as well as their work on updating and modifying the images. To Evan and Cailyn, my amazing kids, who have patiently accompanied me on yet another birding holiday and kept their cool while I check yet another dove's foot. I hope your love for the bush grows and grows.

I am immensely grateful to Maurice van der Merwe for his genuine support, passion, and companionship in the field, and for his willingness to supply snacks; his patience as I experimented with different learning processes has been a great help. In addition, Andrew Wigget and family are thanked for their enthusiasm and spark to keep exploring birding sites.

Sincere thanks to Johan Meyer, Andrew de Blocq and all involved in the INSAB for the assistance with African names, Ernst Retief and Alen Lee and BirdLife South Africa for the assistance on birding key biodiversity areas and status of birds, and to Shannon Conradie for her contributions on climate change.

Thanks to Pippa Parker and the Struik Nature team, in particular Colette Alves for her hard work, calmness and steady hand in refreshing and bringing to life this new edition.

I have mentioned how photography is becoming an integral part of the birder's equipment, and I certainly could not have done this without the kind and generous assistance from the photographers who have contributed to the Newman's Birding Community. Firstly, a big thank you to Brian Robert, Roger Hogg and Rob Cliff, who have supported me from the beginning and who have been unbelievable in their generosity of world-class images. Also, Robyn Soutar and Johan Wandrag, who have been consistent throughout my project requests. Also Per Holmen, Johan van Rensburg, Derek Keats, Paul Ellis, Pieter Verheij, Nigel Voaden, Ken Pinchuck, Andy Wilson and Tinus Lamprecht.

Once again, thank you to everyone who has supported me along the way. Your kindness, generosity, and belief in me have made all the difference, and I am forever grateful.

NICHOLAS NEWMAN

PHOTOGRAPHIC CREDITS

Key: b = bottom, l = left, m = middle, r = right, t = top
AS = stock.adobe.com, BR = Brian Roberts, IOA = Images of Africa, JW = Johan Wandrag, NN = Nicholas Newman,
RH = Roger Hogg, RS = Robyn Soutar, SS = Shutterstock.com, WC = via Wikimedia Commons

p7: vxnaghiyev/AS; **p11**: ward/AS; **p14**: duelune/AS; **p19**: michal/AS; **p20**: henk bogaard/AS; **p21**: Golubev Dmitrii/AS; **p25**: Andrew/AS; **p27**: Jon/AS; **p28**: jacojvr/AS; **p31** tl: rock ptarmigan/SS, tr, bl and br: RH; **p32** tl: RH, tr: Albert Froneman/IOA, m: Andrew Spencer, bl: BR, br: Warwick Tarboton; **p33** tl: Braam/AS, tr: RH, bl: BR, br: AGAMI/AS; **p34** tl: etienne07/SS, tr and m: Kim/AS, bl: BR, br: AGAMI/SS; **p35** tl and br: JAG IMAGES/AS, tr: Daniel Danckwerts/SS, bl: ChrWeiss/AS; **p36** tl: Pascale Gueret/AS, tr: Alta Oosthuizen/AS, bl: Brian Scantlebury/AS, br: David/AS; **p37** tl: Megan Paine/AS, tr: prochym/AS, m: R Cliff, bl: David/AS, br: Rixie/AS; **p38** tl: Jurgens/AS, tr and bl: RH, br: JMx Images/SS; **p39** tl: Hedrus/AS, tr: INGO WASCHKIES, bl: Jane Fourie/AS, br: JMx Images/SS; **p40** tl: Albert Froneman/IOA, tr: Thomas/AS, m: Marc/AS, bl: BR, br: Donal Mullins/SS; **p41** tl: Straystone/SS, tr and br: ondreprosicky/AS; bl: Jurgens/AS; **p42** tl: Kandarp/AS, tr: JAG IMAGES/AS, bl: RS, br: Ian/AS; **p43**: PACO COMO/AS, tr: RS, bl: Karlos Lomsky/AS, br: Warwick Tarboton; **p44** tl: RH, tr: Harry Collins/AS, bl: Charles/AS, br: EcoView/AS; **p45** tl: Riaan van den Berg/AS, tr: Dewald/AS, bl: Roger le la Harpe/AS, br: Kim/AS; **p46** tl: Riaan van den Berg/AS, tr: NN, bl: Warwick Tarboton, br: Neil Ebedes; **p47** tl: cherwoman/AS, tr: Warwick Tarboton, bl: EcoView/AS, br: Frans Vandevalle, CC BY-SA 3.0; **p48** tl: RS, tr: Albert Froneman/IOA, bl: RH, br: BR; **p49** tl: RS, tr: Jp Vd Merwe/Wirestock Creators/AS, bl and br: PACO COMO/AS; **p51** tl: phototrip.cz/AS, tr: AGAMI/AS, bl: BR, br: Eckhard/AS; **p52** tl: Nick Hobgood/AS, tr male and female: RH, m: Thinus/AS, bl: feathercollector/AS, br: phototrip.cz/AS; **p53** tl: Duncan Noakes/AS, tr: Nigel Voaden, bl and br: PACO COMO/AS; **p54**: tl: PACO COMO/AS, tr: Alta Oosthuizen/AS, bl: Frank McClintock/SS, br male: C Raphael Nussbaumer, female: Alex Rocha; **p55** tl: Stacey Ann Alberts/SS, tr: Cathy Withers-Clarke/AS, ml: PACO COMO/AS, mr and br: AGAMI/AS, bl: Albert Froneman/IOA; **p56** tl: David/AS, tr: gallas/AS, ml: RH, mr: Alta Oosthuizen/AS, bl: Walter Summer, br: PACO COMO/AS; **p57** tl: Daniel Danckwerts/SS, tr: JMx Images/SS, bl: Megan Paine/AS, br: Regard van dyk/SS; **p58** tl: Regard van dyk/SS, tr: rock ptarmigan/SS, m, bl and br: RH; **p59** tl and br: BR, tr: RH, bl: JW; **p60** tl: RH, tr: Gareth/AS, m: Lynette Knott Rudman/SS, bl: Daniel Danckwerts/SS, br: David/AS; **p61** tl and br: RH, tr: Jurie/AS, br: Eleanor Esterhuizen/SS; **p62** tl: AGAMI/AS, tr: phototrip.cz/AS, bl: MSM/AS, br: JAG IMAGES/AS; **p63** tl: Supakit/AS, tr: ChrWeiss/AS, m: Walter Summer, bl: RS, br: paulfell/AS; **p64** tl: Boshoff/AS, tr: BR, bl: Alta Oosthuizen/AS, br: Daniel Jara/AS; **p65** tl: AGAMI/AS, tr and m: Erni/AS, bl: EcoView/AS, br: RH; **p66** tl: RH, tr: JAG IMAGES/AS, m: Sergey Ryzhkov/AS, bl: David/AS, br: BR; **p67** tl and tr: AGAMI/AS, bl: Agami Photo Agency/SS, br: vinx83/AS; **p68** tl: Kandarp/AS, tr: JAG IMAGES/AS, m: NN, bl: Frank McClintock/SS, br: Jonathan Oberholster/AS; **p69** tl: phototrip.cz/AS, tr: BR, bl: Jaynes Gallery/Danita Delimont/AS, br: Martin Mecnarowski/AS; **p70**: KikkiaJackson/AS, tr: Nico Smit, bl: RS, br: aussieanouk/AS; **p71**: RS, tr: Bryony/AS, bl: Roger de la Harpe/AS, br: phototrip.cz/AS; **p72** tl: Marius Dobilas/SS, tr: Brian E Kushner/AS, bl: Charles/AS, br: RH; **p73** tl: RH, tr: Ken Griffiths/AS, m: Peter/AS, bl: Riverwalker/AS; **p74** tl: Ian/AS, tr: Jean van der Meulen/AS, bl: EcoView/AS, br: Marek R. Swadzba/AS; **p75** tl: Banu/AS, tr: Nick Dale/AS, m: Eric Isselée/AS, bl: Jp Vd Merwe/Wirestock Creators/AS, br: EcoView/AS; **p76** tl: AGAMI/AS, tr: RH, bl: EcoView/AS, br: wayne/AS; **p77** tl: RH, tr: Erni/AS, bl: EcoView/AS, br: Valerie/AS; **p78** tl: RH, tr: AGAMI/AS, bl: Jurgens/AS, br: Paul/AS; **p79**: WildMedia/AS, tr: PIOTR/AS, bl and br: phototrip.cz/AS; **p81** tl: Paul Ellis, tr: Lars Espeter/AS, bl: selim kaya photography/SS, br: Matthew/AS; **p82** tl: Charl/AS, tr: Peter/AS, bl: RH, br: Johan van Rensburg; **p83** tl: David/AS, tr: NN, bl: C Rob Cliff, br: Regard van dyk/SS; **p84** tl: Derek Keats from Johannesburg, South Africa, CC BY 2.0, WC, tr: Daniel Danckwerts/SS, m: PACO COMO/AS, bl: BR, br: RH; **p85** tl: BR, tr: PACO COMO/AS, bl: Cathy Withers-Clarke/AS, br: Andrew M Allport/SS; **p86** tl: AGAMi/AS, tr: David/AS, bl: geoffsp/AS, br: Oleg Chernyshev/AS; **p87** tl: Regard van dyk/SS, tr: Lynette Knott Rudman/SS, bl: Gareth/AS, br: Alfie/AS; **p88** tl: 2015 Erni/SS, tr: NN, m: Robb Cliff, bl: Simon Stobart/AS, br: Alta Oosthuizen/AS; **p89** tl: phototrip.cz/AS, tr: BR, m: Jurgens/AS, bl: PACO COMO/AS, br: RH; **p90** tl: Jurgens/AS, tr and bl: RH, m: RS, br: BR; **p91** tl: EcoView/AS, tr: AGAMI/AS, bl: Charl/AS, br: Charles J. Sharp, CC BY-SA 4.0, WC; **p92** tl: David/AS, tr and m: Erni/AS, bl: Alta Oosthuizen/AS, br: Joe Ravi/AS; **p93** tl: PACO COMO/AS, tr: Lukas/AS, bl: Gerrit de Vries/AS, br: Tinus Lamprecht; **p94** tl and bl: Erni/AS, tr: AGAMI/AS, br: EcoView/AS; **p95**: PACO COMO/AS, tr: Tarpan/SS, bl: Weranut/AS, br: alan1951/AS; **p96** tl: JW, tr: Tim on Tour/AS, bl: ASakoulis – AS, br: Jurgens/AS; **p97** tl: Jurgens/AS, tr: Roelof Jonkers/SS, bl: MarnaB/SS, br: emranashraf/AS; **p98** tl: StockPhotoAstur/AS, tr: BR, bl: Sergey Ryzhkov/AS, br: slowmotiongli/AS; **p99** tl: Marc/AS, tr: Erni/AS, bl: Agami Photo Agency/SS, br: Hans/AS; **p100** tl: AGAMI/AS, tr: NN, m: RH, bl: RS, br: Designpics/AS; **p101** tl: Sunjoy Monga/SS, tr: Ian/AS, m: RH, bl: BR, br: aussieanouk/AS; **p102** tl: Martin PELANEK/AS, tr: RS, bl: BR, br: dennisjacobsen/AS; **p103** tl and bl: PACO COMO/AS, tr: Riverwalker/AS, br: Ken Griffiths/AS; **p104** tl: Braam/AS, tr: RH, bl: Jurgens/AS, br: RS; **p105**: tl: RH, tr: henk bogaard/AS, bl: JAG IMAGES/AS, br: RH; **p106** tl and bl: BR, tr: Leandro/AS, br: RH; **p107** tl: Dr Ajay Kumar Singh/AS, tr Albert Froneman/IOA, bl: RS, br: EcoView/AS; **p109** tl: Frank Lambert/AS, tr: RS, m: PACO COMO/AS, bl: AGAMI/AS, br: Daniel Jara/AS; **p110** tl and tr: EcoView/AS, m: RH, bl: RH, br: Robert Schneider/AS; **p111**: chungking/AS, tr: Hans/AS, bl: vxnaghiyev/AS, br: Chris/AS; **p112** tl and tr: AGAMI/AS, bl: andreanita/AS, br: Paul/AS; **p113** tl: JAG IMAGES/AS, tr: Albert Froneman/IOA, bl: ondrejprosicky/AS, br: byrdyak/AS; **p115** tl: RH, tr: bennytrapp/AS, bl: Michael Potter11/SS, br: Alta Oosthuizen/AS; **p116** tl: NN, tr: Albert Froneman/IOA, bl: Ian White, br: RS; **p117** tl: Alta Oosthuizen/AS, tr: Jukka Jantunen/SS, bl: creativenature.nl/AS, br: Albert Froneman/IOA; **p118** tl: Alta Oosthuizen/AS, tr: RS, bl and br: RH; **p119**: tl: PACO COMO/AS, tr: Nick Dale/AS, bl: RH, br: BR; **p120** tl: Cat Clarke/AS, tr: JAG IMAGES/AS, bl: Nick Greaves/SS, br: Stan Culley/AS; **p121** tl: Frans Vandewalle (@snarfel), tr: Juan.paz1/AS, bl: JAG IMAGES/AS, br: RS; **p122** tl: Bryony/AS, tr: henk bogaard/AS, bl: RH, br: WildMedia/AS; **p123** tl: Robert Hainer/AS, tr: John/AS, bl: Marie28/Wirestock Creators/AS, br: EcoView/AS; **p124** tl: AGAMI/AS, tr: PACO COMO/AS, bl: Charles J. Sharp, CC BY-SA 4.0, WC, br: RH; **p125** tl: RH, tr: stuporter/AS, bl: BR, br: JAG IMAGES/AS; **p126** tl: SunflowerMomma/AS, tr: Michael de Nysschen/AS, bl: EcoView/AS, br: RH; **p127** tl: KikkiaJackson/AS, tr and br: RH, bl: Gypsey Picture Show/AS; **p129** tl: PIOTR/AS, tr: BR, bl: PACO COMO/AS, br: phototrip.cz/AS; **p130** tl: Thinus/AS, tr: NN, bl: RH, br: AGAMI/AS; **p131** tl: RH, tr: RS, bl: BR, br: tom/AS; **p132** tl: Duncan Noakes/AS, tr: Andrew/AS, ml AGAMI/AS, bl: Daryl Dell, br: EcoView/AS; **p133** tl: Lynette/AS, tr: henk Bogaard/AS, bl: RH, br: PACO COMO/AS; **p134** tl: henk Bogaard/AS, tr: Daniel Danckwerts/SS, m: PACO COMO/AS, bl: Per Holmen, br: JAG IMAGES/AS; **p135** tl: Ward Poppe/SS, tr: BR, bl: ward/AS, br: Stoffel/AS; **p136** tl: Marc/AS, tr: PACO COMO/AS, bl: phototrip.cz/AS, br: RH; **p137** tl: gergo Nagy/SS, tr: Rob Cliff, bl: JW, br: mrallen/AS; **p138** tl: PACO COMO/AS, tr: Albert Froneman/IOA, bl: BR, br: AGAMI/AS; **p139** tl and bl: David/AS, tr: Alta Oosthuizen/AS, ml: Karlos Lomsky/AS, mr: Erni/AS, br: Erni/SS; **p140** tl: Gerrit de Vries/AS, tr: henk Bogaard/AS, bl: RH, br: RH; **p141** tl: Kevin/AS, tr: EcoView, bl: Alta Oosthuizen/AS, br: Gerrit de Vries/AS; **p142** tl: BR, tr: Michael de Nysschen/SS, bl: rugco/AS, br: EcoView/AS; **p143** tl: RH, tr: phototrip.cz/AS, m: Ondrej Prosicky/AS, bl: JW, br: Martin Mecnarowski/AS; **p144** tl: Claude/AS, tr: BR, bl and br: RH; **p145** tl: BR, tr: JAG IMAGES/AS, bl: phototrip.cz/AS, br: ondrejprosicky/AS; **p147** tl: Duncan Noakes/AS, tr: Charl/AS, bl: wonder of birds/Derek Keats, br: Dirk/AS; **p 148** tl, tr and bl: RH, br: Niall Perrins/AS; **p149** tl: RS, tr: Alta Oosthuizen/AS, bl: NN, br: Jukka Jantunen/SS; **p150** tl: creativenature.nl/AS, tr: phototrip.cz/AS, bl: Andre Valadao/SS, br: AGAMI/AS; **p151** tl: phototrip.cz/AS, tr: David/AS, bl: Charl/AS, br: AGAMI/AS; **p152** tl: Michael de Nysschen/AS, tr: Rob Cliff, bl: Evelyn Joubert/SS, br: Charl/AS; **p153** tl: Kim/AS, tr: ingehogenbijl/SS, m: Rob Cliff, bl: RH, br: NN; **p154** tl: Alta Oosthuizen/AS, tr, m and bl: RH, br: RS; **p155** tl: RH, tr: dan/AS, bl: AGAMI/AS, br: Harold Stiver/AS; **p157** tl: Clayton Burne/SS, tr: Eleanor Esterhuizen/SS, bl: BR, br: Duncan Noakes/AS; **p158** tl: Ben's Lens/Wirestock Creators/AS, tr: Derek Keats, bl: RealityImages/AS, br: Regard van dyk/SS; **p159** tl, tr and bl: RH, br: Stéphane Bidouze/AS; **p160** tl: Jesus/AS, tr: AGAMI/AS, bl: fotoparus/AS, br: Peter/AS; **p161** tl: AGAMI/AS, tr and m: RH, bl: PIOTR/AS, br: Alta Oosthuizen/AS; **p162** tl: Albert Froneman/IOA, tr: photoJS/SS, m: Paul Ellis, bl: BR, br:

EcoView/AS; **p163** tl: Ondrej Prosicky/SS, tr: etienneb07/SS, bl and br: Kim/AS; **p164** tl: ChrWeiss/AS, tr: Per Holmen, bl: RH, br: Peter Hawrylyshyn; **p165** tl: Albert Froneman/IOA, tr: EcoView/AS, bl: Charl/AS, br: Roger de la Harpe/AS; **p166** tl: JR Gale/SS, tr: Nathan O'Reilly, bl: Alta Oosthuizen/AS, br: DirkR/AS; **p167** tl: Christopher Sloan, tr: RH, bl: PACO COMO/AS, br: Eckhard/AS; **p168** tl: Nick Hobgood/AS, tr and bl: RH, br: Evelyn Joubert/SS; **p169** tl: JW, tr: JMx Images/SS, bl: PACO COMO/AS, br: Harold Stiver/AS; **p170** tl: Slavia/AS, tr: michaklootwijk/AS, bl: Alta Oosthuizen/AS, br: Kim/AS; **p171** tl: Jurgens/AS, tr: RH, m: Rob Cliff, bl: Charl/AS, br: Mac Two Photography/SS; **p172** tl: Johan Swanepoel/AS, tr: David/AS, m: derek82/AS, bl: RS, br: Cathy Withers-Clarke/AS; **p173** tl: PACO COMO/AS, tr: Charles J. Sharp, CC BY-SA 4.0, WC, bl and br: Villiers/AS; **p175** tl and m: RH, tr: PACO COMO/AS, bl: BR, br: James/AS; **p176** tl: Chris Troch/SS, tr: NN, m: Alta Oosthuizen/AS, b all: RH; **p177** tl: AGAMI/AS, BR, tr: Lars Esppeter/AS, bl and br: RH/AS; **p178** tl: BR, tr: Ward Poppe/SS, m: Kim/AS, bl: RH, br: ward/AS; **p179** tl: phototrip.cz/AS, tr and bl: RH, br: derek82/AS; **p180** tl: Mohit/AS, tr: AGAMI/AS, bl: PACO COMO/AS, br: Richard/AS; **p181** tl: Warwick Tarboton, tr: BR, ml: Robby Holmwood/SS, mr and bl: Warwick Tarboton, br: Dubi Shapiro/AS; **p182** tl: JAG IMAGES/AS, tr: Villiers/AS, m: Warwick Tarboton, bl: Jurgens/AS, br: PACO COMO/AS; **p183** tl: Ellie/AS, tr: PACO COMO/AS, m: Karlos Lomsky/AS, bl: Per Holmen, br: LapTak/AS; **p184** tl: dan/AS, tr: Lynette/AS, m: EcoView/AS, bl: Pappa Pabitra/SS, br: BR; **p185** tl: Lars Buck, tr: Jonthan Sellors/Wirestock Creators/AS, bl: Eduard Drost/AS, br: Jp Vd Merwe/Wirestock Creators/AS; **p187** tl: Francesco Veronesi, CC BY-SA 2.0, WC, tr: mrallen/AS, bl: James/AS, br: amit/AS; **p188** tl: Thinus/AS, tr: BR, bl: Alta Oosthuizen/AS, br: JAG IMAGES/AS; **p189** tl: Cat Clarke/AS, tr: Juan.paz1/AS, bl: Nick Greaves/SS, br: EcoView/AS; **p190** tl: EcoView/AS, tr: Marie28/Wirestock Creators/AS, m: Jurgens/AS, bl: John/AS, br: wolfavni/AS; **p191** tl: Joe Ravi/AS, tr: EcoView/AS, m: stuporter/AS, bl: suerob/AS, br: Michael de Nysschen/SS; **p193** tl: BR, tr: Alta Oosthuizen/AS, bl: Warwick Tarboton, br: dan/AS; **p194** tl: JW, tr: gallas/AS, bl: Alta Oosthuizen, br: Roger de la Harpe/AS; **p195** tl: JMx Images/SS, tr and m: PACO COMO/AS, bl: Milan/AS, br: Jurgens/AS; **p196** tl: Albert Froneman/IOA, tr: Walter Summer, bl: Alta Oosthuizen/AS, br: Markus Lilje; **p197** tl: Regard van dyk/SS, tr: Correia Patrice/SS, bl: RH, br: Paco COMO/AS; **p198** tl: Krista Oswald, tr: Cathy Withers-Clarke/AS, m: Peter/AS, bl: Daniel Danckwerts/SS, br: NN; **p199** tl: AGAMI/AS, tr: BR, bl: RH, br: Hanz/AS; **p200** tl: Jurgens/AS, tr: Robb Cliff, bl: Erni/SS, br: Piyapong Chotipuntu/SS; **p201** tl: Alta Oosthuizen/AS, tr: PACO COMO/AS, m: Szymon Bartosz/AS, bl: Alta Oosthuizen/AS, br: BR; **p202** tl: Kim/AS, tr: phototrip.cz/AS, bl: PACO COMO/AS, br: Adrian De La Paz/Wirestock Creators/AS; **p203** tl: RH, tr: Frank/AS, bl: Kelly Ermis/AS, br: pschoema; **p204** tl: AGAMI/AS, tr and br: RH, bl: Daniel Danckwerts/SS; **p205** tl: prin79/AS, tr: David/AS, bl: RS, br: Jurgens/AS; **p206** tl: Grzegorz/AS, tr: Mike/AS, bl: Tim on Tour/AS, br: PACO COMO/AS; **p207** tl: Per Holmen, tr: Johan van Rensburg, bl: ondrejprosicky/AS, br: gergosz/SS; **p208** tl: Weranut/AS, tr: David/AS, m: EcoView/AS, bl: Jurgens/AS, br: Marc/AS; **p209** tl: Marius Dobilas/SS, tr: Dave Montreuil/SS, bl: Designpics/AS, br: RH; **p210** tl: phototrip.cz/AS, tr: JW, bl: ArtushFoto/AS, br: JAG IMAGES/AS; **p211** tl: Sunflower Momma/SS, tr: Jurgens/AS, m: Albert Froneman/IOA, bl: Marek R. Swadzba/AS, br: Elzet du Plessis; **p212** tl: Neil Lazarus, tr: RS, m: RH, bl: Damian/AS, br: tonymills/AS; **p213** tl: ondrejprosicky/AS, tr: RH, bl: JW, br: Aitor/AS; **p215** tl: BR, tr: David/AS, bl: Alta Oosthuizen/SS, br: AGAMI/AS,; **p216** tl: Pieter Verheij, tr: Daniel Danckwerts/AS, bl: Joris Komen, br: Peter/AS; **p217** tl: AGAMI/AS, tr: Sergey Ryzhkov, bl: Per Holmen, br: Don Reid; **p218** tl: David/AS, tr: AGAMI/AS, bl: Alta Oosthuizen/AS, br: Matthew/AS; **p219** tl: Kim/AS, tr: Regard van dyk/SS, bl: Kelly Ermis/AS, br: Clayton Burne/AS; **p220** tl: Per Holmen, tr: Nigel J. Dennis, bl: Regard van dyk/SS, br: phototrip.cz/AS; **p221** tl and br: BR, m: Jurgens/AS, bl: Regard van dyk/SS, br: Andrew M. Allport/SS; **p222** tl: NN, tr: RH, bl and br: Daniel Danckwerts/SS; **p223** tl: Louis/AS, tr: Paul Ellis, bl: R. Jeff Huth/AS, br: Bouke Atema/SS; **p224** tl: Mariette Vogel/SS, tr and br: BR, bl: AGAMI/AS; **p225** tl: BR, tr: Edward/AS, bl: Tatiana/AS, br: PACO COMO/AS; **p226** tl and tr: RH, bl: NN, br: Kim/SA; **p227** tl: RH, tr: PACO COMO/AS, bl: phototrip.cz, br: JW; **p228** tl: Cathy Withers-Clarke/AS, tr and bl: BR, br: RH; **p229** tl: Kim/AS, tr: RS, bl: Johan van Rensburg, br: RH; **p230** tl: BR, tr: Dylan Vasapolli, bl: Villiers/AS, br: Kim/AS; **p231** tl: AGAMI/AS, tr and bl: Erni/AS, br: Wildlife World/SS; **p232** tl: Jukka Jantunen/SS, tr: Simon_g/SS, bl: OvidiuDaniel/AS, br: Nico Smit/Wirestock/AS; **p233** tl: michaklootwijk/AS, tr: RH, bl: Holger Teichmann, br: poco_bw/AS; **p234** tl: Hanz/AS, tr: Jurgens/AS, bl: wolfavni/AS, br: alan1951/AS; **p235** tl: paula/AS, tr: Derek Keats from Johannesburg, South Africa, CC BY 2.0, WC, bl: Martin Mecnarowski/AS, br: Mark Beckwith/SS; **p236** tl: Hanz/AS, tr: Kim/AS, bl: shams Faraz Amir/AS, br: Martin Mecnarowski/AS; **p237** tl: Claude/AS, tr: Kim/AS, bl: Nigel Key, br: Villiers/AS; **p238** tl: Sander Meertins/AS, tr: Richard Guijt Photography/SS, bl: Riaan van den Berg/AS, br: Thinus van Staden/SS; **p239** tl: BR, tr: Chris Renshaw/SS, bl: Johan van Rensburg, br: Luc van der Biest; **p240** tl: RH, tr: Marius Dobilas/SS, bl: Designpics/AS, br: JW; **p241** tl: Albert Froneman/IOA, tr: selim/AS, bl: Langer/AS, br: Brian E Kushner/AS; **p242** tl: Alberto Torres Castro/SS, tr: Tim on Tour/AS, bl: Martin Mecnarowski/AS, br: Peter/AS; **p243** tl: EcoView/AS, tr: Seymour/AS, bl: Grzegorz/AS, br: JW; **p244** tl: AGAMI/AS, tr: RS, bl: Nick Dale/AS, br: RH; **p245** tl: AGAMI/AS, tr: surassawadee/AS, bl: Louis/AS, br: Erni/AS; **p246** tl: EcoView/AS, tr and br: RH, br: JW; **p247** tl: Peter/AS, tr: Gunter/AS, bl: RH, br: EcoView/AS; **p249** tl: dennisjacobsen/AS, tr: Gunter/AS, bl: RH, br: Beate/AS; **p250** tl: BR, tr: PACO COMO/AS, bl: Duncan Noakes/AS, br: Alta Oosthuizen/AS; **p251** tl and br: Alta Oosthuizen/AS, tr: MK Oosthuizen, bl: Nigel Voaden; **p252** tl: Andrew M. Allport/SS, tr: PACO COMO/AS, bl: Albert Froneman/IOA, br: Steve Byland/AS; **p253** tl: PACO COMO/AS, tr: Stacey Ann Alberts/SS, bl: giedriius/AS, br: slowmotiongli/AS; **p254** tl: Wirestock Creators/AS, tr: PACO COMO/SS, m: Michael Potter 11/SS, bl: wolfavni, br: NN; **p255** tl: Piyapong Chotipuntu/SS, tr: Frank Lambert/AS, bl: Jurgens/AS, br: geoffsp/AS; **p256** tl: NN, tr: ondrejprosicky/AS, m: BR, bl: Denielle/AS; **p257** tl: Bernard DUPONT from FRANCE, CC BY-SA, WC, tr: Simon Stobart/AS, bl: Braam/AS, br: JAG IMAGES/AS; **p258** tl: RH, tr: David/AS, m: Ar Ajay Kumar Singh/AS, bl: Roger de la Harpe/AS, br: EcoPrint/SS; **p259** tl: AGAMI/AS, tr and br: BR, br: mattiaath/AS; **p260** tl: Karlos Lomsky/AS, tr: Lukas/AS, bl: Alta Oosthuizen/SA, br: Gerrit de Vries/AS; **p261** tl: PACO COMO/AS, tr: Albert Froneman/IOA, bl: Adrian/AS, br: Graeme Hatley/AS; **p262** tl: pschoema/AS, tr: Clayton Burne/SS, ml: PACO COMO/AS, mr: Romas Vysniauskas, bl: NaturalWorldLover, br: Shumba138/AS; **p263** tl: RS, tr: Kelly Ermis/AS, m: EcoView/SA, bl: RH, br: Bryony/AS; **p264** tl: Frank/AS, tr: Nigel Forrow, bl: Alta Oosthuizen/AS, br: irinabal18/AS; **p265** tl: Wim/AS, tr: Jandre Verster, bl: Thomas/AS, br: Sergey Ryzhkov/AS; **p266**: tl: Erni/AS, tr: EcoView/AS, bl: Petr Šimon/AS, br: Angela/AS; **p267** tl: Selim_KAYA/AS, tr: BR, bl: Alta Oosthuizen/AS, br: Ondrej Prosicky/SS; **p268** tl: RH, tr: ann gadd/AS, bl: massimhokuto/AS, br: Albert Froneman; **p269** tl: VOLODYMYR KUCHERENKO/AS, tr: Per Holmen/AS, bl: nwdph/SS, br: Johan van Rensburg; **p270** tl: phototrip.cz/AS, tr: Michael Potter 11/SS, bl: Bryony/AS, br: RS; **p271** tl: Cathy Withers-Clarke/AS, tr: EcoView/AS, bl: Shumba138/AS, br: Riaan van Berg/SA; **p272** tl: Seymour/AS, tr: Hans/AS, bl: Nick Dale/SA, br: EcoView/AS; **p273** tl: Aitor/AS, tr: wayne/AS, m: RH, bl: Jurgens/AS, br: EcoView/AS; **p275** tl: Beate/AS, tr: Jim Hulley, m: Warwick Tarboton, bl: Stefan Hirsch, br: Kim/AS; **p276** tl: AGAMI/AS, tr: Alfie/AS, bl: BR, br: Edward/AS; **p277** tl: Warwick Tarboton, tr: Graeme Hatley/AS, m: dennisjacobsen/AS, bl: Alta Oosthuizen/AS, br: pschoema/AS; **p278** tl: PACO COMO/SA, tr: EcoView/AS, m: Romas Vysniauskas/AS, bl: RachelKolokoffHopper/AS, br: RH; **p279** tl: Clayton Burne/SS, tr: wolfavni/AS, m: RH, bl: Danilo Collini/As, br: Wim/AS; **p280** tl: FotoRequest/AS, tr: Erni/AS, bl: Thomas/AS, br: Alta Oosthuizen; **p281** tl: NN, tr: Riaan van den Berg/AS, bl: RH, br: nwdph/SS; **p282** tl: Cavan/AS, tr: Erni/AS, m: Kim/AS, bl: Villiers/AS, br: RH; **p283** tl: Victor Tyakht, tr: shams Feroz Amir/AS, bl: Michael Ninger, br: Jordan Confino Photography/AS; **p285** tl: NickVorobey/AS, tr and bl: Alta Oosthuizen/AS, br: NN; **p286** tl, tr and br: RH, bl: AGAMI/AS; **p287** tl: Peter/AS, tr: Albert Froneman/IOA, bl: Stacey Ann Alberts/SS, br: PACO COMO/AS; **p288** tl: Alta Oosthuizen/AS, tr: RH, bl: Regard van dyk/SS, br: Karlos Lomsky/AS; **p289** tl: Lynette/AS, tr: phototrip.cz/AS, bl: Dirk/AS, br: RH; **p290** tl: Piyapong Chotipuntu/AS, tr: David/AS, m: Lynette Knott Rudman/SS, bl: RH, br: Marc/AS; **p291** tl: Daniel Danckwerts/SS, tr: RH, bl: BR, br: Jurgens/AS; **p292** tl and tr: David/AS, bl: Kim/AS, br: Rob Cliff; **p293** tl: Johan Swanepoel/SA, tr: Bryony/AS, bl: Alta Oosthuizen/AS, br: Nigel Forrow; **p294** tl: irinabal/AS, tr: prin79/AS, bl: WildlifeWorld/AS, br: Chris/AS; **p295** tl: RS, tr: phototrip.cz/AS, bl: dennisjacobsen/AS, br: Erni/SS; **p296** tl: Thinus Lamprecht, tr: Sheril/AS, bl: Bryony/AS, br: PACO COMO/AS; **p297** tl: Alta Oosthuizen/AS, tr: Inna Madeeva/AS, bl: Erni/AS, br: Simon Venables/SS

INDEXES

GERMAN NAMES

HERERO NAMES

NAMA NAMES

Gungwa 72
Hunyi 68
Khitsha Homu 170
Khopola 92, 295
Khoti Mavalanga 245, 273
Khoti Mfumo 75, 246
Khoti Mpenyani 75, 245
Khwezu Elimhlope 89, 109
Kwenyana 101
Lokoloko 124, 140
Mabyitana 173, 227
Madzukuya 235
Man'An'Ani 104, 246
Mandzamandza 178
Mangatlwana 241
Mangoko 70
Manole 75, 111, 244, 272
Manon'wana 69, 143
Manteveni 69, 236
Masemgahomu 110
Matsinyani 215
Mavolwane 259, 276
Mghubhana Lowu Kulu 201
Mhangela 70, 101
Mithisi 77, 273

Mjonjo 257
Mpyempye 269, 281
Musoho 235
N'wancakini 68, 210
N'warikwenyana 64
N'warimakokwe 141
N'watimhakweni 271
N'watshekulana 224
Ncilongi 68
Ncivovo 93, 140, 260
Ncocololo 90
Ndzandza 138, 228, 259
Ngalakana 190, 234, 279
Nghondzwe 239
Nghunghwa 213, 243
Nghututu 144
Nghwari 205
Nghwari Ma Ntshengwhayi 142, 232, 279
Nghwari Ya Xidhaka 141, 233
Ngulukwani 76, 247
Ngwafalantala 93
Ngwamhlanga 79, 145
Nhlazi 93, 261
Njenjele 263, 278

Nkata Mangovo 68
Nkonyana Leyi Kulu 140
Nkorhondlopfu 70
Nkorhonyarhi 69, 143, 236
Nkuhunsi 103
Nqcunu 147
Ntsaviya 212
Ntsukwani 270
Nwarikapanyana 64, 96, 109
Nwatsekutseku 99, 141, 234
Phuphuphu 204
Qandlopfu 79
Qigwana 70
Rikolwa 106, 212
Ripetani 238
Sekwamhala 211
Sekwanyarhi 185
Serhu 92, 139
Thungununu 148
Tlulutlulu 142, 191
Tsheketani 296
Tshembyana 264, 293
Vhevhe Nkomo 182, 190, 205
Vontiyo 56
Wariba 260

Xiavava 89, 203
Xicololwa Leyi Kulu 71
Xighigwa 63
Xighwaraghwara 261, 277
Xigidavusiku 269
Xikhodlane 225, 276
Xikhunguba 43
Xikotlwa 225, 276
Xikuvikuvi 75
Xime-memee 83
Ximhungwe 144
Ximinta Ntsengele 145
Xindzinghiri Mbandi 130, 177
Xintsingiri 129
Xinwavulombe 188
Xinyankakeni 238
Xisekwana 155
Xithaklongwa 73, 243
Xitsemahangoni 59, 169
Xitserere 153
Xivhambalana Xa Ncila 64, 260
Xiyahkokeni 74, 211
Xiyinha 236, 283
Yhokwe 182, 234
Yinca 79, 107, 247

isiXHOSA NAMES

Amabalengwe 34, 163
Ibengwana 235
Icelekwane 92, 139
Icola 61
Igolomi 126, 142, 184, 191
Igotyi 58, 221
Igqubusha 63
Igwabalelunga 42, 68
Igwangwa 70
Ihashe 265
Ihem 105
Ihlanga 245, 273
Ihlolo 89, 199
Ihlungulu 43
Ihoye 49, 75, 185, 247
Ijiza 215
Ikhalakandla 227
Ikhalukhalu 71, 270
Ikhwehula 173, 227
Ikreza 161
Ilanda 110
Ilithwa 70, 127
Ilowe 211
Imbombo 201
Impinzi 132, 147, 157
Incede 81, 218
Inchaphe 54, 193
Inciniba 79, 107, 247
Indlasidudu 92, 295
Indlazi 93, 261
Indwe 105, 127
Indweza Eluhlaza 166
Ing'ang'ane 104, 246
Ingcungcu Eluhlaza 176

Ingegane 203, 264
Ingqanga 48, 144, 242
Ingqembe 198
Ingqwangi 91, 172, 293
Ingxangxosi 105
Ingxexe 51
Injwiza 161, 215
Inkwali 141, 233
Inkwaza 213, 243
Inkwili 180
Inqatha 224, 258, 291
Inqathane 158, 175
Inqilo 153, 170, 292
Intakomlilo 34, 134
Intendekwane 183
Intenenengu 120, 181
Intengu 39
Intengwana 39
Intibane 256
Intsasa 56, 167
Intshatshongo 141, 183
Intshili 93, 140, 260
Intshiyane 132, 249
Intsikizi 49, 144
Inxanxadi 61
Inyakrini 120, 181, 188
Iqabathule 198, 256
Iqaqolo 105
Iqiyogiyo 40, 64, 232
Irulumente 32, 58, 286
Isagqukhwe 204
Isahomba 34, 134
Isakabula 35
Isakhwehle 142, 232, 279

Isavukazana 64, 260
Isichukujeje 33, 56
Isicibilili 129
Isigoloda 240
Isihlahlane 162
Isikhwenene 182
Isikretyane 222
Isiphunguphungu 44
Isiqola 135
Isitshisane 64, 96, 109
Ivukazana 260
Ivuzi 48, 212
Izuba 190, 234, 279
Ubikhwe 209
Udwetya 199
Ugaga 150
Ugagasisi 151
Ugxakhweni 159, 286
Ujejane 89, 125, 203
Ujobela 134
Ujojo 134, 291
Ukhetshe Womlambo 207, 269
Ukholo 100, 239
Umbankro 91, 152, 171
Umbese 159
Umganto 88, 153
Umhlantonono 159, 177, 286
Umkholonjane 76, 112
Umkholwane 69, 143, 236
Umkro 170
Umkulunga 41, 124, 140
Umlonji 165
Umnqangqandola 137
Umsimpofu 89

Umswi 154, 229
Umvila 219
Umxwiqa 48, 76, 247
Undenjenje 56, 194
Ungcuze 215
Unocel' Izapholo 115, 285
Unocofu 49, 79
Unogandilanga 51, 167
Unogushana 81, 147
Unolwilwilwi 202, 226
Unomanyuku 83
Unomaphelaphelane 220
Unomaswana 59
Unomaweni 88, 154, 201
Unomyayi 43
Unondlwane 53, 85, 195, 252
Unondyola 55, 196, 287
Unongubende 218
Unonkqayi 45
Unotelela 258
Unowambu 89, 109, 111
Untamnyama 92, 139
Untloyiya 241
Untsho 48
Unyileyo 165
Uphendu 267
Uphezukomkhono 93, 296
Usasa 39, 171
Usilwangula 79, 106
Uthebethebana 96, 206
Uthekwane 239
Utsoyi 81, 132, 177
Uxomoyi 68, 210

isiZULU NAMES

Abayeni 62
Amadojeyanabomvu 51, 193
Amadojeyanajwayelekile 51
Ibhada 170
Ibhakelimsilosihlaku 36, 257
Ibhaku 35, 134
Ibhaku Lehlanze 36
Ibhobhonelisisesibomvu 137
Ibhobhoni Lethafa 63
Ibhoboni 63
Ibhoyi 83, 176
Ibomvana 34, 134
Idadelibomvu 104, 211
Idadelikhandamnyama 126, 155, 211, 237
Idadelimlomobomvu 143, 268, 281

Idadelimlomophuzi 173, 185, 237, 282
Idadelimnyama 45, 237, 282
Idadelincane 125, 267, 281
Idlanga Lentaba 245, 273
Idonsi 162, 223
Ifefelibomvu 123, 190
Ifefelihle 123, 177
Ifefeliluhlaza 122
Ifefemidwa 123, 190, 205
Ifefenomsilasantshengula 123
Ifubesi 103
Igedezi 227
Igelesha Lehlathi 163
Igelesha Logu 162
Igeleshelimqalonsundu 161
Igwababa 43, 70

Igwababa Ledolobha 42, 101
Igwalagwala Lehlanze 126, 142, 184, 191
Igwalagwala Logu 159
Igwalagwalaleliluhlaza 126, 142, 184, 191
Igwedlamanzi 143, 238
Igwigwi 224, 258, 291
Ihelkehle 230
Ihhoye 49, 75, 185, 247
Ihlabahlabane 64, 295
Ihlalanyathi 138, 228, 259
Ihlekehleke 84, 197
Ihlekehleke Lasehlane 84
Ihlekehlelimhlophe 63, 109
Ihlokohlokelibubende 193
Ihlokohlokelikhulu 162

Ihlokohloko Lomuzi 162
Ihlokohlokwana 161
Ihobhelililayo 92, 139, 295
Ihobhelimehlabombu 92, 139, 295
Ijikanyawo 103, 271
Ijiyankomelimlotha 31, 218
Ijuba Ledolobha 92, 183, 191
Ijubantondo 183
Ikhwelemarsheni 88, 153, 201
Ikhwelentabeni 36, 60, 86, 223
Ikhwezelikhulu 121, 182, 189
Ikhwezelimacwebi 188, 277
Ikhwezelimsilomude 121, 182, 189
Ikhwezi 120, 181, 188

314 INDEXES

AFRIKAANS NAMES

ENGLISH NAMES